2—

The Stranglers

The Cult of Thuggee and Its Overthrow in British India

"Bring tobacco!" says the prosperous Brahmin merchant to his companions, and the timorous traveler who has taken refuge in their party smiles with anticipation. A moment later a yellow-and-white scarf flashes around his neck from behind, and he is jerked to the ground with the life throttled out of him. This is no kindly company of merchants, but a party of death-dealing Thugs, the ritual murderers who terrorized the roads of early 19th-century India in the name of the bloodthirsty goddess Kali.

This book tells in grim yet fascinating detail the story of the cult of Thuggee in British India during the years 1828 to 1841 and of the young Bengal Army officer who finally managed to suppress its bloody activities. William Sleeman was one of those rare Englishmen who came to the East without an Occidental chip on his shoulder. Alert, versed in Hindustani and in the labyrinths of the Hindu religion, he was one of the first to suspect how deeply Thuggee had penetrated all of Indian life, and almost alone in the struggle to bring its menace to the attention of an indifferent administration. In the process Sleeman learned the Thugs' secret language, recorded their confessions, and involved his life inextricably with theirs.

George Bruce has created this engrossing book from Sleeman's own reports to Governor-General Bentinck of India and from the confessions of the Thugs themselves, in which these proud, fatalistic assassins divulged the grisly secrets of their trade. Both as history and as crackling true adventure, this book provides an unforgettable glimpse of a society in which the cult of death was deeply rooted in life.

Photograph by Tom Hanley

George Bruce brings to his work on British India an intimate firsthand knowledge and lifelong study of the Far East. He has traveled on foot through the Malayan jungles and in a dugout canoe up the rivers of Borneo. During World War II he served in the British Army, later reported the last stages of the Malayan war and received a State Department grant for travel in the United States. He has published several books, including *A Family Called Field, Retreat from Kabul,* and *The Anglo-Sikh Wars.*

Mr. Bruce presently lives in London with his wife and children.

The Stranglers

The Cult of Thuggee and Its Overthrow in British India

GEORGE BRUCE

HARCOURT, BRACE & WORLD, INC., NEW YORK

First American edition 1969
Library of Congress Catalog Card Number: 69-12029
Printed in the United States of America

ACKNOWLEDGEMENTS

The Publishers and author are indebted to Brigadier John Sleeman, C.B.E., for his permission to reproduce copyright material from previously unpublished collections on Thuggee and Dacoitee by Captain James Paton and letters from William Sleeman to the Fraser family in India; and to the Secretary of State for Commonwealth Affairs for his permission to reproduce unpublished Crown-copyright material from the India Office Records.

Contents

List of Illustrations

(Between pages 118 and 119)

Preface

This book tells in detail the ghoulish and sinister story of the secret Thug societies of India and how 150 years ago William Sleeman, a young Bengal Army officer, led the twelve-year campaign that broke them up and suppressed them.

Controlled only by the Hindu goddess Kali, the brutality of the Thugs was unique. Merciless and indiscriminate assassination was their aim, and for centuries they murdered thousands of people a year. No other secret society has ever menaced the ties of trust that bind human society together and enable it to function as did the Thugs in their day. Yet the British in India denied their existence until Sleeman forced the truth upon the Government.

I have drawn for this book mainly from Sleeman's reports to Lord Bentinck, the Governor-General of India at the time, on the religious beliefs of the Thugs, their ways of murdering their victims, and how they were finally detected and put down. All this is to be found in detail in the manuscript volumes of Bengal Political Proceedings, 1829 to 1835; and India Political Proceedings, 1835 to 1842. Sleeman was a meticulous recorder and his verbatim reports of his conversations with captured Thugs throw much light on the motives and beliefs of this strange sect of killers.

This hitherto unpublished material also shows the boldly unorthodox methods William Sleeman used to press the Governor-General to authorise a campaign against the Thugs. An appendix of extracts from Sleeman's vocabulary of the Thug secret dialect will be found on p. 219, and a list of his published works is included in the Bibliography (p. 225), which records also the sources of quotations from other authorities.

The remarkable drawings reproduced in this book were, according to Captain James Paton, one of Sleeman's assistants, drawn at his request by an Indian artist about 1836, and were based on the artist's talks with Thug prisoners.

I wish to thank Brigadier John Sleeman, C.B.E., for lending me the now very rare books published by his great-great-grandfather; S. C. Sutton, Librarian, and the staff of the India Office Library, the staff of the British Museum Library, and, most important, my wife for her help in editing the book.

G. B.

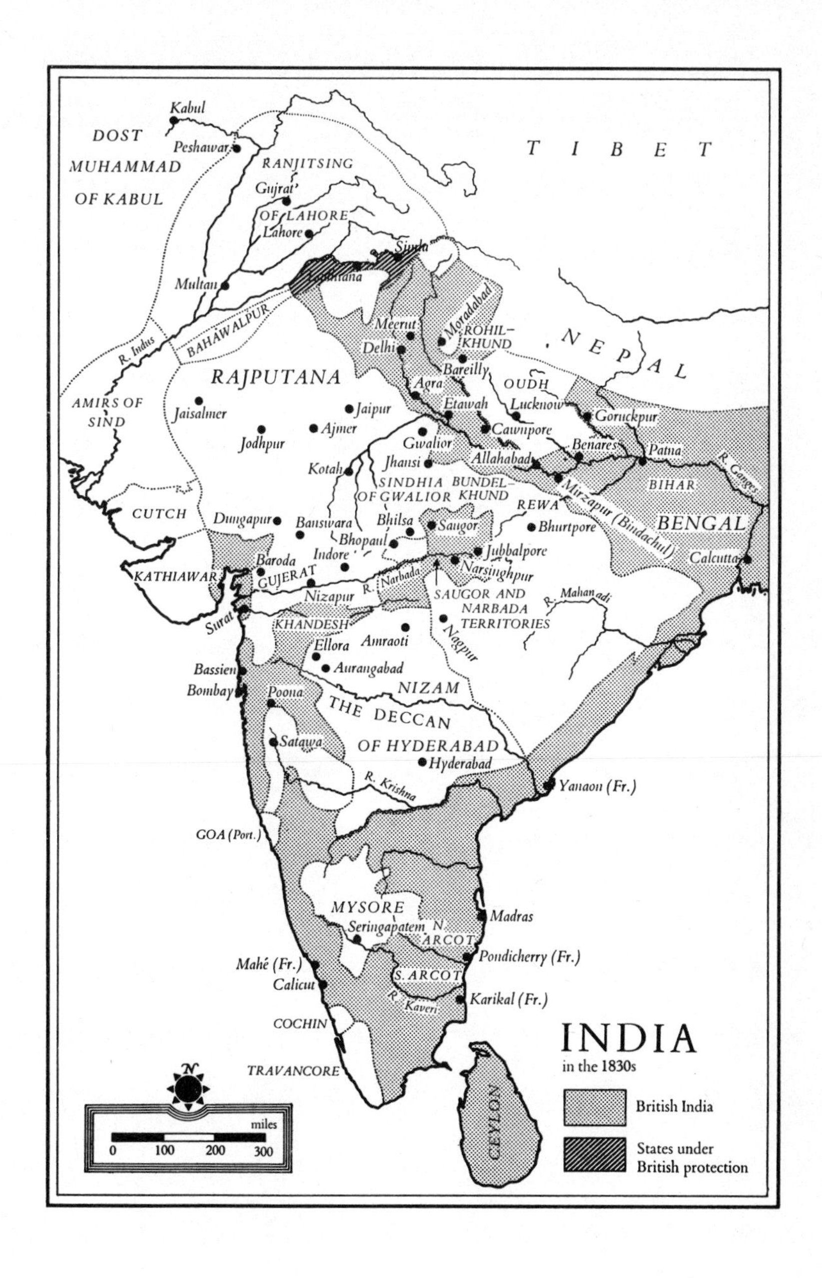
INDIA
in the 1830s
British India
States under British protection
miles
0 100 200 300
TIBET
Kabul
DOST MUHAMMAD OF KABUL
Peshawar
RANJITSING OF LAHORE
Gujrat
Lahore
Simla
Multan
BAHAWALPUR
R. Indus
NEPAL
Meerut
Moradabad
ROHILKHUND
Delhi
Bareilly
RAJPUTANA
Agra
OUDH
AMIRS OF SIND
Jaisalmer
Jaipur
Etawah
Lucknow
Goruckpur
Ajmer
Jodhpur
Gwalior
Cawnpore
Benares
Patna
Kotah
Jhansi
Allahabad
R. Ganges
SINDHIA OF GWALIOR
BUNDELKHUND
BIHAR
Mirzapur (Bindachul)
REWA
CUTCH
Dungapur
Banswara
Bhilsa
Saugor
Bhurtpore
BENGAL
Bhopaul
Indore
Jubbalpore
Calcutta
Baroda
Narsinghpur
KATHIAWAR
GUJERAT
R. Narbada
Nizapur
SAUGOR AND NARBADA TERRITORIES
R. Mahanadi
Surat
KHANDESH
Amraoti
Nagpur
Ellora
Aurangabad
Bassien
Bombay
NIZAM
Poona
THE DECCAN OF HYDERABAD
Satawa
Hyderabad
R. Krishna
Yanaon (Fr.)
GOA (Port.)
MYSORE
Madras
Seringapatem
N. ARCOT
Mahé (Fr.)
Pondicherry (Fr.)
S. ARCOT
Calicut
R. Kaveri
Karikal (Fr.)
COCHIN
TRAVANCORE
CEYLON

I

A Savage Jest

India in the nineteenth century was no place for a weakling. Heavy eating and drinking in stifling heat and humid monsoon weighted the scales against the survival of all but the strongest. "These frequent deaths make one tremble," wrote one frightened lady. And Emily Eden, sister of Lord Auckland, Governor-General in the late 1830s, lamented: "It is melancholy to think how almost all the people we have known at all intimately have in two years died off, and that out of a small society. None of them turned fifty: indeed all but Mr S. between thirty and forty."

Hot dusty winds rattled the palm leaves, mosquitoes buzzed, malaria, cholera, dysentery and smallpox struck down nearly half the debilitated white residents before their time. Many of the military who survived sickness were too often killed by sabre gashes, or the surgeon's amputation. But the death of John Maunsell, son of a small landowner in Ballywilliam, County Limerick, was altogether different—a violation of secret custom, or at heart, a savage jest.

Maunsell, a lieutenant in the 23rd Native Infantry of the Bengal Army set out on horseback in October 1812 from Agra, in what were then called the North-western Provinces, on a visit of inspection to Ettawah, seventy-five miles south-east, accompanied by two sepoy orderlies and a horse carrying his belongings and equipment. All three were armed, Maunsell with sword and holster pistols, the sepoys with the Brown Bess musket and bayonet.

On the second day of his journey Maunsell had camped near the village of Sindhouse in one of the wayside groves known as *choultries* in common use then by travellers, with a well, a few lime trees, a little grass and a shrine. It is easy to visualise the scene after the hot and dusty ride—the horses tethered, the tents pitched in the shade out of the late afternoon's blaze, the green paroquets chattering and the small monkeys shrieking in the branches. Maunsell, according to custom, would have pulled off his hot red broadcloth uniform with relief and splashed in buckets of cool well water in the enclosure behind his tent. In imagined security, he probably stretched out on his camp bed in the hot night and slept soundly after his long day in the sun.

Three days later when neither he nor his orderlies had reached Ettawah, a troop of cavalry was ordered out to search the road. In a wayside grove they found among the ashes of a recent fire, charred regimental buttons and badges that were identified as those of Maunsell and the sepoys. They were assumed to have been murdered, but the bodies were not found. This added to the mystery of what was already an unusual affair; fear of reprisals had for some time discouraged attacks upon Army officers.

Had exceptional qualities or influential friends brought Maunsell's name before the eyes of the great in India, the outcome could have been different, because the evidence would have been sifted more thoroughly, the suspects questioned severely and the truth might have come to light. Instead, a punitive force attacked and destroyed the villages near by, seizing at random any inhabitants thought likely to have taken part in the murder and handing them over to the Indian local authorities for trial. And in the East India Register for 1812 Maunsell was reported to have died in action against banditti on 22 October.

Some forty thousand people, of whom Maunsell was the only white person, died mysteriously while travelling through India that year—as indeed they had done as long as records were kept. They set out, on foot or on horseback, on journeys of up to several hundred miles between cities, and were never seen again. Misadventure was the officially recorded cause of their deaths, though sinister rumours did reach the Government and would have been investigated had the East India Company been interested in anything but trade and money.

These had been the sole reasons for the British presence in India ever since in 1615 Sir Thomas Roe, James the First's

Ambassador to the Emperor Jahangir, then ruler of much of India, spent three years negotiating trading privileges for the Company, whose merchants and seamen were soon rounding Cape Cormorin, sailing up the east coast and founding trading stations.

Francis Day, in 1639, leased a four-mile-long strip of sand on the south-east coast for £600 a year, built Fort St George and laid the foundations of the great city of Madras. Bombay was acquired from the Portuguese by the English Crown in 1661 in exchange for the promise of support against the Dutch, and as part of Catherine of Braganza's dowry on her marriage to Charles II, but with royal disdain for such a trifle, Charles leased it to the Company for £10 a year. Together with Calcutta, founded in 1690 by a thrusting and aggressive merchant, Job Charnock, on a swamp leased to him by Ibrahim Khan, then Nawab of Bengal, it became the twin bastion of the Company's power in India.

A century later, clever diplomacy backed by superior armed forces had enabled the East India Company to acquire the whole of Bengal and, after defeating the French, to make itself the acknowledged paramount power in India. In 1805, when Governor-General the Marquis Wellesley's ruthless programme of annexation ended, the Company, or its allies the Princes, ruled two-thirds of the sub-continent.

In the early nineteenth century, the Government and the Company's Board of Control in London appointed the Governor-General to rule India's millions with an army of some 300,000 British-officered sepoys backed by a few home regiments. But the Company's administration and its sense of justice were those of a peremptory military despotism. Administrative refinements were considered too costly.

Commercial preoccupation with revenue, dissociation from India's civilisation, and the habit of tolerating the less pleasant features of her life led to the expedient policy of non-interference with religion. And so—because those in authority generally turned a deaf ear to rumour and report—India's grim secret was kept. The mysterious society of murderers had never seemed more secure than in the chaotic early years of the nineteenth century.

But in 1802 Captain Philip Sleeman died seven thousand miles away in Cornwall. He left little money and so his son William was obliged to join the Bengal Army instead of the King's Army at home, in which William had hoped his father would purchase him a commission. The Bengal Army must have seemed a much less glorious alternative to fighting Napoleon in Europe, but it was not necessary to raise money to purchase a commission.

In 1809 William Sleeman sailed for India on board the East Indiaman *Devonshire*.

2

A Sword, a Noose and a Club

William Sleeman landed at Calcutta in October 1809, aged twenty-one, and was posted as an infantry cadet to the 2/12 Native Infantry, 400 miles north-west at Dinapore, on the Ganges near Patna in Bihar. Ambitious and energetic, he had chosen direct entry to a regiment rather than join the Company's cadet college at Baraset, which at that time was notorious for creating young rakes with a greater liking for the gambling tables and the Calcutta stews than military studies. Sleeman had spent three years studying Arabic and Hindustani in England until he reached the minimum age for direct entry, and he surprised his commanding officer by his fluency when he joined the regiment.

He must have stood out among his brother cadets in a not altogether favourable light. Hard drinking and Indian mistresses were powerful distractions from the excitements of war and the boredom of peace in the Bengal Army. Sleeman didn't smoke, drank very little—he was soon to abstain from alcohol for life—and at this time had no contact with women beyond the demands of formal social occasions. But he redeemed himself among his fellows by his skill at field sports, excelling at tiger-shooting and at pig-sticking—the hunting of wild boar with a lance, on horseback.

A formal portrait of him in blue, high-collared tunic with gold lacings shows him with sidewhiskers and short auburn hair brushed forward in the style of the day, cool, friendly blue eyes and resolute, rather handsome features. An unpretentious and hard-working rather than a brilliant officer, one would say, warm-hearted towards his fellow men: but the artist seems most to have tried to portray moral and intellectual firmness, qualities which could coalesce into something near to ruthlessness.

Sleeman's thirst for work was unquenchable. Apart from concentrated attention to his military studies, he applied himself, says Vincent Smith,* who later edited his papers and journals, "with exemplary diligence to the study of the Arabic and Persian languages, and the religions and customs of the country".

Here perhaps lies the key to Sleeman's later penetration of one of India's secrets: the study of languages (in a few years he spoke five oriental languages fluently) and religions. But, at least as a young man, he was not religious himself, more rationalist in outlook, often quoting in his writings the English philosophers Hobbes and Locke. The effect of religious beliefs on men rather than the nature of man's relationship to God appears to have interested him. India in the early decades of the nineteenth century was a fertile field for such studies and inquiries.

Complete social and political breakdown had followed the collapse of the Mughal Empire fifty years before. Extending British rule at this time, the officers of the East India Company found northern India ravaged and exhausted—sacked palaces, vanishing roads, toppled fortresses, smashed reservoirs and ruined towns were all that remained of past glories. A present-day Indian writer, Yusuf Ali, quotes, as symbolic of India then, part of a poem by the Urdu poet Sauda (1712–1780) named *City of Terror and Confusion*:

> If I speak of the city—its silence and ruin,
> Even the senses of the owl would take flight:
> No house but resounds to the bark of the jackal:
> If you go in the evening to a mosque to pray,
> Not a light will you find but the light of the ghoul.

Political stability was restored in the British-ruled areas, but in the Indian states grim and bloody anarchy prevailed, every raja regarding large-scale robbery and predatory raiding as his birthright. Sleeman summed up the situation thus:

In India, the difference between the army of a prince and the

* Author of the first *Oxford History of India*.

gang of a robber was, in the general estimation of the people, only in *degree*—both were driving an 'imperial trade'. Both took the auspices and set out on their expedition after the festival of *Dasahara*, when the autumn crops were ripening; and both thought the Deity propitiated as soon as they found the omens favourable; one attacked palaces and capitals and the other villages and merchants' store-rooms.

The worst among the robbers were the Pindaris, mounted bands totalling some 30,000, who rode forty or fifty miles a day in bodies of two or three thousand with neither baggage nor tents, wasting and destroying like locust swarms whatever province they invaded, seizing all the cattle and property they could find, burning what they could not take away.

Pindari cruelties were of nightmare proportions. Women and children were raped and murdered under the eyes of husbands and parents. People of either sex who looked as if they possessed a little money were tortured until they produced it and then tortured again in case they had more. A common method was to put hot ashes into a bag, tie it over the mouth and nostrils of the victim and then thump him on the back until he inhaled the ashes. Not many people survived the lung injuries this torture caused. Pindari women accompanied their menfolk on these savage forays, but far from having a restraining effect they gave a lead in cruelty—she-devils mounted on small ponies who were more feared than the men.

Dacoits too added their bit to this pattern of bloodshed and violence. Mainly tribes of hereditary criminals, they ranged over the whole of India—Buduks, Sanseeas and others, linked by intermarriage, common religious observances and the same language. Often they were brave and skilful enough to attack strong parties of regular troops and mounted police and carry off huge amounts of public funds under escort across the country. Their skill in attacks after dark and in vanishing with their loot was supreme. No magistrate could hope to catch or trace a gang of Buduk Dacoits with the limited forces he had at his command.

In the regions of north-east and north-west India ruled early in the nineteenth century by the East India Company, the magistrates and police believed there were four to five thousand Dacoits at large, most of whose families had been in the trade for as many as twenty generations. Murder and terrorism they used as a matter of course and Sleeman tells a story that throws some light on their attitude to it:

> A friend of mine one day asked a leader of a band of Dacoits, or banditti, whether they did not often commit murder. "God forbid," said he, "that we should ever commit murder; but, if people choose to oppose us, we, of course, *strike and kill*; but you do the same. I hear there is now a large assemblage of troops in the upper provinces going to take foreign countries; if they are opposed they will kill people. We only do the same."

Sir John Malcolm, Governor of Bombay from 1827 to 1830, wrote of these terrible conditions:

> Never had there been such intense and general suffering in India; the native states were disorganised and society on the verge of dissolution; the people crushed by despots and ruined by exactions; the country overrun by bandits and its resources wasted by enemies; armed forces existed only to plunder, torture and mutiny; government had ceased to exist; there remained only oppression and misery.

The economic situation was no better than the social and political. Pindaris and Dacoits paralysed intercity trade and around this commercial stagnation the East India Company tightened its own control. The textile markets were stacked with cheap manufactured goods from Britain; Bengal's ancient hand-loom weavers' industry was impoverished. "Inconceivable oppressions and hardships have been practised towards the poor manufacturers and workmen of the country, who are, in fact monopolised by the Company as so many slaves. . ." wrote an English visitor.

Then as perhaps now, one of the causes of India's troubles was the beliefs and practices of popular Hinduism. Its principal gods were Vishnu, the creator, and Shiva, the destroyer. Shiva's female consorts included Parvati, Sakti, Devi, Durga and Kali; but, because the male is unproductive without the female, the goddesses were believed to be the element of fertility in nature and were worshipped more widely than Shiva himself. Elaborate temple rituals with a large sexual and fertility element marked this worship, including temple prostitutes, or *devadassis* at the service of the priests and worshippers, and, up to the end of the eighteenth century, human sacrifice.

Sleeman visited the temples of the goddess Kali, and saw the black, naked, deliberately hideous image of the goddess; and how on festival days the precincts were carpeted in the blood of ritualistically slaughtered animals; for Kali thirsted for blood, and the animals were substitutes for the human sacrifices of half a century earlier. Kali's devotees tried to satisfy her, sometimes offering in a frenzy of adoration their own blood and agony in the ritual of hook-swinging. Priests beat the worshipper's back until it was numb, then passed hooks through his muscles and attached them to ropes, which in turn were attached to the top of a tall pole, the other end of which was embedded in the ground. The pole was swung round and round, the victim was lifted aloft and whirled, streaming with blood, above the heads of the ecstatic devotees, all shouting—"Victory to Mother Kali!"

Sleeman would have heard the awful invocation addressed to her by worshippers seeking her favours: "Terrific-faced Kali, holding a drawn sword and a noose and a club, wreathed with human skulls, lean, emaciated and terrible, wide-mouthed, tongue dreadfully protruded, maddened, blood red-eyed, and filling the four quarters of the globe with hideous cries . . ." And probably, the echoes of death and destruction in a haunting and oft-sung Bengali hymn to Kali:

Because thou lovest the Burning-ground
I have made a burning-ground of my heart—
That thou, Dark One, haunter of the Burning-ground,
Mayest dance thy eternal dance.
Nought else is in my heart, O Mother:
Day and night blazes the funeral pyre:
The ashes of the dead all strewn about
I have preserved against thy coming,
With death-conquering Mahakala 'neath thy feet.
Do thou enter in, dancing Thy rhythmic dance
That I may behold Thee with closed eyes.

Sakti, another goddess, stood for the essence of life as represented by the naked female form. Her devotees were called Sakts. Members of this cult met in secret in specially dedicated temples in their homes, but in public they worshipped Kali, so no outsider knew who was a Sakt. They included two sects, called the right- and the left-handed, the former worshipping the Linga, or erect male phallus of Shiva and the Yoni or female organ of Sakti. The most devout among this sect, the Lingayats, both men and women, carried about with them a phallus-shaped charm made of bronze, silver or gold, some of which were realistic in form, with veins and indentations clearly shown; others fantastic, topped with grotesque faces, bizarre little fertility symbols for personal adornment.

More realistically, left-handed Sakts worshipped a beautiful young woman and, as that tireless researcher Sir George Macmunn explains, "especially in the cult of *yoni-parast* (yoni-reverence) their adoration of her genital is active and realistic". The object of worship—a physically perfect female devotee of the Brahman caste, a dancing-girl, or a flower-girl—was naked, adorned with jewels and made pure by repetition of mantras. She was then sprinkled with wine and initiated, and the rites, or orgies, began. Much of the teaching was taught verbally, but they were said to involve every form of sexual variation that frenzied ingenuity could devise.

Priests of the higher Hinduism, who scorned these licentious rites, regarded them as being based on a literal and misconceived interpretation of the Veda, or sacred book. In modern terms they could best be called an offshoot of the mother-cultus, similar in character to the Phrygian Cybele and the Diana of the Ephesians. They were all part of the background of religious mysteries that Sleeman studied. Unlike the average Englishman of the day, he was free of the sense of personal superiority that stemmed from evangelical Christianity. Rather than revolted by these rituals and ceremonies, he was objectively interested and critical, seeking, as this passage shows, an understanding of Hindu motivation:

> With the Hindoos . . . the greater the improbability, the more monstrous and preposterous the fiction, the greater is the charm it has over their minds; and the greater their learning in the

> Sanskrit the more they are under the influence of this charm. . . . They go on through life reading and talking of these monstrous fictions which shock the taste and understanding of other nations, without once questioning the truth of one single incident, or hearing it questioned.

But for many months, during the Ghurka War, in which he commanded a company of infantry, Sleeman's researches were interrupted; until finally, the fighting ended with victory over Nepal, at great cost, in 1816. With the regiment, he left the wilds, marched down the Himalayan foothills, over the dusty plains, past the barley and the poppy fields, the mud and cow-dung hovels, to the city of Allahabad, at the junction of the Ganges and the Jumna rivers. At last, he would have hoped, he could continue in his leisure with his researches, but instead he found himself obliged to help in the round of pleasures and ceremonies of European society. Impatiently, he complained:

> In India this duty devolves entirely upon the young civil and military officers of the Government, and at large stations it really is a laborious one, which often takes up the whole of a young man's time. The ladies must have amusement and the officers must find it for them because there are no other persons to undertake the arduous duty.

Helping at balls and theatricals was too much; Sleeman grudged the time he could not give to his work. It was beginning to be concentrated on one subject—a secret society of murderers and their links with the goddess Kali.

Members of this brotherhood were called *thags* in Hindustani, meaning deceivers, from the verb *thag-lana*, to deceive. The English eventually called them Thugs, so coining a new word. Thugs were said to believe that their art of murder was depicted in eighth-century stone carvings in the subterranean temple of Kailasa at Ellora, in central India, hewn out of a mountain by Krishna I (*c.* A.D. 760–800), but the earliest mention of Thugs in literature is found in the thirteenth-century writings of Jalalu-d din Firoz Khilji, Sultan of Delhi. The brotherhood was certainly well-established then—a thousand Thugs were seized and brought before him, but possibly believing them a supernaturally inspired occult body, he refused to execute them and exiled them instead to Bengal, where they promptly introduced a crueller form of Thuggee.

But in the Army Sleeman was ill-placed for researches into the activities of Thugs in his day—he knew none of the handful of magistrates who had acquired some knowledge of the brotherhood in their duties. He might have made slow and laborious progress indefinitely and perhaps, as his youthful idealism evaporated, turned to more profitable interests. But in the autumn of 1816 an article by Dr Robert C. Sherwood was published in Madras about a secret brotherhood of murderers named *phansigars** who were rabidly at work in the mists of despair that covered India.

* The word for Thugs in southern India.

3

Sherwood and the Phansigars

Sherwood, of the Madras Medical Service, was a close friend of William Wright, a magistrate who in 1815 had arrested a gang of suspect Thugs only to see, with humiliation and despair, their release by an incredulous judge. Like Sleeman, Sherwood was a student of Hinduism, and Wright disclosed to him the confessions of some of the gang awaiting trial. Sherwood questioned these prisoners exhaustively. Doubtless hoping for clemency, those who had already confessed broke their society's oaths anew and told him all. Sherwood wrote it down, prepared it for publication and sent it, somewhat surprisingly, to the *Madras Literary Gazette*, in which it appeared under the title "Of the Murderers called Phansigars".

An important report, one can only guess why it appeared in what must have been a fringe publication. Either the editor was a friend whom Sherwood wished to help; or, more likely, the strict press censorship the East India Company imposed prevented publication in every paper but the obscure *Madras Literary Gazette*. The style of the report is decidedly period, but because of its significance and because few copies exist either of the *Gazette* or of *Ramaseeana*, a book by Sleeman in which subsequently Sherwood's report was also published, it is given verbatim except for minor editing where the detail is a little too much:

While Europeans have journeyed through the extensive

territories subject to the Government of Fort St George, with a degree of security no where surpassed, the path of the Native traveller has been beset with perils little known or suspected, into which numbers annually falling, have mysteriously disappeared, the victims of villains as subtle, rapacious and cruel as any who are to be met with in the records of human depravity. The Phansigars, or stranglers, are thus designated from the Hindustani word *Phansi* a noose. In the more northern parts of India, these murderers are called *Thugs*, signifying deceivers: in the Tamul language, they are called *Ari Tulucar*, or Mussulman noosers: in Canarese, *Tanti Calleru*, implying thieves, who use a wire or cat-gut noose. . . .

There is no reason to believe that Europeans were aware of the existence of such criminals as Phansigars until shortly after the conquest of Seringapatem in 1799, when about 100 were apprehended in the vicinity of Bangalore. They did not engage general attention; nor would it appear that they were suspected to belong to a distinct class of hereditary murderers and plunderers, settled in various parts of India, and alike remarkable for the singularity of their practice and the extent of their depredations. . . .

While they lived under the protection of the Polygars (Indian chiefs) and other petty local authorities . . . it was unnecessary to dissemble that they subsisted by depredation. They and their families lived peaceably with their neighbours, whom they never attempted to molest and between whom there subsisted a reciprocation of interest in the purchase and disposal of the plunder which the Phansigars brought with them on returning from their expeditions.

Afterwards, on the extension of the English Government, it was usual for the Phansigars, while they continued their former practices, ostensibly to engage in the cultivation of land or some other occupation, to screen themselves from suspicion. . . .

Phansigars never commit robbery unaccompanied by murder, their practice being first to strangle and then to rifle their victims. It is also a principle with them to allow no one to escape of a party however numerous, which they assail, that there may be no witnesses of their atrocities. The only admitted extension to this rule is in the instance of boys of very tender age, who are spared, adopted by the Thugs and on attaining the requisite age, initiated into their horrible mysteries.

A gang of Phansigars consists of from ten to fifty, or even a greater number, a large majority of whom are Musselmans; but Hindus, and particularly those of the Rajput tribe, are often associated with them. Bramans too, though rarely, are found in the gangs. Emerging from their haunts they sometimes perform long journeys, being absent from home many months, and prowl along the eastern and western coasts to Hyderabad and Cape Cormorin. . . .

Their victims are almost exclusively travellers whom they fall in with on the road. Each gang has its leader, who directs its movements. Of a numerous gang some usually remain at home, while the rest are engaged in the work of pillage and murder. Those that are abroad are often divided into separate parties of ten or fifteen persons, who either follow each other at some distance, or, the parties taking different routes, they rendezvous at an appointed place in advance, measures being at the same time taken to secure a speedy junction of the gang, should this be requisite for the purpose of attacking several travellers at once. Different gangs sometimes act in concert, occasionally apprising one another of the approach of travellers whose destruction promises a rich booty. Phansigars have the appearance of ordinary inoffensive travellers and seldom assume any particular disguise. They indeed not unfrequently pretend to be traders. . . . Phansigars are accustomed to wait at Choultries (resting places) on the high roads or near to towns where travellers are wont to rest. They arrive at such places and enter towns in straggling parties of three or four persons, appearing to meet by accident and to have had no previous acquaintance.

Some of the gang on such occasions are employed as emissaries to gather information and especially to learn if any persons with property in their possession are about to undertake a journey. They are often accompanied by children of ten years of age and upwards, who, while they perform menial offices are initiated into the horrid practices of the Phansigars and contribute to prevent suspicion of their real character.

Skilled in the arts of deception, Phansigars enter into conversation and insinuate themselves, by obsequious attentions, into the confidence of travellers of all descriptions, to learn from them whence they come, whither and for what purpose they are journeying and of what property they are possessed:

> . . . under the pretence of friendly ends,
> And well placed words of glozing courtesy,
> Baited with reasons not unplausible,
> Wind them into the easy-hearted man;
> And hug them into snares.

When the Phansigars determine . . . to attack a traveller, they usually propose to him, under the specious plea of mutual safety or for the sake of society, to travel together, or else they follow him at a little distance and on arriving at a convenient place and a fit opportunity presenting . . . one of the gang suddenly puts a rope or sash round the neck of the unfortunate persons, while others assist in depriving him of his life.

Two Phansigars are considered indispensable to effect the murder of one man, and commonly three are engaged. There is some variation in the manner in which the act is perpetrated. While travelling along, one of the Phansigars suddenly puts the cloth round the neck of the person they mean to kill, and retains hold of one end, while the other is seized by an accomplice; the instrument crossed behind the neck is drawn tight and the two Phansigars pressing the head forwards. At the same time the third villain, in readiness behind the traveller, seizes his legs and he is thrown forward upon the ground.

In this situation he can make little resistance. The man holding the legs of the miserable sufferer now kicks him in those parts endowed with most sensibility and he is quickly despatched.

Some of the gang are sent in advance, and some left in rear of the place, to keep watch and prevent intrusion by giving notice . . . to those engaged in the act. Should any persons unexpectedly appear on the road, before the murdered body is buried, some artifice is practised to prevent discovery, such as covering the body with a cloth, while lamentations are made professedly on account of the sickness or death of one of their comrades: or one of the watchers falls down, apparently writhing with pain, in order to excite the pity of the intruding travellers and to detain them from the scene of murder. Such are the perseverance and caution of the Phansigars that a convenient opportunity not offering, they will sometimes travel in company with or pursue persons whom they have devoted to destruction several days before they execute their intention.

If circumstances favour them, they generally commit murder in a jungle or in an unfrequented part of the country and near to a sandy place or water-course. A hole three or four feet in depth in such a spot is dug with facility, in which the body being placed with the face downwards, it is shockingly mangled.

Deep and continued gashes are often made in it in both sides, from the shoulders to the hands and to the feet, which lay open the abdomen and divide the tendons at the heel. Wounds are also made between the ribs into the chest, and sometimes if the hole be short, the knees are disjointed and the legs forced back upon the body. The hole is then filled with earth.

The body is thus cut and disfigured to expedite its dissolution, as well as to prevent its inflation, which, by raising or causing fissures in the superincumbent sand might attract jackals, and lead to the exposure of the corpse. When the amount of the property is less than they expected to find, the villains sometimes give vent to their disappointment in wanton indignities on the dead body.

If, when a murder is perpetrated, a convenient place for interring the body be not near, or if the Phansigars be apprehensive of discovery, it is either tied in a sack and carried to some spot where it is not likely to be found, or it is put into a well, or, which is frequently practised, a shallow hole is dug, in which the corpse is buried, till a fit place for interring it can be discovered, when it is removed and cut in the manner already mentioned.

If the traveller had a dog it is also killed, lest the faithful animal should cause the discovery of his murdered master. The office of mangling the dead body is usually assigned to a particular person of the gang. The Phansigars are always provided with knives and pickaxes, which they conceal from observation. From the foregoing account it will be obvious that the system of the Phansigars is but too well adapted for concealment. The precautions they take, the artifices they practice, the mode of destroying their victims, calculated at once to preclude almost the possibility of rescue or escape—of witnesses of the deed—of noise or cries for help—of effusion of blood—and, in general, of all traces of murder: these circumstances conspire to throw a veil of darkness over their atrocities. I now proceed to notice various particulars, more fully illustrating the practices, habits and character of these criminals.

It is not improbable that formerly a long string, with a running noose, might have been used by the Phansigars for seizing travellers and that they robbed on horseback. But be this as it may, a noose is now, I believe, never thrown by them from a distance in this part of India. They sometimes use a short rope with a loop at one end but a turban or a dhoti are more commonly employed for strangling travellers. When such a cloth is used it is doubled to the length of two or two and a half feet and a knot is formed at the double extremity, and about 18 inches from it a slip knot is tied.

In regulating the distance of the two knots, so that the space between when tightly twisted may be adapted to embrace the neck, the Phansigar who prepares the instrument ties it upon his own knee. The two knots give the Phansigars a firm hold of the cloth and prevent its slipping through their hands in the act of applying it.

After the person they attack has been brought to the ground . . . the slip knot is loosed by the Phansigar who has hold of that part of the cloth, and he makes another fold of it round the neck, upon which, placing his foot, he draws the cloth tight, in a manner similar to that (to use the expression of my Phansigar informer) "of packing a bundle of straw".

Sometimes, the Phansigars have not the time to observe all the precautions I have mentioned in cutting and interring a body, apprehensions for their own safety inducing them to leave it slightly buried. Sometimes, also, when a murder is perpetrated in a part of the country which exposes them to the risk of observation, they put up a screen or the wall for a tent and bury the body within the enclosure, pretending if inquiries are made, that their women are within the screen. On such occasions these obdurate wretches do not hesitate to dress and eat their food on the very spot where their victim is buried.

If, which scarcely ever happens, a traveller escape from the persons attempting to strangle him, he incurs the hazard of being dispatched by one of the parties on the watch. Should he finally escape, or should any other circumstances occur to excite alarm or apprehensions of being seized, the gang immediately disperses, having previously agreed to reassemble at an appointed time, at some distant place.

Travellers resting in the same grove as Phansigars are sometimes destroyed in the night and their bodies conveyed to a distance and buried. On these occasions a person is not always murdered when asleep, as when he is in a recumbent posture the Phansigars find difficulty in applying the cloth. The usual practice is first to awaken him suddenly with an alarm of a snake or scorpion and then to strangle him.

In attacking a traveller on horseback . . . one of the gang goes in front of the horse, and another in the rear: a third, walking by the side of the traveller, keeps him engaged in conversation till, finding that he is off his guard, he suddenly seizes the traveller by the arm and drags him to the ground, the horse at the same time being seized by the foremost villain. The miserable sufferer is then strangled in the usual manner. Against Phansigars it must be obvious that arms and the ordinary precautions taken against robbers, are unavailing. When a person is armed with a dagger it is usual for one of the villains to secure his hands. It sometimes happens that a party of several persons possessed of valuable effects, are, while journeying in imagined security, suddenly strangled, and the lifeless and despoiled bodies being removed and interred, not a vestige of them remains. Instances are said to have occurred of twelve and fourteen persons being simultaneously destroyed. The booty . . . is usually shared as follows: to the leader two shares; to the men actually concerned in the murder and to the person who cuts the dead body, each one share and a half; and to the remainder of the gang each one share.

The plunder was almost always carried home by the Phansigars and sold greatly below its value. It was never disposed of near to the place where the person to whom it belonged was murdered, nor where it was likely to be recognised, of which the Phansigars were enabled to judge by the information imparted to them by the credulous sufferers.

Their system seems to be founded on superstition. They pay the most servile regard to omens; and they never leave their abodes to go on an expedition without a previous persuasion derived from modes of divination in use among them, that it will be attended with success. . . .

Kali . . . is regarded as their tutelary deity and is the object of their adoration. Before an expedition is determined on, an entertainment is given, when the ceremony of sacrificing a sheep is performed; and though perhaps not always, it would seem generally in the following manner:

A silver or brazen image of the goddess, with certain paraphernalia pertaining to her; and the images of a lizard and a snake, reptiles from which presages are drawn; together with the implements of Phansigari, as a noose, knife, and pick axe, being placed together, flowers are scattered over them, and offerings of fruit, cakes, spirits, etc., are made; odiferous powders are burned, and prayers are offered for success.

The head of the sheep being cut off, it is placed with a burning lamp upon it and the right forefoot in the mouth, before the image of Kali, and the goddess is entreated to reveal to them, whether she approves of the expedition they are meditating. Her consent is supposed to be declared should certain tremulous or convulsive movements be observed during the invocation in the mouth and nostrils, while some fluid is poured upon those parts. But the absence of those agitations is considered as indicating the disapprobation of the goddess and the expedition is postponed. . . .

White and yellow being considered the favourite colours of their patroness Kali and those in which she is arrayed, the cloths for strangling are of one or other of these. . . .

Ridiculous as their superstitions must appear they are not devoid of effect. They serve the important purposes of cementing the union of the gang; of kindling courage and confidence; and, by an appeal to religious texts deemed infallible of imparting to their atrocities the semblance of divine sanction.

To the same superstitious feeling is also to be ascribed the curious circumstances that Phansigars are accustomed to refrain from murdering females and persons of the Camala caste, which includes gold, iron and brass-smiths, carpenters and stonecutters, washermen, potmakers, pariahs, lepers, the blind and mutilated, a man driving a cow or a female goat. These persons appear to be regarded as either the descendants or the servants of Kali; or as having claims to her especial protection. . . .

When this rule is respected, any one of these persons, travelling with others of different castes, proves a safeguard to the whole party; the same principle which prompts Phansigars to destroy every individual of a party, forbidding them to kill any unless the whole. Many Phansigars, who have become informers, have declared that they never knew any of these persons to be destroyed and thought that no pecuniary temptation could be sufficiently powerful to cause a violation of this rule. Others have stated that they had heard of a gang of Phansigars who, having murdered a woman, never afterwards prospered and were at length destroyed.

The utility to such criminals as Phansigars of signs and of words and phrases not understood by others must be obvious. . . . Some of them in more frequent use I shall mention. . . .

Drawing the back of the hand along the chin, from the throat outwards, implies that caution is required—that some stranger is approaching. Putting the open hand over the mouth and drawing it gently down implies that there is no longer cause for alarm. If an advance party of Phansigars overtake any traveller whom they design to destroy, but have need of more assistance, they make certain marks on the roads, by which those of the gang who follow understand that they are required to hasten forward. A party in advance also leaves certain marks where a road branches off, as intimations to those who follow on the route their comrades have taken. Phansigars bring up all their male children to the profession unless bodily defects prevent them from following it. The method of initiating a boy is a very gradual one. At the age of ten or twelve years he is first permitted to accompany a gang of Thugs. One of the gang, generally a near relation, becomes his *ustad* or tutor, whom the child is taught to regard with great respect, and whom he usually serves in a menial capacity, carrying a bundle and dressing food for him. Frequently, the father acts as the preceptor to his son.

In the event of being questioned by travellers whom he may meet, the boy is enjoined to give no information further than that they are proceeding from some one place to another. He is instructed to consider his interest as opposed to that of society in general and to deprive a human being of life is represented as an act merely analogous and equivalent of killing a chicken or a sheep. . . .

After his initiation a Phansigar continues to greet his tutor with great respect. He occasionally makes him presents and assists him in his old age. On meeting him after a long absence, he touches his feet in token of reverence.

Such is the effect of the course of education I have described, strengthened by habit, that Phansigars become strongly attached to their detestable occupation. They rarely if ever abandon it. Some, narrowly escaping the merited vengeance of the law and released from prison under security, could not refrain from resuming their old employment; and those who, bending under the weight of years and infirmities, are no longer able to bear an active or principal part, continue to aid the cause by keeping watch, procuring intelligence, or dressing the food of their younger confederates.

The bonds of social union among Phansigars are drawn still closer by intermarriages. Though not of frequent occurrence instances are not wanting in which they have married into families deemed honest and respectable. The women are not ignorant of the proceedings of their husbands. . . .

To the influence of personal character are Phansigars usually indebted for becoming heads of gangs. Like others who follow lawless and abandoned courses, the Phansigars are profligate and improvident, and addicted to the use of bang,* so that the wealth they may acquire, though considerable is soon wasted. . . .

Unfortunately, few of the numerous Phansigars that have at different times been apprehended could be convicted in accordance with the evidence required by the Mohammedan criminal law; which admitting not the testimony of accomplices, and rarely the sufficiency of strong circumstantial evidence unless confirmed by the confession of the culprits, their adherence to protestations of innocence has alone, but too frequently, exempted them from punishment. Those that have been tried

* An opium drink.

and released becoming greater adepts in deceit have . . . carried with them a knowledge of the form of trial, and of the nature of the evidence requisite to their conviction.

I have heard of no instance in which a European was murdered by Phansigars.* The manner in which they are accustomed to travel in India is perhaps generally sufficient to exempt them from danger; added to which apprehension of strict enquiry and search should a European be missing, may be supposed to intimidate the Phansigars, at least in the dominions of the Company. . . . That the disappearance of such large numbers of natives should have excited so little interest and enquiry as not to have led to a general knowledge of these combinations of criminals will naturally appear extraordinary. Such ignorance, certainly, could not have prevailed in England, where the absence, if unaccounted for, of even a single person, seldom fails to produce suspicion, with consecutive investigation and discovery.

In India, the case is far otherwise: and unless occurring to a person of some consequence, such an event would scarcely be known beyond the precincts of the place of residence or the village of the unfortunate sufferer. Many that fall victims to the Phansigar are the subjects of other and distant states, many have no settled abodes. It must also be remembered that Phansigars refrain from murdering the inhabitants of towns and villages near to which they are halting; neither are they accustomed to murder near their own habitations, circumstances which not only prevent suspicion attaching to them as the murderers, and to the local authority as protecting and sharing the booty with them, but tend to throw it upon others, who reside near the spot whither a traveller may have been traced, and where he was last seen. Besides, a person setting out on a journey is often unable to fix any period for his return; and though he should not revisit his home at the expected time, his delay will for a while excite little alarm in the minds of his friends. He is supposed to be unexpectedly detained—to be ill—to have met with some ordinary accident—to have deserted his family—to have died. Should suspicion arise that he has been murdered, the

* Maunsell was the exception.

act is attributed to ordinary highway robbers; and it is but seldom that minute enquiries can be instituted by his bereaved relatives. But supposing that this is done, the progress of the missing travellers traced to a particular place and not beyond it, still suspicion would be apt to any, rather than to a few apparently inoffensive travellers, journeying either for the purpose of traffic, as is imagined; or, as is often pretended, to see their relations, or to be present at some marriage, and who, if ever noticed, have been long since forgotten. If notwithstanding all these improbabilities, suspicion should fall upon the actual perpetrators, where could they be found?

Thus with respect to Sepoys who, having obtained leave of absence, never rejoined their corps, the conclusion generally formed has been that they had deserted—when, in various instances, they had fallen sacrifices to the wiles of the Phansigars. The same observation is applicable to treasure bearers, charged with the conveyance of money and valuables; many of whom having disappeared, no doubt was entertained that they had absconded, and appropriated the property to their own use.

Even the fear, which an indistinct idea of danger tends to create in the minds of these and other travellers would render them only more liable to fall into the snare. Less persuasion would be needed to induce them to join a party of Phansigars, prompted by the belief that they were thus providing in the most effectual manner for their own safety.

Phansigars are equally strangers to compassion and remorse—they are never restrained from killing by pity for the unfortunate traveller—and they are free from the visitings of conscience, which usually follow, sooner or later, the steps of guilt. "Phansigari," they observe with cold indifference, blended with a degree of surprise when questioned on this subject, "is our business." By an application of the same doctrine, they have compared themselves, not inaptly, to tigers, maintaining that as these ferocious beasts are impelled by irresistible necessity and fulfil the designs of nature in preying on other animals, so the appropriate victims of the Phansigars are men, and that the destiny of those whom they kill "was written on their foreheads".

It ought not to be forgotten that, unlike many who adopt criminal courses, the Phansigars had not previously to divest themselves of upright principles, to oppose their practice to their feelings; but that, on the contrary, having been trained up from their childhood to the profession, they acquired habits unfitting them for honest and industrious exertion: that a detestable superstition lent its sanctions to their enormities: and that they did but obey the instructions, and imitate the examples of their fathers. . . .

Thévenot [a seventeenth-century traveller], in the following passage, evidently alluded to the Phansigars or Thugs: "Though the road I have been speaking of from Delhi to Agra be tolerable, yet hath it many inconveniences. One may meet with tigers, panthers, and lions upon it and one had best also have a care of robbers and above all things not to suffer any body to come near one upon the road. The cunningest robbers in the world are in that country. They use a certain slip with a running noose, which they can cast with so much sleight about a man's neck, when they are within reach of him, that they never fail, so that they strangle him in a trice.

"They have another cunning trick also to catch travellers with. They send out a handsome woman upon the road, who with her hair disshevelled seems to be all in tears, sighing and complaining of some misfortune which she pretends has befallen her. Now, as she takes the same way as the traveller goes, he easily falls into conversation with her, and finding her beautiful, offers her his assistance, which she accepts, but he hath no sooner taken her up behind him on horseback, but she throws the snare about his neck and strangles him, or at least stuns him, until the robbers (who lie hid) come running to her assistance and complete what she hath begun."

It may also be a question whether to the Hindus or to the Musselmans ought to be considered as attaching the reproach of inventing this detestable system of pillage and murder. The respect paid by the Musselman Phansigars to the omens and modes of divination and to the religious and idolatrous rites of the Hindus—a respect apparently not accidental, but which pervades and seems interwoven with their whole system—affords grounds for the belief, that to them, rather than to the Musselmans, is to be ascribed the invention.

On the other hand it may be argued that had these bands of

murderers consisted primarily of Hindus, it would probably have appeared that the practice was of considerable antiquity; in which case there could hardly have been that prevailing ignorance among the Hindus with regard to it, which is found to exist. . . .

Thus the credit for first revealing Thuggee's evil story goes to Richard C. Sherwood. But to read his report about the most deadly society of secret assassins ever known to the world is still to wonder why it did not create an outcry at the time. For if Sherwood and Wright hoped that this revelation of murders done daily under the very noses of magistrates and police could bring about an anti-Thug campaign they must have been bitterly disappointed. There is no official record of any reaction whatsoever. The truth about Thuggee, brought into the open by a respected medical man, was ignored.

Admittedly, Lord Hastings, the Governor-General, was at that time busy with threats to the peace and security of the territories under his rule. From 1812 onwards the Pindaris had been making sporadic raids on Company territories, but in 1816, just before Sherwood's article appeared, they had launched a series of fierce attacks on that part of the east coast of India today known as Orissa. Riding, murdering, plundering, in twelve days they killed 182 people, sacked 400 villages, tortured 3603 men and women and wounded 600 more. Hastings at once prepared an army big enough to defeat both them and the even more formidable Maratha chiefs with whom he knew them to be in league. Thus, it could rightly be claimed that he was then too concerned with what amounted to a challenge to the security of the Company's territory to bother with an article in an obscure literary magazine that presumed to give chapter and verse about a secret society of assassins who were making a graveyard of India.

But there was another reason, too, for this official silence: the policy of non-interference—of "taking the country as we find it"—supported by Lord Hastings and those brilliant soldier-administrators Sir John Malcolm and Sir Thomas Munro, both of whom held strongly the Utilitarian view that "progress" rather than legislation would set India to rights. "Great and beneficial alterations in society, to be complete", wrote Malcolm, "must be produced within society itself; they cannot be the mere fabrication of its superiors, or of a few who deem themselves enlightened."

Munro's intolerance of betterment by legislation was still more resolute:

> I have no faith in the modern doctrine of the improvement of the Hindoos, or of any other people. The character of the Hindoos is probably much the same as when Vasco da Gama first visited India, and it is not likely that it will be much better a century hence.
>
> When I read, as I sometimes do, of a measure by which a large province had been suddenly improved, or a race of semi-barbarians civilised almost to Quakerism, I throw away the book.

If the Government did not believe it should interfere with social customs in India, still less did it believe in interfering in popular religion. Indeed, without ever having looked into its practices and rituals the Government had committed itself wholeheartedly to its support, including the patronage of religious festivals and the administration of temple funds. British military bands, of all things, played at these festivals; officers were detailed to attend them, as a mark of esteem. And the probable consensus of opinion among civilians who read the report was—"It all sounds much exaggerated and rather unlikely, but if it is really true that the Indians, these poor benighted Natives, are murdering each other in this way, let them get on with it. This is how they've lived for centuries. To interfere and try to civilise them would be useless. And besides it would be bad for trade."

As for the officers of the Bengal Army, fewer still would have raised an eyebrow had they been told of Sherwood's report, for it is unlikely that more than a handful would have bothered to read it. Apart from coaxing what enjoyment they could out of their stay in India, they were, with a few very notable exceptions, concerned only with imposing the Company's will by military force when other means had failed. Never theirs to wonder why. But William Sleeman read it and understood its meaning. Added to his own knowledge of the Thugs, and their religious background, the impact of the report upon him was so strong that the whole course of his life was changed. He was soon to dedicate it to overcoming them.

4

Murder for Kali

Sleeman began to face in 1817 the issue of whether he should try to transfer from the Bengal Army to the Civil Service—the system of magistrates, judges, police and revenue collectors who administered the Company's territories. Only as a magistrate would he hear of murders which might be the work of Thugs and meet the villagers, and the oppressed dwellers in the cow-dung hovels, who could tell him what was happening.

The issue cannot have been easy. It meant for one thing a break with family tradition. Three of William's brothers were in the Navy and another in the Army; he himself had always dreamt of being a soldier. It also meant abandoning a promising career, for he had already distinguished himself in the line, had for his known fairness and impartiality been made an adjudicator of the Ghurka War prize money and was, moreover, in demand as an interpreter. He had every chance of rapid promotion to senior commander.

To be seconded to the Civil Service might well lose him the best of both worlds. Being still on the Army List he would necessarily lose promotion to those actively soldiering; and promotion in the civil field would inevitably go soonest to those on the books. So he faced a painful struggle about which way to turn. But in the months that followed Sherwood's report the dreadful dangers of the Thug grip upon India seem to have become clear to him, posing unavoidable questions.

In this social and economic upheaval might not Kali's inspiration, the release she gave from moral and human restraints, make the cult of great appeal? Were not the hereditary Thugs on the roads looking for recruits of suitable character for the lower ranks of their gangs? Might it not offer a livelihood to many workless Indians?

A goddess of the first rank in the Hindu pantheon of deities had commanded Thugs to kill in her name. Would not this command mean as much to her votaries as the known will of the Virgin Mary to Roman Catholics? The implications of Sherwood's report were very clear. But had he not under-estimated the numbers of these secret murderers? Was it not likely that from the cool foothills of the Himalayas to the burning plains of central India and the jungles of the south, India lay at the mercy of the Thug gangs? Though secret and denied, might they not already rival the Pindaris in their potential for evil? Kali's black and hideous image must have taken on a more horrible meaning for Sleeman as he faced these questions.

Finally, in 1818, he decided that he could no longer stay in the Army, and he sent in his application to be seconded to the Civil Service. It was forwarded to Government House, Calcutta, but the administrative machine moved slowly and it was not until December 1819 that a letter came from the office of Lord Amherst, then Governor-General, advising him that he had been seconded and appointed junior assistant magistrate to Mr Molony, in the Saugor and Narbada Territories, with effect from February 1820. These were part of the lands ceded to the Company by the Maratha princes after their military defeat by an army commanded in the field by Lord Hastings.

All Sleeman's subsequent writings make it clear how delighted he was with his appointment, yet equally they show his eventual awareness that the structure of the Company's administration was anything but ideal for his purpose. It had divided the provinces of British India into 258 districts, with an average population of about one million. To rule these districts—to administer justice and to enforce the law—it appointed as magistrates men who had earlier received some training for the purpose, and a few suitable seconded army officers.

The magistrate, who was also a judge, had, as well as his English junior assistant, from twelve to sixteen *thanadars*, or Indian officials equivalent in rank to police sergeants, each in charge of a subdivision of the district, with a population of about 100,000 people. The senior magistrate was paid from 2000 to 2500 rupees (£250) a month; the *thanadars* no more than 25 rupees a month each. Each *thanadar* had assigned to him four or five Indian policemen paid 8 rupees monthly, and thirty or forty mounted irregular troops on four rupees a month. Finally, there was in each village a watchman, and in large villages two or more, paid, not by the government but by the community a few grains of rice or wheat daily. For this, they were required regularly to report all police matters to the *thanadar*.

The *thanadars*, who formed the basis of this pyramid of justice, had much responsibility and endless work for pay it was impossible to live on. A *thanadar* needed two horses; and the magistrate would tell him he must have two horses, or resign. "The people," Sleeman remarked, "seeing how much we expect from the *thanadar*, and how little we give him, submit to his demands for contributions without murmuring, and consider almost any demand trivial from a man so employed and so paid."

Corruption in these circumstances flourished like the tropical rain forest; and most magistrates knew nothing at all about it. Sleeman tells a revealing story of an attempt to apply the squeeze by one of his *thanadars*:

> In a village which he had purchased and let in farms, a shopkeeper was one day superintending the cutting of some sugar-cane which he had purchased from a cultivator as it stood. His name was Girdhari and the boy who was cutting it for him was the son of a poor man named Madari. Girdhari wanted to have the cane cut as near to the ground as he could, while the boy, to save himself the trouble of stooping would persist in cutting it a good deal too high up. After admonishing him several times, the shopkeeper gave him a smart clout on the head. The boy, to prevent a repetition, called out—"Murder, Girdhari has killed me—Girdhari has killed me!" His old father who was at work carrying the cane at a little distance out of sight, ran off to the village watchman, and, in his anger, told him that Girdhari had murdered his son. The watchman went as fast as he could to the Thanadar, who resided some miles distant. The Thanadar ordered off his subordinate, the Jemadar, with six policemen, to arrange everything for an inquest on the body by the time he should reach the place with all due pomp.

The Jemadar went to the house of the alleged murderer and dismounting, ordered all the shopkeepers of the village, who were many and respectable, to be forthwith seized and bound hand and foot. "So, you have been aiding and abetting your friend in the murder of poor Madari's only son," said the Jemadar. "May it please your excellency, we have never heard of any murder." "Impudent scoundrels," roared the Jemadar, "does not the poor boy lie dead in the sugar-cane field, and is not his highness the Thanadar coming to hold an inquest upon it? And do you take us for fools enough to believe that any scoundrel among you would venture to commit a deliberate murder without being aided and abetted by all the rest?"

The village watchman began to feel that perhaps he had been too precipitate and entreated the Jemadar to go first and see the body of the boy. "What do you take us for," said the Jemadar, "a thing without a stomach? Do you suppose that government servants can live and labour on air? Are we to go and examine bodies upon empty stomachs? Let his father take care of the body and let these murdering shopkeepers provide us with something to eat."

Materials for a feast were forthwith collected at the expense of the shopkeepers, who stood bound awaiting the arrival of his highness the Thanadar, who was soon after seen approaching majestically upon a richly caparisoned horse.

"What!" shouted the Jemadar, "is there nobody to go and receive his highness in due form?" One of the shopkeepers was untied, and presented with 15 rupees by his family and those of the other shopkeepers. This he took up and presented to his highness who deigned to receive them through one of his train and then dismounted and partook of the feast that had been provided. "Now," said the Thanadar, "we will go and hold an inquest on the body of the poor boy." And off moved all the great functionaries of government to the sugar-cane field, with the village watchman leading the way. The boy's father met them as they entered and was pointed out by the watchman. "Where is your poor boy?" said the Thanadar. "There," said Madari, "cutting the canes." "How! cutting the canes? Was he not murdered by the shopkeepers?" "No," said Madari, "he was beaten by Girdhari and richly deserved it I find."

Girdhari and the boy were called up and the urchin said he called out murder merely to prevent Girdhari giving him another clout. His father was then fined nine rupees—about two month's earnings—for giving a false alarm, and Girdhari 15 for so unmercifully beating the boy. They were made to pay on the instant, under the penalty of all being sent off forty miles to the magistrate. Having thus settled this very important affair his highness the Thanadar walked back to the shop, ordered all the shopkeepers to be set at liberty, smoked his pipe, mounted his horse and rode home, followed by all his police officers, pleased with the day's work.

The outcome, wrote Sleeman, was that the owner of the land protested to the *thanadar* that if his tenants were subjected to such oppressive fines he would never get any rents and that he would take the earliest chance of mentioning the facts to his friend the magistrate, who was Sleeman. Having ascertained that this land-owner was in fact friendly with the magistrate, the *thanadar* hushed the affair up by paying back all but the expenses of the feast.

Such tricks were commonplace, but corruption went far deeper. Sleeman found out that "managed" robberies brought the under-paid *thanadars* a rich harvest. The procedure was simple. Stolen property found in one man's house would by a little police jugglery turn up in the home of another. Both men, Sleeman observed, and all the members of the village community would be summoned to the court of the *thanadar* to give evidence as to what they had seen or heard, or about anyone remotely associated with it, or the arrests of the supposed offenders, the search of their houses, the character of their grandparents. And they were told that they would be sent 100 miles away to the magistrate's court, where they would be made to stand at a door among 150 pairs of shoes—witnesses and accused alike had to enter the court barefoot—till his *excellency* the Nazir, under-Sheriff of the court, announced them to his highness the magistrate, which he would not do without a bribe.

To escape all these costly evils the villagers generously compensated the *'hanadar* for his trouble in over-seeing the security of their village. More significantly, the *thanadars* allowed gangs of robbers, and even suspected Thugs to live within their jurisdiction. In return for this consideration the *thanadars* received a promise never to rob or kill on home territory plus a share of what the gang brought back from distant expeditions elsewhere, and of this Sleeman noted:

> The police officers employed on our borders find it very convenient to trace the perpetrators of all murders and gang robberies into the territories of native chiefs, whose subjects they accuse often when they know that the crimes have been committed by our own. They are, on the one hand, afraid to seize or accuse the real offenders, lest they should avenge themselves by some personal violence, or by thefts or robberies, which they often commit with a view to get them turned out of office as inefficient. . . .
>
> Their tenure of office is far too insecure and their salaries are far too small. They are often dismissed summarily by the magistrate if they send him in no prisoners; and also if they send in to him prisoners who are not ultimately convicted, because a magistrate's merits are too often estimated by the proportion that his convictions bear to his acquittals among the prisoners committed for trial to the Sessions.
>
> Men are often acquitted for want of judicial proof when there is abundance of that moral proof on which a police officer or magistrate has to act in the discharge of his duties; and in a country where gangs of professional and hereditary robbers and murderers extend their depredations into very remote parts . . . the most vigilant police officer must often fail to discover the perpetrators of heavy crimes that take place within his range.

Sleeman must soon have learned the size of the problem he had set himself in believing that he could be the nucleus of an anti-Thug campaign in India. Apart from constant alertness for clues leading to Thugs, there was an enormous amount of work for him to do in these circumstances. In the wealth of corruption that surrounded him it would have been all too easy to forget what was for him the major task. But he must have clung to his dream to rid India of Thugs with all the tenacity of which he was capable.

After barely two years as assistant, he was promoted in 1822 to magistrate in charge of the Narsinghpore district in the valley of the Narbada river. He could now not only rule in accord with the ideas he had developed, but pursue his inquiries into Thuggee more thoroughly.

He started what for a magistrate was an innovation—riding from village to village on horseback with mounted escort and servants cantering along behind him, and hearing at the *thanadars'* courts where they originated cases which had been referred to his headquarters. It had the merit of saving the peasantry and small merchants the cost of travel to his court and preventing *thanadars* intimidating them. Normally, with magistrates never venturing out of their headquarters *thanadars* ruled the districts solely for their own profit; but by riding out to the villages Sleeman ruled as he wished. The peasants, and small landholders, or zemindars, he believed, rewarded him by taking him a little into their confidence, as far as it paid them to do so.

Most important, by degrees, from this person and that, Sleeman gradually established certain confirmation of what most magistrates regarded as rumour—that in areas where the fields were irrigated from wells the peasants continually found bodies at the shaft bottoms, always with the same telltale injuries to throat and neck. He learned too that these grim discoveries, far from being something new or surprising were a part of peasant life; similar bodies had been found in their fathers' time and in the time of their grandfathers, too. Secretly, they hoisted the bodies out of the wells and buried them, never daring to tell the police or the village watchman; nor did they even talk together about these killings. It was better not to, for they knew them to be the work of a mysterious brotherhood of murderers protected by the goddess Kali, who rewarded their friends and destroyed their enemies. They were content to know nothing, to ask no questions, but to help by lies and by silence and in return to be generously rewarded. Thus, through the centuries the peasantry and the zemindars had been drawn into the net. They dare not look this way or that, or over their shoulders, or step out of line, in case they saw something not for their eyes and, as occasionally happened, mysteriously disappeared.

Confirmation, after this, that the lower ranks of the police frequently found bodies in the dry season in ravines and dried-up river beds called *nullahs* was not hard to get. A *thanadar*, frightened by Sleeman's persistent questioning, confessed the whole truth, admitting that he and his colleagues knew by the telltale signs that these murders were the work of Thugs, even though they reported otherwise.

Sleeman had discovered a great deal. Perhaps he obtained from his *thanadars* and from his friends the peasants the promise that henceforward when bodies were found strangled, either in a shallow grave or at the bottom of a well, correct reports would be made of the event, so that he himself could report them to his superiors, until the numbers of murders in his district compelled the authorities to take notice. But in believing that he had won the confidence of the people, he was deceived. Thugs were at work all around him, literally within a hundred paces of the shadow of his court-house. He discovered this only years later, when he had been posted elsewhere. For despite his benevolence, the villagers still saw him as a representative of the despotic rulers, whose regime had brought only mixed blessings.

True, in and around the villages, the lives of the peasants were now safe from the seasonal attacks of local chiefs, but errors in land policy, rapacious taxation, the milking of the country's economic life by avaricious Company officials—all these had contracted Indian standards of living so disastrously that for many peasants mere survival was hard. And this very poverty undermined Sleeman's efforts to find out the truth. The Thugs made it worth while to keep their secrets—and murdered those who talked.

Proof was needed before anyone at Government House would believe the macabre and shocking truth behind the smooth façade of the much-vaunted system of law and order. It would be of little use merely to write without supporting evidence and say: "Many of these people reported to have died from cholera, smallpox and snake-bite on the roads have in fact been strangled by Thugs."

The difficulty was that proof meant uncovering the identity and details of the recent murders of at least one gang of Thugs—an almost impossible task for a magistrate burdened with daily work, criminal and civil—with the hordes of pleaders, litigants, accused and witnesses milling around his court and calling for justice. And to so fine a pitch of skill had Thugs through generations raised their power to deceive, that few if any villagers or *thanadars* knew any details of the murders in their localities.

Worst of all, Sleeman found himself up against a British wall of avowed disinterest, even hostility towards any organised investigation. Government House, and most of his fellow magistrates, argued that if Thugs existed, and there was no proof, they were members of a religious fraternity; and Company policy was not to interfere. Thus, apart from a few notable exceptions among fellow magistrates Sleeman was almost alone in his determination to stem the flood of murders.

Of this early investigation we know little beyond his word that these years at Narsinghpore were "by far the most laborious of my life"; while Vincent Smith refers to his "unremitting reports" to the Government about Thuggee. We can only guess at the chronic frustration he had to endure. We do not even know when it was that he caught the first Thug; only that information given to him by one of his police officials about the presence of a gang of thirty in the near by district of Jubbulpore led to their arrest by Sleeman's friend Charles Fraser. They were tried not by one of the sessions judges, but by Mr Wilder, Agent to the Governor-General for the region, and possibly for this reason convicted, for the judges at that time would rarely convict Thugs on the evidence obtainable. Compared with what was to come, they were dealt with leniently, two being hanged, the remainder either transported for life or given limited imprisonment. Sleeman questioned closely those of them willing to talk about their secrets and it was from these first captive Thugs that he obtained the information for his reports to the Government.

Analysing the conditions that enabled Thugs to flourish, he also pointed out in these reports that bankers and merchants sent huge amounts of gold and silver across India to wherever the rate of exchange made for profit—usually by bearers without arms or escort; and sepoys going on leave with savings in their belts criss-crossed the country on the way home. These and other wayfarers entered towns only to buy their provisions, which they cooked under the shade of trees in wayside groves. They made no social contact with townsfolk which would have enabled them to be traced when they vanished. The roads passed through long stretches of jungle, and bypaths led away into the Thugs' chosen places of murder. It was the custom for travellers of the same caste to mix and talk freely. Thugs were used to feigning almost any caste and so they easily established confidence and led these victims into lonely places to be killed. Another factor was the willingness of landholders and rajahs to help Thugs by turning a blind eye to what went on in their domains if they were paid well enough for their trouble.

Sleeman also discovered that Thugs did not strangle with a sling, as Sherwood had said in his report, but, at least in central and northern India, usually with a strip of twisted yellow or white silk knotted in one corner with a silver coin consecrated to Kali. The strangler held the other end in his left or right hand. With a rapid flick of the wrist he threw the weighted end around the victim's throat from behind, caught it, tightened it, the knuckles pressing inwards, jerked with iron wrists born of long use, and within a few seconds the victim was dead.

Individual prowess as a strangler, or *bhutote*, was highly respected, speeding a Thug's ascent through the hierarchy to the rank of *jemadar*, but less daring Thugs upheld traditional methods needing two or three accomplices for holding the victim. Brahmins, the Hindu priestly caste, were often Thugs too, and they strangled like any others, even when their victims were also Brahmins. In the princely states Thugs made a point of becoming friendly with officials of high rank about the Court, freely admitting they were Thugs, ingratiating themselves by handsome presents and sometimes even revealing the names of travellers of rank whom they intended to kill.

Their methods of snaring unsuspecting travellers were elaborate. If the traveller suspected one small party he soon fell in with another, who seemed to enter into his feelings of distrust. The first party was apparently shaken off and the second then strangled him. If there was only one party of Thugs, or the travellers suspected and avoided them all, two or more Thugs whom they had not yet seen were ordered to keep them in sight, while contact was made with other members of the fraternity in an operation that might last a week or more before the victims were finally ensnared by the most practised inveiglers, and strangled.

When known to police or magistrates Thugs sometimes obtained sanctuary by enlisting in the armed forces of princes, or rajahs, or engaging in some other service until the danger was over. A great many of the most noted Thugs in India, Sleeman later discovered were in Scindia's regiments at Gwalior, and in those of the rulers of Oudepore, Jodpore, Jypore. It was impossible to seize them, because they made friends of the commandants by their presents, and their manners. Equally, Hindu princes hardly ever punished Thugs unless they had by some accident murdered some priest or public officer of the Court in whom they felt particularly interested. While their grief or resentment lasted the Thugs were punished, but no longer.

Thugs would never kill a tiger. They believed that no man who had violated this rule ever survived long afterwards. Equally, they believed that no tiger would ever kill a Thug, unless he had broken the rules by cheating some of the gang out of their just share of loot. Just possibly, a tiger might kill a tyro Thug not of good descent.

But most significant of all the information Sleeman gained was the Kali legend, the mainspring of Thuggee, the holy writ that inspired them to kill without fear. Thugs, who addressed Kali with the greatest reverence, called her Kankali, or the man-eater, representing her as swallowing huge drafts of blood from men and demons. Alone, she was shown as black and hideous, but in company with her husband always fair and beautiful, and, Sleeman continues:

> Once on a time the world was infested with a monstrous demon named Rukt Bij-dana, who devoured mankind as fast as they were created. So gigantic was his stature, that the deepest pools of the ocean reached no higher than his waist. This horrid prodigy Kali cut in twain with her sword, but from every drop of blood that fell to the ground there sprang a new demon. For some reason she went on destroying them, till the hellish brood multiplied so fast that she waxed hot and weary with her endless task. She paused for a while, and, from the sweat brushed off one of her arms, she created two men, to whom she gave a *rumal*, or handkerchief, and commanded them to strangle the demons. When they had slain them all, they offered to return the *rumal*, but the goddess bade them keep it and transmit it to their posterity, with the injunction to destroy all men who were not of their kindred.
>
> A tradition is current among Thugs, that about the period of the commencement of the Kali Yug [the nineteenth century],

Kali co-operated with them so far as to relieve them of the trouble of interring the dead bodies, by devouring them herself. On one occasion, after destroying a traveller, the body, as usual, was left unburied; and a novice, unguardedly looking behind him, saw the naked goddess in the act of feasting upon it, half of it hanging out of her mouth. She, upon this, declared that she would no longer devour those whom the Thugs slaughtered, but she condescended to present them with one of her teeth for a *pickaxe*, a rib for a knife, and the hem of her lower garment for a noose, and ordered them, for the future, to cut and bury the bodies of whom they destroyed.

White and yellow being considered the favourite colours of their patroness and those in which she is arrayed, the cloths for strangling are one or other of these to the exclusion, I believe, of all other colours.

Sleeman had already written of popular Hinduism's monstrous fictions and their uncritical acceptance by devotees. Now he had hit upon one that inspired an age-old society of assassins, Muslims as well as Hindus, despite the Prophet's law against murder. Later, he found out a great deal more about the almost occult hold Kali maintained over adherents of both faiths.

All the facts that he unearthed about the Thugs and their beliefs were presumably incorporated in the early reports he forwarded to the Government. But there is no evidence in the official records that their contents were circularised to magistrates and police in India; nor was anyone appointed to direct action against the Thugs. Sleeman's reports must have been pigeon-holed and destroyed, as were so many official records, by the white ants that infested Fort William, Calcutta.

From 1822 until 1828 was the period of Lord Amherst's undistinguished Governor-Generalship. Of him, Vincent Smith in the *Oxford History of India* noted that he "was not intellectually fit for his high office and ought not to have been appointed". And a qualified observer of the time remarked that the motto in Government circles, apart from revenue collection, appeared to be—"Do nothing, have nothing done and let nobody do anything".

Sleeman therefore grew to be regarded as a magistrate with a bee in his bonnet. Somewhat scornfully, he was nicknamed "Thuggee"

Sleeman. But being a man of unusually steadfast convictions, he was not discouraged. He had made up his mind that Thugs should as soon as humanly possible be seized, and the roads of India be made safe. And despite official discouragement he spoke of it as "a great undertaking" which would be "so beneficial to the people of India". But though he added to his knowledge of Thugs he made only isolated arrests of the fraternity, as year after year, the blazing heat of the dry season gave way to the steamy warmth and endless deluge of the monsoon months. In 1825, shortly after he was promoted Captain, aged thirty-seven, after fifteen years in India, Sleeman fell victim to malaria and became seriously ill.

5

Some Recognition

Sleeman's strong constitution saved him from an early grave. He recovered, took sick leave and sailed south to Mauritius, in the Indian Ocean, which, taken fifteen years earlier in the Napoleonic Wars, was still mainly French in language and customs. To his lifelong friend Charles Fraser in India he wrote a letter dated 17 August 1825 which speaks of the return of his energy: "I live here as comfortably as I could anywhere . . . but I should be infinitely more comfortable among you, for I abhor an idle life. . . ." Not for Sleeman the delights of lotus-eating, or the pleasures of love in this lush tropical island, for referring in a characteristically dispassionate tone to the other sex he continues:

> . . . there really is a vast number of pretty girls here and they all dress better than English girls of the same class in society, though they may fall short of them in more essential points. The morals are very lax and a man who has been much upon the town will perhaps point out half a dozen women of easy virtue in the most respectable ball room of the island—indeed, at a ball at Government House.

Sleeman was still little attracted by women and in no hurry to marry; but a later event adds a touch of irony to this comment.

His return to health and work coincided with a major swing in the British attitude to the responsibilities of governing India. In England, the followers of the Evangelical movement, led by William Wilberforce, and by Charles Grant, chairman of the

Company's directors, argued that India could and should be reformed by conversion to Christianity. In this view, they found themselves strange bedfellows with their normal opponents, the agnostic Radicals, who also believed in reform, but through western science and humanism. Both were in opposition to the conservative Utilitarians, who held that reform in India by outside agencies was an impossible dream.

By 1827 the Radicals and Evangelicals had won the day. The Company's refusal to allow Christian missionaries into India on the grounds of religious interference was reversed. The President of the Board of Control was actually advising the incoming Governor-General, Lord William Cavendish Bentinck: "We have a great moral duty to perform in India."

Many of the Company's officials in India responded to these remarkable developments. They began to realise the shame and disgrace of the Thug gangs, waging their secret warfare against society along India's dusty roads and in her humid jungles. Soon the Company's ledger men were in stubborn retreat, reformist views were fashionable and some attention was given at last to the secret, disregarded sore of Thuggee. As a result, in 1827 special responsibility for anti-Thug operations over a wide area of central India was given to Sleeman, but without any more authority or troops than he had already, while he still had to carry out his ordinary duties as a magistrate. In effect, the only change was that his office became a clearing house for information from other magistrates about Thugs. But at least there was official recognition that Thugs existed.

Perhaps the greatest problem facing Sleeman or any other magistrate who tried to arrest and try suspected Thugs was the attitude of the judges, most of whom invariably released the suspects on the grounds of lack of evidence. An extreme case was the reaction of Judge Elliot, the circuit judge then at Jubbulpore, central India, to a case of Thuggee sent for trial by W. A. Pringle, a magistrate. Even when the Government had at last shown signs of being opposed to Thugs, Elliot responded with blind prejudice and scorn.

Back from his usual early morning ride one day in May 1827, the judge entered his court. One can imagine the scene—litigants wrangling in Urdu, Hindustani and Persian; Hindu and Muslim lawyers plucking at his sleeve and entreating him to spare their clients from ruin, police pushing files of statements across his table and the prisoners clanking into the court in irons. Judge Elliot read out the facts of the case.* The servant of a magistrate, W. A. Pringle, returning from Calcutta with his master, had been murdered during the night by Thugs and thrown into the Ganges. The alleged Thugs, he read on, went into a godown, or grog shop, where they were said to have got drunk and to have quarrelled over the distribution of the loot. Three of them went to the police, confessed and accused the other four of murder and the entire gang was arrested on the orders of Mr Pringle by a police official, the Nazir Abdoloo Ullee. The statements of the informers and the testimony of the murdered man's widow were the only evidence against the accused.

The widow was called—a slight, shrinking figure in a drab sari with a shawl over her head—who was so frightened that she nearly dropped the cup of Ganges water when she whispered the oath. Judge Elliot began his judicial day by warning her that she had better speak the truth and if she did not she would be punished. These words made the widow tremble violently. Articles found on the accused—a ring, a necklace and some clothing, all of which she had already in the lower court testified as her husband's—were thrust before her.

"Were these articles your husband's property or were they not?" Judge Elliot demanded, but the widow was so frightened, both of him and the four accused Thugs glowering at her, that she lost all power of speech and sat mute and trembling.

The judge loudly repeated the question, translated into both Urdu and Hindustani, but again there was no reply. He repeated it once more and when there was still no answer he ordered the widow to be taken away and confined at his discretion. He read the statements of the informers of the court, then seeing that there was no further evidence, he gave the verdict that the case was not proved and released the four accused Thugs unconditionally.

He then ordered the three informers to be brought before him and, without, apparently, the formality of a charge, told them that they were Guilty of giving false evidence and that they had

* Reported in *Ramaseeana*, by William Sleeman.

created alarm in the country by spreading stories about an alleged sect called Thugs. He sentenced them each to five years' imprisonment—with fifteen lashes and the public humiliation of a five days' ride round the city of Jubbulpore mounted on an ass, facing the animal's behind. Warning them not to spread more rumours about Thugs when eventually they were released, he sent them off to the cells.

Judge Elliot then called for the Nazir, the Indian official who at the magistrate's orders had arrested the Thugs. To that innocent man's wonder he was first denounced for his part in the proceedings, even though it was Pringle's express order, then severely punished. "You are ruining the country by seizing innocent people in this manner," Judge Elliot said, and sentenced him to fourteen years' imprisonment, plus the indignity of exposure on an ass round the city.

Pringle later told Sleeman that his efforts in the case were "visited with the severest censure and both the Government and the Nizamut Adawlut (district high court) were led into the belief that there was no such gang of Thugs and that the crime, if it existed at all, was very limited in extent". Pringle said he had gathered much information about Thug gangs in his district, had started operations against them which at that time promised well, but which were subsequently baffled by Mr Elliot.

> All I then brought to light has proved to be true, and much more [he wrote], though it is melancholy to reflect on the loss of human life, which might have been prevented, had I obtained the credit of my assertions, and been allowed to prosecute my researches . . . which must have led to an exposure of Thuggee and to the apprehension of many of the Thugs themselves.

This conflict between magistrates and senior judges was of long standing. Quite early in the nineteenth century one or two energetic magistrates had arrested a few score Thugs and sent them for trial at the higher criminal court. Even though several Thugs had confessed and loot was found in their homes, the judges still declared that there was not enough evidence to prove them guilty. The judges regarded legal procedure as of supreme importance and were united in opposing changes to make it less liable to be rigged. Sleeman wrote later of these legal obstacles:

For some years we had been trying men accused of Thuggee, but they had almost invariably escaped. It had been difficult, to a degree perhaps not readily appreciable by English lawyers . . . to convict men upon clear judicial evidence of acts of Thuggee. The migratory character of the murder gangs—the vast extent of country which they traversed—the number of local screens and fences—the difficulty of personal identification—the craft and subtlety of the offenders themselves—the unlimited amount of false swearing and of false impersonations which, at any time, they could bring into our criminal courts, were obstructions to the course of justice, under a strict interpretation of the existing law, which were seldom or never overcome.

A timid, or even a cautious—perhaps I ought to write a "conscientious"—judge would be sure to acquit even a notorious Thug for want of satisfactory evidence. . . . Some of the causes I have mentioned contributed largely, also to the embarrassment of the question of jurisdiction. A murder is committed in one part of the country and the murderers are apprehended in another, perhaps some hundreds of miles distant from the scene of the atrocity. To limit jurisdiction in such a case to the particular district in which the crime was committed was to throw up all sorts of difficulties and delays, and to ensure the prisoner's escape. These impediments to the strict and prompt administration of justice were wonderfully protective of Thuggee.

The more complicated the machinery and the more formal the procedure of our courts, the better for these professional stranglers. They thrived upon the legal niceties and the judicial reserve of the English tribunals and laughed our regulations to scorn.

Sleeman tried to force the hand of the government against the judiciary by reporting what he had discovered about the social links of Thuggee—how many Indian landholders, from zemindar to raja, gave Thugs good character references when they were charged; how they paid the financial security without which the Thugs faced indefinite imprisonment. These protectors of Thugs usually knew little or nothing about the mass murders and had no wish to know.

In return Thugs paid the landholders huge rents for small plots of land they leased to camouflage themselves as cultivators. On returning from a safari, they gave valuable presents from their loot—pearls, rubies, diamonds, fabulous swords, fine horses: and they assured their patrons they would not compromise them by killing too near home.

Many Indians of rank pretended to punish Thugs but in fact practised extortion. When one of his zemindars arrested a Thug gang, the Maharajah of Gwalior sent two field guns and the equivalent of a brigade of troops against him. Men on both sides were killed and the fighting lasted several hours before the Thugs were surrendered. Later the Maharajah himself released them after payment of a heavy ransom. Another chief seized a gang, flogged the youngest to make him say who had been murdered and what loot had been taken, then blackmailed gang leaders.

Inevitably, Sleeman's progress was slow. By 1827 only some 300 Thugs—two large gangs—had been convicted, and the Thugs admitted later that they had not been in the least disturbed at the efforts the British were mounting against them. To so fine a pitch of skill had they through generations raised their power to deceive that few if any villagers or *thanadars* knew any details about the murders in their localities. Here is a description, based on the official record, of the murder of an Indian official and his family, in Sleeman's district, at this time.

> Bunda Alee, together with his wife and year-old baby, was escorting his fourteen-year-old daughter to her wedding to a young landowner at Indore, 300 miles away to the west. He was accompanied by a retinue of six servants and bodyguards.
>
> They had crossed dusty plains and dark jungles and by the fifth day it had become wearisome. Fond of his wife and daughter as he was, Bunda Alee felt the need for lively company. A party of prosperous-looking merchants overtook him, and after a respectful greeting stayed to talk. By coincidence, the merchants were travelling to the city of Indore as well. Bunda Alee was delighted—these urbane and sophisticated strangers would help to make the time go quickly. They rode together for the next two days and like people on holiday who might never normally meet, the two groups became friends.

On the third evening they camped together in a small grove curtained by tall trees between a jungle of plumed white grass and an open sun-baked plain. It was nearly dusk when Bunda Alee had eaten and, with his sword at his side, had seated himself at his tent door, while his wife and daughter busied themselves within. Here he was joined by several of the merchants. Two of them twanged a stringed instrument, the sitar, and sang songs. Bunda Alee saw with an increased sense of security a company of red-coated sepoys and their mounted British officers marching towards them across the plain. About 100 yards away they halted and, bugles shrilling, began to pitch camp. The merchants played their instruments louder. Their companions at the far end of the grove joined in the song at the tops of their voices. Grooms shouted angrily at two horses which had strayed towards the military lines. It was a noisy scene.

Suddenly, one of the travelling companions sitting beside him seized Bunda Alee's sword, and from behind two others gripped his arms. Bunda Alee managed to shake off the grip and sprang up, shouting loudly for his servants as he turned to the tent for another weapon. One man seized his legs, another grabbed his arms, like a whip something flashed round his throat and tightened. "Murder! Murder!" his servants shouted, but they too were seized. Bunda Alee struggled convulsively, gave a frantic last heave for life and fell dead.

A man named Ghubbil Khan flicked the *rumal* round the throat of Bunda Alee's wife as she ran out of the tent with her baby in her arms. She fell with her baby beside her husband's body. Ghubbil Khan admired the pretty child as he tucked his *rumal* in his waistband. He picked it up and held it in his arms. From the tent door two more Thugs emerged dragging the body of Bunda Alee's fourteen-year-old daughter, the bride of tomorrow, her long black hair trailing in the dust. The sitar twanged loudly and the rest of the Thugs sang the haunting songs at the tops of their voices. Suspecting nothing, 100 paces away the soldiers were still pitching their tents.

Gravediggers in the Thug gang, had dug two holes a few yards away in the tall grass, to which they now dragged mother, father, daughter and servants. They then robbed their victims, stripped them, broke their joints, pressed them down into the holes and made great gashes in the bodies—blood could be spilt in the grave, though not outside it, Kali had decreed. Ghubbil Khan still held the baby girl. "She is mine," he is reported to have said. "I'll bring her up and marry her to my son."

The Thugs shook their heads disapprovingly. "A child from parents of such exalted rank would be recognised and lead to our discovery," warned Durgha Jemadar, chief of the gang. Ghubbil Khan threw the child down on to the bodies of its parents and the earth was hastily shovelled down.

The Thugs burnt the tell-tale possessions of their victims which had no value and stole off before dawn. The company of sepoys and British officers camping only one hundred yards away saw and heard nothing, so efficiently and quietly was the murder executed. Nor were the Thugs in the least disturbed by the arrival of the troops. Murder was for them a fine art, with its own rules, spontaneously brought into play as circumstances changed.

Sleeman was cut off from all knowledge of killings like these, carried out during Thug expeditions which operated on lines based on centuries of experience—even when they occurred within sight of his own court house. Thuggee, as its Hindu meaning of *deceivers* implies, signified not merely to kill, but first to deceive, an almost hypnotic power that dominated in Thugs all normal human qualities. It was reinforced by callousness, or mindlessness, allied to emotional and moral insensibility, that schizoid state which makes men sometimes like lumps of clay and at other times capable of normal behaviour. Thugs, in the towns and villages where they lived as normal social beings were, Sleeman noted, "commonly the most scrupulous in the discharge of their duties in all relations of life—the most liberal promotors of social enjoyment, and the most rigid observers of everything relating to caste and religion".

They were among the most devoted husbands and fathers, yet they murdered women and children without turning a hair. Sleeman once asked a prominent Muslim Thug named Sahib Khan, among those in prison, how this was possible. "From the time that the omens have been favourable", came the reply, "we consider them as victims thrown into our hands by the deity to be killed—and that we are the mere instruments in her hands to destroy them—and that if we do not kill them she will never again be propitious to us and we and our families will have to endure misery and want." Religious fanaticism combined with material need underlay this answer, yet if Thugs had been really pious devotees of Kali, they would have obeyed her order never to strangle priests and holy men. Sometimes they disobeyed.

A gang commanded by Cheyne Jemadar and Runjeet Jemadar rested in the village of Kurnal to perform their devotions in the sacred waters. Later, riding out of the village, they overtook two holy men with long unkempt beards and emaciated bodies covered with rags and white ash, both riding on ponies. As they rode ahead the Thugs discussed whether to strangle them.

Cheyne Jemadar said: "Were we not taken in by the fine clothes of the party we murdered near Mooltan? What profit then can we expect from travellers dressed in rags?"

"Such heresy!" said Runjeet Jemadar. "The goddess has put them into our hands and we have no right to let them go."

"True—there is no reason to spare them," nodded Bukshir, a celebrated strangler. "I will give 100 rupees for their ponies and whatever other property they possess." The ponies being worth about half this sum, the offer was thought sportsmanlike. The death of the holy men was decreed.

The party slowed down to allow the victims to catch up and Cheyne Jemadar began talking to them. Together they rode into the village of Turowlee where both parties took lodgings for the night in the serai (accommodation for man and beast). Cheyne Jemadar invited the holy men to a lavish dinner, and since a few grains of rice were the normal daily ration of these fakirs, they gratefully accepted, blessing their benefactors for their goodness. Thugs dearly loved time spent in relaxed enjoyment with victims about to die, behaving as if their lives stretched years ahead. They sat now on the rush-carpeted floor relishing the taste of death more than food. It made them feel like gods to have the fate of men like these in their hands. Seduced by the array of tempting dishes, the holy men's restraint slipped away and they ate heartily. The Thugs caught each other's eyes and guffawed inwardly. Towards midnight the holy men belched out a blessing and staggered off to bed, agreeing with their hosts to set out together early in the morning.

The Thugs had already chosen the murder site—a narrow track bordered by high grass two miles out of the village. Just before dawn they set off. Cheyne Jemadar assigned four Thugs to each victim—one beside the bridle, two beside the right-hand stirrup to seize the victim and one in reserve beside the left stirrup. The party neared the chosen spot, but the Thugs' easy talk flowed on. Bukshir was praising the holy men for unremitting devotion to their beliefs when Cheyne Jemadar gave the *Jhirnee*, or signal to kill. Bukshir whipped his *rumal* round the neck of the fakir he was flattering and stopped talking only when some seconds later the victim lay dead on the ground beside his companion, killed by Runjeet Jemadar.

Bukshir distributed his 100 rupees among the gang, taking for himself an unexpected 75 rupees found on the bodies, and the two ponies.

Everyone was satisfied, and even those Thugs who stubbornly brought up the fact of Kali's law were persuaded by Cheyne Jemadar that they had undoubtedly brought the holy men a speedy passage to Paradise, so that no blame could be attached to the murder.

Killing thus became insensate, beyond faith or feeling. No pity, or mercy, broke this solidarity for death, not even, when faced by youth and beauty—by boys on life's threshold.

One evening in 1826, Nuthee Khan lodged his Thug gang in a serai near Jypore for the night. Shortly before dark, a handsome Muslim boy aged about fifteen and wearing gold earrings set with pearls, took rooms for the night. He had four young male attendants with him. The physical attractiveness of the boy and his companions, their costly clothes and their youthful charm alike fascinated Nuthee Khan and excited in him an overwhelming desire to kill them all.

Adept at insinuating himself with strangers, establishing friendly terms with these boys was child's play, and soon he found out that the boy who attracted him so much was the son of a landowner some distance away, returning with his four attendants from a visit to his uncle. Gravely, he warned them of the dangers of the roads and suggested that they should travel with him and his friends, all of whom, he said, were honest merchants.

The boys trusted him without question and for two days, while seeking a suitable time and place for the murder, Nuthee Khan and his gang rode with them, enjoying their youthful high spirits, listening to what they said of their hopes and dreams. On the third evening, Nuthee Khan found lodgings for them in a shop whose owners secretly helped Thugs and shared in their loot—the shopkeepers kept an eye on the boys that night while the Thugs went off to the serai to meet a party of dancing-girls.

By late evening, a Thug named Bikka had found a suitable murder place and Nuthee Khan had chosen as stranglers himself, Bikka, Kureema and three others, with several assistants. Nuthee Khan awoke the boys before daylight and hurried them on to the road, with the excuse that the next stopping place was far distant and they must make haste. He wanted the murder done in the safety of darkness. An hour later they reached the place and Nuthee Khan suggested it was time to rest and eat. A carpet was spread, the boys sat down and the stranglers arranged themselves suitably, chatting as they did so about the journey ahead. Dawn filtered through the trees and the landowner's young son, whose physical attractiveness Nuthee Khan still admired as he sat beside him, remarked upon the beauty of the scene. He had his last glimpse of it, for Nuthee Khan shouted: "If the lads are here give them tobacco!" Nuthee Khan's *rumal* and those of his helpers flashed round the boys' necks and though they struggled with all terrible desperation of youth, within seconds they lay dead, face downwards.

Apart from the perverted pleasure they got out of their kill, the Thugs acquired a fine horse, a pair of earrings set with two large pearls in each, and 250 rupees (£25). Nuthee Khan paid the gang 40 rupees for the boy's mare and sold her for 60.

The outcome of this story shows how little Thugs had to fear from relatives, for a few weeks later, the uncle of the murdered boy set out in search of him, tracing him as far as the shop in the village of Dowsa where the party had stayed the night. A week afterwards, the Thugs returned and saw a man sitting weeping in front of the shop. He was the boy's uncle, and he had been sitting there for the past week. Eventually, jackals dug up the bodies and death by strangulation was established. The father of one of the boys refused ever to eat again and died within a few days. But not until years later was the identity of the murderers established by Sleeman.

More than most of the numerous reports of Thug murders this one shows what a terrible scourge—what a cruel enigma—was Thuggee, whose baffling silence about its victims distilled human grief throughout a lifetime.

Still denied any real aid from the Government, despite its apparent recognition of the fact of Thuggee, Sleeman meantime questioned one after the other all the Thugs who were arrested in central India, so as to build up as thorough a picture of their customs and habits as possible.

6

Thug Lore

How was it that young men were drawn into Thuggee? What kept it alive through the centuries? How were the leaders, or jemadars, chosen? And how much attention was really paid to Kali's rituals, omens and signs among Thugs? These were a few of the questions Sleeman put to those captured Thugs willing to talk. He had their answers carefully recorded, translated into English and eventually published in India in 1836, with the title *Ramaseeana.*

A Thug whom Sleeman asked how the rank of Jemadar was acquired explained that first and foremost he would be a strong and resolute man whose ancestors had been Thugs for generations and who also knew how to raise enough money to provide for a gang for a month or two. He would have influence over local authorities, or the Indian officials at courts of justice and it would be desirable for him to be of good presence and appearance, so that he could pose as a man of rank.

While such a man could gather around him the fifty or so Thugs needed for a gang, much higher qualifications were required for the rank of Subahdar of Thugs. A Muslim Thug named Nasir Khan whom Sleeman questioned on this point named Sheikh Amed as the most able leader:

> He has sixty fully initiated Thugs (Borkas) who pretend to be recruits for regiments. He is thoroughly acquainted with the drill of the Company's regiments and their military terms and can speak English. Other Thug leaders generally display their wealth in an ostentatious appearance that betrays them. Sheikh

Amed is 60 years of age, and willing to go about for months cooking his own food, walking and living like the poorest man, while he can command the services of a hundred.

Among hereditary Thug families, sons were initiated slowly and carefully. They were kept completely ignorant of their fathers' trade at first, but as they grew older and stronger were allowed to accompany expeditions, though kept away from the actual scene of murder. Gradually, by a method of brainwashing perfected through generations an adolescent would be drawn into the net.

Sleeman asked a Thug informant named Sahib Khan:

"At what age do you initiate them?"

"I was initiated by my father when I was only 13."

"Have you any rule as to the age?"

"None. A father is sometimes avaricious and takes his son out very young merely to get his share of the booty, for the youngest boy gets as much in his share as the oldest man."

"How soon do you let them see your operations?"

"The first expedition they neither see nor hear anything of murder. They don't know our trade, they get presents, bought out of their share, and become fond of the wandering life, as they are always mounted on ponies. Before the end of the journey they know that we rob. The next expedition they suspect that we kill and some of them even know it. And in the third expedition they see all."

"Don't they become frightened?"

"Not after the second or third expeditions."

Another Thug interposed with a different story:

"About twelve years ago my cousin Aman Subahdar took with us for the first time my cousin Kurhora, a lad of fourteen. He was mounted on a pretty pony and Hursooka, an adopted son of Aman's, was given charge of him. We fell in with five Sikhs and before we set out before daylight, Hursooka was ordered to keep the boy out of sight and hearing. Kurhora became impatient, got away from Hursooka and galloped up at the instant the *Jhirnee* [the leader's signal to murder] was given. He heard the screams of the men and saw them all strangled. He was seized with trembling, fell from his pony and became delirious. He was terrified at the sight of the turbans and the murdered men and when anyone touched or spoke to him he talked about the murders and screamed exactly like a boy in his sleep.

"We couldn't get him to move and after burying the bodies Aman and I and a few others sat by him while the gang went on. We were very fond of him and tried all we could to tranquillize him, but he never recovered his senses and before evening he died. I have seen many instances of feelings greatly shocked at the sight of the first murder, but never one so strong as this. Kurhora was a very fine boy. Hursooka took his death much to heart and became a monk. He is now at some temple on the bank of the Narbada river."

The contrast between this Thug's trade of murder and his affection for the unhappy boy must have caused Sleeman to wonder how Thug children and fathers felt towards each other, for he then asked: "Do your children reverence their Thug fathers, like other sons, even after they know about their trade?"

The answer was brief and emphatic: "The same. We love them and they love us the same."

Such apparent conflicts and inconsistencies were part of the Thug personality. Whatever his feelings about his son's intellectual capacities or the heights to which he might rise as a normal member of society, a Thug father had no other course but progressively so to degrade and brutalise him that Thuggee would seem the best and easiest life.

Boys in their teens would first be employed as scouts, then as sextons, both grave-digging and butchering the victims. After this they became *shumseeas*, or hand-holders, and finally *bhurtotes*, or stranglers, who were, if well born, regarded as members of the Thug aristocracy. Only those youths who were naturally courageous enough and who had also, in the course of their bloody apprenticeship, become inhuman or demented enough not to be put off by the horror of being steeped in murder for life were candidate stranglers.

Such a youth sought out the oldest and most experienced strangler in the gang with the request that he would become his *guru*, or teacher, instruct him in the art of the *rumal* and preside over the religious rites by which he was to be confirmed in his unholy calling. When the *guru* was satisfied that this teenager was of the stuff of which man-killers were made, he agreed, and began the course of instruction—first, in tying the silver rupee with the classic knot in one end of the strip of yellow silk. The strangler who learned this correctly tied a knot with the end of the *rumal* hidden in it, while the badly taught one left the end out—it was more secure for his less skilful hand.

Having mastered the art of the lightning-like handling of the *rumal*, the young strangler was ready for his first murder, of perhaps hundreds, and the jemadar of the gang was so told. Careful precautions were taken to make sure that there was no bungling—he would be told to choose an elderly traveller or some other weakling. While the traveller slept, with the gang waiting at their places round him, the teacher took his disciple a little distance away, with three or four older members. Together they took the auspices. If they had no sign the candidate would have to wait and some other Thug would strangle the weakling traveller, but if they had a favourable sign within thirty minutes, Kali was believed to have given her sanction. They would then return in high spirits to where the sleeping traveller awaited his death. The *guru* quietly twisted a new strip of yellow silk and tied the knot himself around the consecrated silver rupee. Respectfully, the disciple received it in his right hand, took up his position slightly behind and to one side of the victim. The *shumseeas* now shook the sleeper vigorously to rouse him for slaughter. As he sat up his hands were seized, the apprentice whipped the *rumal* round his neck and killed him.

Far from feeling remorse or pity, the killer was said to feel only the delight. He had become one of those privileged to murder for Kali, the Black Mother, and, says Sleeman, it was the most memorable day of his life:

> He bows down before his *guru* and touches his feet with both hands and does the same to all his relations and friends present, in gratitude for the honour he has attained. He opens the knot . . . takes out the rupee and gives it with all the other silver he has, to his *guru*, as a *nuzur* (gift); and the *guru*, adding what money he has at the time, purchases a rupee and a quarter's worth of *goor*

> (coarse sugar) for the ceremony of the *tuponee*, and lays out the rest in sweetmeats. . . . On his return home after the expedition, the newly qualified strangler gives a feast to his *guru* and all his family; and if he has the means, to all his relations; and he presents his *guru* with a new suit of clothes for himself and one for his wife. . . . The *guru* after a certain interval returns the compliment to him and his family, and the relationship between them is ever after respected as the most sacred that can be formed. A Thug would often rather betray his father than the *guru* by whom he had been knighted.

The *tuponee* was a sacrificial ritual to Kali performed as soon as possible after every murder. The coarse yellow sugar was placed on a carpet spread upon a clean, fresh spot in the jungle or forest. The Thugs placed on it a consecrated pickaxe and a piece of silver for an offering, which would in due course be handed over to Kali's priests. The most esteemed Thug, who was also believed to be most in favour with Kali, and learned in the ways of propitiating her, sat down on the edge of the carpet with his face to the west. The most accomplished stranglers in the gang sat down on each side of him looking in the same direction. The rest of the gang arranged themselves on the ground surrounding the carpet.

The leading Thug then made a hole in the ground, and having put into it a little of the sugar, clasped his hands in a devotional attitude, and raising his eyes heavenwards prayed to Kali to "fulfil our desires". The gang fervently repeated the words of the prayer after their leader, who, sprinkling a little water on the pickaxe and in the hole, put a little of the sugar into the hand of every Thug seated beside him. One of the gang then gave the signal for strangling, just as if they were about to kill. The Thugs on the carpet ate in solemn silence and the most perfect stillness prevailed until these privileged killers had swallowed the sugar and drunk a little water. The sugar was then distributed as consecrated food to all the gang entitled by rank to it and they ate it with silent reverence. Only Thugs who had strangled with their own hands were thought worthy of sugar that had been blessed by the prayers of celebrated stranglers. For those outsiders whom youth or fear or incapacity had denied the honour of strangling their trusting fellow men, some unconsecrated sugar was set aside.

The effects of the consecrated sugar were believed to be irresistible. Although only practised stranglers were authorised to eat it, if there was any young disciple whose advance was desired, a little of it would be secretly given him in the belief that he would progress rapidly thereafter. Sleeman once asked a Thug if, after a particularly treacherous murder, he had not felt pity, and the answer came: "We all feel pity sometimes, but the *goor* of the *tuponee* changes our nature. It would change the nature of a horse. Let any man once taste of that *goor* and he will be a Thug, though he know all the trades and have all the wealth in the world."

Fantastic though this belief may seem, intensity of religious belief, as we know, can dominate men's actions. Christians celebrating Holy Communion believe that the wine and the water they partake of is changed into the flesh and blood of Christ, which should make them become like Him in their lives.

Thugs worshipped the monstrous Kali. It has been suggested that she was the man-eating tiger of India deified during the development of religion from animism to anthropomorphism. In this we find a possible meaning for the *goor*. It might be thought to confer on them the same cruelty and savagery for which they could hope after eating tiger's flesh and assimilating the animal's nature. Only in the most exceptional circumstances would Thugs hunt down, kill a tiger and eat its flesh; it would need more time and risk than for Thuggee. The sugar, yellow like the tiger, could in the distant past have been accepted as a suitable substitute until in the course of time its origin was forgotten.

Other rites and sacrifices besides the *tuponee* were offered to Kali by the worshipping Thugs. Most important was the ritual of consecrating the pickaxe with which they dug their victims' graves. A curved blade of wrought iron about ten inches long, it was sharply pointed at one end and had a round hole for a wooden shaft at the other. The Thug most skilled in ceremonies received it on a brass dish while sitting on a carpet in front of a shallow pit. He then would pour water from a brass jug over it into the pit, take more water sweetened with consecrated sugar and pour this over it. The turbaned Thugs would sit silent and motionless watching him mark seven red spots on the blade and then place it on the brass dish beside incense, sandalwood and a coco-nut. He would light a fire of dried cow dung, throw on it melted butter, the sandalwood, herbs and incense. The aromatic smoke would rise and the Thugs inhale it with satisfaction.

As the flames leapt up the master of ceremonies would take the pickaxe blade and boldly pass it several times through the fire. He would remove the shell of the coco-nut, place it on the ground and shout—"Shall I strike?" There would be a loud cry of approval and he would then shout in a devout voice: "All hail mighty Kali, great mother of us all!" With the butt end of the pickaxe, he would strike the coco-nut and shatter it in pieces. "All hail mighty Kali—and prosper the Thugs!" was the correct response then.

He would next wrap the pickaxe blade in a piece of clean white cloth, place it on the ground facing west and bow low it to. All in turn would then salaam to the consecrated blade—Kali's tooth. They then shared the coco-nut—it was probably a substitute for the flesh of a human sacrifice offered to Kali up to the beginning of the nineteenth century. Finally, everyone washed hands and faces and made ready to take the auspices. The ritual of the pickaxe related to one safari only. At the outset of every fresh safari it would be repeated.

Not every Thug was trusted with the safe-keeping of the pickaxe. It was highly venerated and given to the Thug most noted for sobriety, shrewdness and caution. During a journey he carried it concealed in his waistband, but in camp it was buried pointing in the direction in which the gang were going. Thugs firmly believed that if another direction was more likely to bring victims, the point would by morning be found to be pointing this way.

This veneration of the pickaxe would seem to have its roots in the animistic belief that tools and weapons achieve their ends owing to inherent qualities of their own, rather than those built into them by whoever designed and made them, or the strength and skill of the human hand using them. Thugs believed that after Kali had blessed their pickaxe it was a living thing. When it was buried nobody dared tread on the ground above, nor might it be touched by any unclean man or by an animal. It was purified after every grave made with it.

Formerly, they used to throw it into a well at night rather than bury it and believed that when summoned with the proper rites it would come up of itself, but since they began to neglect Kali's orders it had lost this virtue. Sleeman doubted whether anyone had ever seen this happen. The Thug he was interrogating replied:

> "It is true—quite true. We have seen the sacred pickaxe spring in the morning from the well into which it had been thrown overnight, and come to the hands of the man who carried it, at his call. Nay, we have seen the pickaxes of several gangs all come up of themselves, from the same well at the same time, and go to the hands of their bearers."
>
> "Yes [Sleeman said], and you have all seen the common jugglers by sleight of hand appear to turn pigeons into serpents and serpents into rabbits, but all know that they do it by their skill and not by the aid of any goddess. The man who carries your pickaxe is chosen for his skill, and earns extra. No doubt he can, in the same way, make it seem that the axe appears of itself when he draws it out by his sleight of hand."
>
> "What?" cried a Thug named Nasir. "Cannot a hundred generations of Thugs tell the tricks of man from the miracles of God? Is there not the difference of heaven and earth between them? Isn't one a mere trick and the other a miracle—witnessed by hundreds assembled at the same time?"
>
> "Sahib Khan—you are more sober than Nasir—have you ever seen it?"
>
> "On one expedition only."
>
> "Who were the pickaxe bearers?"
>
> "Imman Khan and his brother. During this expedition I repeatedly heard them call in the morning at the well into which they had thrown the pickaxes overnight. I saw the pickaxes come up of themselves from the wells and fall into their aprons, which they held open *thus*."
>
> "And you never saw any of your own gang do this?"
>
> "Never. I have thugged for twenty years and never saw it."
>
> "How do you account for it?"
>
> "That they attend more to omens and regulations than we do."

The Thug regulations and omens affecting the pickaxe were strict. Should anyone drop it, the omen was dreadful—the gang believed that he would either be killed that year or they would suffer some great misfortune. He was deprived of office at once and the gang went back home and reconsecrated the pickaxe. But the wrath of Kali was hard to assuage. Thugs belonging to such a gang were regarded as "doomed ones" and among the fraternity were ostracised.

Only an oath sworn on the pickaxe was capable of binding a Thug irrevocably. Compared with it, oaths sworn by Muslims on the Koran and by Hindus by the Ganges water were, strange to relate, far less binding.

> "Tell me—now, while you are in custody [Sleeman asked], which oath do you Muslim Thugs think the strongest—that upon the Koran, or that upon the pickaxe?"
>
> "If we could be allowed to consecrate the pickaxe in the proper way," answered Nasir, "neither the Koran nor anything else on earth could be so binding. But it would be of no use without consecration."
>
> Sahib Khan said: "If any man swears a falsehood upon a properly consecrated pickaxe, he will die a horrid death. His head will turn round, his face towards the back and he will writhe in agony until he dies."
>
> "Have you seen this?"

All those present, even the most intelligent and educated, agreed that they had seen it happen to Thugs who had been foolish enough to underrate the power of such an oath. Thugs even venerated this implement of burial above the *rumal*, the instrument for strangling, thinking of it with enthusiasm as the greatest source of their prosperity and security. The *rumal*, after all, only represented the hem of Kali's garment, but the pickaxe represented one of her own teeth. Another Thug demanded,

> "Do we not worship it every seventh day? Is it not our standard? Is its sound ever heard, when digging the grave, by any but a Thug?"
>
> "No other tool would answer, you think, for making the graves?"
>
> "How could we dig graves with any other instrument? This is the one appointed by Kali, and consecrated. We should never have survived any attempt to use anything else. No man but a Thug who has been a strangler and is remarkable for his cleanliness and personal decorum, is permitted to carry it."

The pickaxe was the great symbol of the Thug secret society, but their veneration for it was only one of the superstitions by which they steeled themselves to face the continuous horror of their lives, and became, in their own words "hard-breasted enough to Thug".

No Thug gang ever set out on a safari without first solemnly taking the auspices. For this purpose they engaged one of Kali's priests, who sat on a carpet kept for these rituals with the gang leader and four Thugs whose fellows regarded them as men of the highest character—though killing, the worst of crimes and the biggest sin, was their sacred duty, oddly enough lesser moral lapses disgraced Thugs. The rest of the gang sat around outside the carpet, doubtless watching the fateful ritual with no less anxiety than gamblers the croupier's hand on the roulette wheel.

The jemadar handed a brass plate with rice, wheat and two silver coins on it to the priest, and respectfully asked him what would be the proper day to start the safari. After due search and ceremony the priest disclosed the day, the hour and the direction. On the day, they again assembled. In his right hand the jemadar held a brass jug of water by the lip and in his left hand, against his breast, a clean white handkerchief containing one silver and two copper coins, five pieces of turmeric and the consecrated pickaxe.

The priest now led the way to a field or garden outside the village and stopped in a secluded place. The jemadar, still holding the pickaxe and the brass jug, while facing in the same direction, with his mind abstracted from earthly things—concentrated on the goddess—cried: "Great Goddess! Universal mother! If this our meditated safari is fitting in thy sight, vouchsafe us help, and the signs of thy approbation!"

All the Thugs present repeated this prayer after the leader and joined in the praises and worship of the goddess. They then waited anxiously and if within thirty minutes they saw or heard a favourable omen from the left, it meant that she had taken them by the left hand to lead them on. If it was followed by one on the right, they rejoiced, because it signified that Kali had taken them by the right hand too. But despite the priest's choice of the day, if they heard a bad omen the gang went home, the priest chose another day and the auspices were taken again.

After getting favourable omens, the leader sat meditating on the goddess for seven hours while the gang made preparations for the safari. When all was ready, they set out in the precise direction and accomplished the first stage of their journey by nightfall. Here they awaited good omens from right and left. They rode or walked next morning to the nearest water and there ate a little coarse sugar and dal. From then on any bad omen could be averted by sacrifices and offerings, but any bad omen before this meant returning home and opening the safari anew. If the jemadar were to drop the brass water jug, all were certain he would die within a year.

The sound of weeping for the dead on leaving the village or the funeral of anyone there threatened overwhelming evil, though a corpse from any other village augured good, as did a party of friends weeping round a woman leaving her parents' house to go to her husband's. It was fatal to start a safari in July, September or December, or on a Wednesday or Thursday, and forbidden by Kali to kill Brahmins, religious mendicants or holymen and bards, for their sanctity; sweepers, washerwomen, maimed or sick people for their impurity. A traveller wearing gold ornaments was protected from strangling during the first week of a safari by the metal's sacred character.

Even after surmounting these initial hurdles, Thugs were still not free to kill and rob as they pleased, for from moment to moment good and bad omens checked or encouraged them. No Thug ever went without his turban—for primitive people believed the head held the soul. If a turban caught fire, of all things, great evil threatened and the gang went back home and waited seven days, though if they were a few hundred miles away, an offering could be made and the guilty one alone returned. Even if a Thug's turban fell off it was a bad omen needing sacrifices to propitiate Kali.

Belief in the significance of omens, though it may seem absurd in the twentieth century, is quite logical and reasonable in the primitive religious context of animism, with its notions that all things—rocks, trees, mountains and rivers as well as birds, reptiles, insects and animals—had souls that influenced the lives of men. As R. V. Russell reminds us in *Tribes and Castes of the Central Provinces of India*:

> Animals such as the tiger and the cow and imposing objects such as sun, moon, high mountains were the principal gods and later their spirits developed into anthropomorphic gods. Even lesser animals and birds were revered and thought able to affect the lives of men. Hence, their appearance, flight, and cries were naturally taken to be direct indications afforded by the god to worshippers.

Augury, or the science of omens, was the interpretation of these signs given by the divine beings surrounding man. Thugs thought the ass the most meaningful source of omens—it was the sacred animal of Sitala, the Hindu goddess of smallpox, who was associated with Kali. And it was a maxim of augury that an ass was equal to 100 birds in importance, just as it was more significant than any of the other quadrupeds. If they heard it bray on the left at the start of a safari and soon after repeated on the right, they believed that nothing on earth could prevent their success. While they were hunting human victims the ass was a valuable guide. If while they were in camp it brayed from the left they must go on at once, but if from the right all was well. If it approached them braying from the front it was a very bad omen and was called *mathaphore*, the "head-breaker".

Four-footed animals thronged the jungles and forests of central India, in particular the Saugur and Narbada Territories where Thugs were so very active. The movements and cries of almost any of them could send a Thug in the opposite direction, or stay his hand when about to strangle. Wolves crossing the road from left to right threatened great evil, but from right to left they promised good. Their howling during the day signalled danger and Thugs had at once to quit the region. Called the *weeping of the wolf*, this howling was particularly dangerous between midnight and daylight. Jackals were even worse—a pair of them crossing the road in front of the gang, from whatever direction, threatened prison and chains, yet oddly enough a single one going from right to left promised good fortune. The cries of jackals in daytime, especially a short call, like a bark, threatened so much evil that a gang would fly from the place in which they heard it, turning their backs on victims however much loot they promised. No less evil was the noise of jackals fighting, for this evil animal, which made its lair among ruins and played the part of a scavenger, naturally foretold great harm.

Yet the harmless hare, strangely enough, threatened even more harm than the jackal. It was a bad omen should one run across the road from either direction, yet contrariwise good if its call were heard on the left at night. If coming from the right, it was sinister; all travellers for whom death was intended were let go. So complete was this prohibition that were Thugs to disobey, it was said that they would find no loot on their victims, or what they did find would aid their ruin. More than this—Kali promised that they would in punishment die in the jungle and the hare would lap the rain water out of their skulls. The noise of wild cats fighting was good only during the first watch of the night. If heard later it was called "Kali's temper" and threatened the inevitable evil, while heard in daytime it was a warning of still greater misfortune.

Birds figured in the farago of Thug augury no less than animals. Two owls calling one to the other was a signal of ill, warning that intended victims should be allowed to live, while the gurgling cry of a large owl meant that they should suspend their journey for a few days. When they heard it on the left it indicated danger behind and they fled as far ahead as possible for two or three days; heard on the right it meant danger ahead and they should retreat. The loud chirping of the small owl while sitting promised good, but heard when the bird was flying it meant the opposite. A low soft call of this small owl, known as the *chireya*, always threatened great evil.

The kite's cry, heard in camp between the first watch and daybreak, was a dreadful omen, so bad that Thugs would get up and ride off at once, leaving untouched anyone, however rich, they had planned to kill. The croak of the large mountain crow was more complicated to interpret. Heard from a tree while the gang were in camp it promised a rich traveller there and they waited confidently for him to arrive. But were the crow to croak while on the back of a pig or buffalo or from any carcass or skeleton, the omen was evil. The partridge too did its bit with a warning cry. "If the partridge call at night or the jackal during the day, quit that country, or you will be seized," Thugs warned each other.

Various events involving blood and believed by primitive peoples to be unclean were believed to contaminate Thugs and bring them under the *itak*, or sign of ill-fortune, after which they would go back home and start afresh. If a mare dropped a foal while they were in camp they were contaminated. The birth of a child in a Thug family, the first periods of a Thug's daughter, the circumcision of a boy, marriage and the defloration of a virgin, and a dog, cat, cow or buffalo giving birth—all these events contaminated Thugs.

Thus, no Thug who heeded omens could ever think of himself as a free agent while his every act was dominated by the movements, cries and flight of the brute creation. He was in Kali's hands from start to finish of the safari. Other rules too, no pious Thug (that strange contradiction in terms) neglected. During the first week of a safari Thugs were forbidden to dress any food in ghee, eat any animal food except fish, have sexual intercourse, indulge in benevolent feelings or charity towards animals, have their clothes washed, shave, bathe or clean their teeth. But were they to kill within the first seven days Kali as a reward freed them from these restraints.

Even though they frequently transgressed their goddess's rules, they still believed themselves to be in her hands and hoped that gifts to her priests and frequent sacrifices would propitiate her anger and ensure her protection. Sleeman asked a number of convicted Thugs whether they were not troubled by the spirits of the people whom they murdered.

> "Never—they cannot trouble us," said Nasir Khan.
>
> "Why? Do they not trouble other men when they commit murder?"
>
> "Of course, the man who commits murder is always haunted by spirits. He has sometimes 50 at a time upon him and they drive him mad."
>
> "How do they not trouble you?"
>
> "Are not the people we kill killed by the orders of Kali?"
>
> "Yes," said another Thug, "it is by the blessing of Kali that we escape that evil."
>
> "And is there no instance of a Thug being troubled by a spirit?" All present cried—"None!"

Thugs in captivity argued without exception that observance of omens was the foundation of successful Thuggee and that their misfortunes were due to disregarding them. All, even the most sensible, believed that their good or ill success depended always upon the skill with which the omens were interpreted, and, Sleeman says:

> A Thug of the old Sindhouse stock told me . . . that had they not attended to these omens they could never have thrived as they did. And that in ordinary cases of murder, a man seldom escaped while they and their families had, for ten generations, thrived though they had murdered hundreds of people. "This," said he, "could never have been the case . . . had not omens been intended for us. There were always signs around us, to guide us to rich booty, and warn us of danger, had we been always wise enough to discern them, and religious enough to attend to them." Every Thug concurred . . . from his soul.

While questioning captive Thugs on the power of omens, Sleeman asked whether any of them could recollect any misfortune caused by going on when a hare crossed the road before them.

> "Yes," said Nasir. "When General Doveton commanded the troops at Jhalna we were advancing towards his camp. A hare crossed the road. We disregarded the omen, though the hare actually screamed in crossing, and went on. The very next day I and seventeen of the gang were seized and we only got our release after much difficulty. We had killed some people belonging to the troops, but fortunately none of their property was found upon us."
>
> "And do you think these signs are all mandates from the deity, and if properly attended to, no harm can befall you?"
>
> "Certainly, no one doubts it—ask anybody. How could Thugs have otherwise prospered? Have they not everywhere been protected as long as they have religiously attended to their rules?"

Sleeman's next question—an attempt to assess how strictly Thugs obeyed the omens—showed divided opinion. He asked:

> "When you have a poor traveller with you, or a party of travellers who seem to have little of value with them—and you hear or see a very good omen—do you let them go in the hope that the virtue of the omen will guide you to better prey?"

"Let them go?" cried the Thug named Dorgha—"Never, never!"

"How could we?" said Nasir. "Is not the good omen the order from Kali to kill them and would it not be disobedience to let them go? If we didn't kill them, should we ever get any more?"

A Brahmin Thug contradicted: "I have known the experiment tried with good effect. I have known travellers who promised little let go and the virtue of the omen brought better."

"Yes," a Thug named Inaent said, "the virtue of the omen remains and the traveller who has little should be let go, for you are sure to get better."

This brought an angry denial from Sahib Khan, a Muslim. "You could never let him go without losing all the fruits of your expedition. You might get property but it could never do you any good. No success could come from your disobedience."

"Of course not," pronounced Morlee, a Hindu. "The travellers who are in our hands when we have a good omen must never be let go, whether they promise little or much. The omen is unquestionably the order, as Nasir says."

"The idea of securing the good will of Kali by disobeying her order is quite monstrous," Nasir said. "We Deccan Thugs do not understand how you got hold of it. Our ancestors were never guilty of such folly."

"Do you believe then that if you were to murder without the observance of the omens and rules you would be punished both in this world and the next like other men?"

"Certainly," Sahib Khan replied. "No man's family ever survives a murder. It becomes extinct. A Thug who murders in this way loses the children he has and is never blessed with more."

"And when you observe the omens and rules you never feel a dread of punishment here nor hereafter?"

"Never."

"And do you never feel sympathy for the persons murdered—never pity or compunction?"

"Never," Sahib Khan said.

"And can you sleep as soundly by the bodies or over the graves of those you have murdered, and eat your meals with as much appetite as ever?"

"Just the same. We sleep and eat just the same unless we are afraid of being discovered."

"And when you see or hear a bad omen you think it is the order of the deity not to kill the travellers you have with you or are in pursuit of?"

"Yes—we dare not disobey."

Despite these confident arguments, in a further effort to assess the strength of their convictions, Sleeman tried to throw doubt on the significance of Thug lore and on the standing in the fraternity of learned members. He asked Sahib Khan:

"You believe that a *Borka* (fully initiated Thug) could form a gang in any part of India to which he may be forced to flee?"

"Certainly."

"Do you know any instance of this?"

"A great number. Mudee Khan was from the old Thug stock and had to emigrate after an attack upon his home country. I met him many years afterwards in the Deccan. He had then a gang of fifty Thugs of all castes and descriptions—weavers, braziers, bracelet-makers and all kinds of ragamuffins whom he had scraped together in his new abode."

"Did they find the same patrons among the landholders and other heads of villages?"

"They made friends everywhere in the same way. Without patrons they couldn't have thrived. They had to give them a liberal share of the loot."

"But these men have all been punished, which doesn't indicate the protection of Kali."

"It shows the danger of scraping together such a set of fellows for Thuggee. They killed all people indiscriminately, women and men, of all castes and professions and knew so little about omens that they killed people despite warnings that the most ignorant should have known were hostile. They were punished, as all knew they would be. We used to think it dangerous to be associated with them for even a few days. Ask any of them who are now here whether this is not true—whether they ever let go even a sweeper if he had a rupee on him."

"And you think that if they had been well instructed in the signs and omens and attended to them, they would have thrived?"

"Undoubtedly—so should we all."

"You think that a *Kuboola* (amateur) couldn't form a Thug gang anywhere for himself?"

"Never. He could know nothing of our rules of augury or proceedings so how could he possibly succeed? Doesn't all our success depend upon knowing and observing omens and rules?"

"It would therefore never be very dangerous to release such a man as a *Kuboola*?"

"Never," Sahib Khan said, "unless he could join better instructed men. Everyone must be convinced that it is by knowing and attending to omens that Thuggee has thrived."

"I am not convinced, nor are any of the Indian officers present [Sleeman said]. We do all we can to put down what you call an institution of the deity and without any fear of her anger."

"They may say so, but they all know that no man's family can survive a murder committed in any other way. Yet Thugs have thrived through a long series of generations. We all have children and we are never harmed."

Doggedly Sleeman ploughed ahead with this meticulous research, material for his official reports, but with little result. Lord Amherst, Governor-General, was at this time deeply involved in war against Burma and opium troubles with China, for his conduct of which he was lucky not to have been recalled. The last thing he sought was an onslaught on the socio-religious fabric of India which could possibly have brought tensions within the country to breaking point.

So Sleeman's was still a voice crying in the wilderness. Anyone else's zeal but his could well have been blunted by the constant frustrations of the years following his appointment as magistrate. Some day, he must have felt, his work would bear fruit; and at least he was doing his best to fulfil his resolve to rid India of the criminal secret society of Thuggee.

But early in 1828 Lord Amherst resigned. He was succeeded in July by Lord William Bentinck. Captain Sleeman no doubt hoped that this reformist Whig peer would turn a more sympathetic ear to his demands that a campaign should be mounted against the Thug secret society.

7

Sleeman Tells the Press

Lord William Cavendish Bentinck, aged fifty-six, was the second son of the Duke of Portland and a member of England's Whig oligarchy. Active and ambitious, he was appointed Governor of Madras when only thirty, but he was recalled when the sepoys mutinied in 1806 over new regulations about the cut of beards and the shape of turbans, which, they felt, infringed their religious beliefs. Bentinck had always said that he had been treated unjustly in being held responsible for this, and boldly demanded that he should be recompensed by being appointed Governor-General. Only a clever and confident man could transform dismissal into a reasoned justification for reinstatement in the highest rank, but Bentinck eventually achieved it. Having spent the intervening years mostly as a military commander, he returned to India triumphantly in 1828.

It was recalled that his career had foundered some twenty years before on the rocks of so-called religious interference and therefore it was expected that if he moved at all on this course it would be with extreme caution. Yet the new climate of opinion in England looked for reform; and Bentinck doubtless had this in mind when soon after his arrival he said that it was the duty of a civilised government to forbid all acts which violated humanity's normal feelings. The government of India, he asserted, should certainly not for the sake of the principle of non-interference put up with inhuman behaviour—not even when, like suttee, it was believed to have the sanction of immemorial custom and the gods. He made no mention of Thuggee; nor did he take any action against suttee at the time. He was probing, assessing public opinion, noting the stir of mild indignation his speech had caused.

Suttee was the ancient custom of Hindu widows burning themselves to death upon their husbands' funeral pyres, and public opinion was believed to be firmly united in upholding it. But shortly before Bentinck took office Sleeman made his promotion to civil charge of the Jubbulpore district in March 1828 the occasion for a bold proclamation forbidding this cruel rite, without Government sanction—a thing no other magistrate had dared to do.

He made the prohibition effective, he believed, by rendering anyone who had brought even an ounce of wood for the fire liable to punishment, but more than a year later, after Bentinck had arrived, Sleeman was embarrassingly caught up in the toils of the issue. He describes how on 24 November 1829 one of the most respected Brahmin families in the district asked permission for an aged widow to burn herself on the banks of the Narbada river with the body of her husband, who had died that morning. Sleeman refused.

> I threatened to enforce my order and punish severely any man who assisted, and placed a guard for the purpose of seeing that no one did so. She remained sitting by the edge of the water without eating or drinking. The next day the body of her husband was burned to ashes in a small pit of about eight feet square, and three or four deep, before several thousand spectators. . . . Her sons, grandsons and some other relations remained with her, while the rest surrounded my house, the one urging me to allow her to burn, the other urging her to desist. She remained sitting on a bare rock in the bed of the Narbada, refusing every kind of sustenance and exposed to the intense heat of the sun by day, and the severe cold of the night, with only a thin sheet thrown over her shoulders. On Thursday, to cut off all hope of her being removed from her purpose, she put on the *dhaja*, or coarse red turban, and broke her bracelets in pieces, by which she became dead in law, and forever excluded from caste. Should she choose to live after this she could never return to her family. . . .
>
> I became satisfied that she would starve herself to death if not allowed to burn, by which the family would be disgraced, her

miseries prolonged, and I myself rendered liable to be charged with a wanton abuse of authority, for no prohibition of the kind I had issued had as yet received the formal sanction of the government.

Sleeman, it seems, had deliberately tried to force the government's hand, as he was soon to do over Thuggee. But, courageous though his move was, this case of suttee brought him hard up against a human problem in the shape of this frail old lady and defeated his best intentions:

On Saturday, the 28th, in the morning, I rode out ten miles to the spot and found the poor old widow sitting with the *dhaja* round her head, a brass plate before her with undressed rice and flowers, and a coco-nut in each hand. She talked very collectedly, telling me that "she had determined to mix her ashes with those of her departed husband, and should patiently wait my permission to do so, assured that God would enable her to sustain life till that was given, though she dared not eat or drink".

Looking at the sun, then rising before her over a long and beautiful stretch of the Nerbudda river, she said calmly: "My soul has been for five days with my husband's near that sun, nothing but my earthly frame is left, and this, I know, you will in time suffer to be mixed with the ashes of his in yonder pit, because it is not in your nature or usage wantonly to prolong the miseries of a poor old woman. . . ."

Satisfied myself that it would be unavailing to attempt to save her life, I sent for all the principal members of the family and consented that she should be suffered to burn herself if they would enter into engagements that no other member of their family should ever do the same. This they all agreed to, and the papers having been drawn out in due form about midday, I sent down notice to the old lady, who seemed extremely pleased and thankful. The ceremonies of bathing were gone through before three o'clock, while the wood and other combustible materials for a strong fire were collected and put into the pit. After bathing, she called for a "pan" (betel leaf) and ate it, then rose up, and with one arm on the shoulder of her eldest son and the other upon that of her nephew approached the fire. I had sentries placed all round, and no other person was allowed to approach within five paces. As she rose up fire was set to the pile and it was instantly in a blaze. . . . She came on with a calm and cheerful countenance, stopped once and casting her eyes upwards, said, "Why have they kept me five days from thee, my husband?" On coming to the sentries her supporters stopped; she walked once round the pit, paused a moment, and, while muttering a prayer, threw some flowers into the fire. She then walked up deliberately and steadily to the brink, stepped into the centre of the flame, sat down and leaning back in the midst as if reposing upon a couch, was consumed without uttering a shriek or betraying one sign of agony.

A few instruments of music had been provided, and they played, as usual, as she approached the fire, not, as is commonly supposed, in order to drown screams, but to prevent the last words of the victim being heard, as these are supposed to be prophetic, and might become sources of pain or strife to the living. It was not expected that I should yield, and but few people had assembled to witness the sacrifice. . . .

Regard for his status might have persuaded Sleeman not to yield, had he not been guided by affection and respect for the peoples of India—the same feelings that inspired him to fight Thuggee. And there could have been another reason. Had indignation at his refusal to let the woman burn herself flared into trouble, the effect upon his future of having acted independently might have been serious.

There is no record of any reproof of Sleeman by George Swinton, Chief Secretary of the government—a post comparable with that of Home Secretary—for having acted thus in this sensitive issue. It might well have been that Bentinck, at this time still uncertain of what to do, was secretly grateful to Sleeman for showing that no public outcry followed a total ban. At all events, in December 1829 Bentinck risked another accusation that he was interfering with religion and passed a law making the burning or burying alive of Hindu widows punishable as manslaughter. In extreme cases, if, for example, the victim's will had been paralysed by drugs, or if priests or relatives had used compulsion, it was to be treated as murder. The change was accepted calmly and the sacred cow of religious interference was exposed at last as a hollow sham.

But someone else had very probably influenced Sleeman over the prohibition of suttee. Fate had at last sent into his life a woman who changed the lack of interest he had so far shown in the opposite sex. In 1828, at the fairly ripe age of forty, he had met Amélie de Fontenne, the strikingly attractive daughter, born in Mauritius, of a French nobleman, the Comte Blondin de Fontenne, who had fled France during the revolution and settled in the East. A portrait shows her with high forehead, dark hair and eyes and self-possessed expression in an oval face. Clearly, to William Sleeman Amélie must have seemed as different as could be from the normal run of English misses then in India, in character, appearance and intelligence, and this she proved to be. He was captivated by her.

Amélie responded and in June 1829, Sleeman, who up till then had shunned women, married this girl who was twenty-one years younger than he. The marriage was totally successful, a love match; they rarely left each other's side during the next twenty-five years. From the first days of their life together Amélie showed herself to have an original and independent mind. The trite interests of European women in India, the bustling round of tea, card and dinner parties, the preoccupation with trivia, with clothes, gossip, scandal and other women's husbands, she disdained. It seemed that she had decided for herself the kind of life she wanted and however it clashed with convention she would lead it. Practical intelligence, in the French way, was one of her main qualities. When still in her teens she had mastered all the details of her father's sugar-cane plantation in Mauritius. He had sent her to India later to assess whether the local plant would be suitable for cultivation in Mauritius. Then it was that she met her future husband. She shared soon his vision of freeing India from the scourge of Thuggee.

One day, not long after they were married, Sleeman was about to set off on a journey of some 200 miles on horseback to question arrested Thug suspects. As we can be sure he would never have considered involving her, we must assume that Amélie asked him to take her with him, pleading her deep interest in his work and her wish to get to know the country. On horseback, she probably argued, she was the equal of any man and she would relish camping by the roadside with him.

Doubtless Sleeman pointed out the dangers—poisonous snakes and insects, wild animals, oppressive heat, the bad water, discomfort, risk of sickness—worst of all Thug assassins; but Amélie went on the trip. Necessary arrangements were made—servants for her, carpets, camping equipment, furniture, more tents, everything to make life in the wilds comfortable, as well as horses and bullock wagons to carry it.

That his beloved young wife should insist upon sharing these unrewarding conditions must have been a milestone in the dangerous and macabre task Sleeman had set himself. For this first expedition together became the pattern for the future. She too saw something of the grim work of the Thugs and one night two years later it would be horrifying.

Perhaps owing to Amélie's additional will and energy behind him, Sleeman's one-man drive against Thugs and, no less, his attempt to bring the Governor-General round to starting a full-scale campaign began to have results. In the summer of 1829 he learned from informers that fifty Thugs had arrived in the Jubbulpore district, his own, to murder on the roads there. He had no troops able to arrest such a gang—the handful of police at his command would swiftly have been overcome had they attempted it. He then heard that the 73rd Regiment, under Captain Oliver, was marching through the district. Sleeman arranged for some informers to march slightly ahead of the column and to call for military aid should they recognise any Thugs.

The plan succeeded, the entire gang were arrested, and Sleeman put all his energies into the long and demanding task of preparing a summary of evidence relating to the fifty accused. The Thug informers—they were called approvers—testified to the identity of each Thug whom they knew, and the travellers, if any, whom they had seen them murder. Thus:

> "This is Bola Khan. He resides at the village of Seronge. I swear that he has been a professional Thug all his life and that his father was a Thug before him. I was with a gang two years ago and saw him strangle two merchants, a carrier of Ganges water and three sepoys. The bodies were buried in wayside groves on the road to Indore."

The testimony of one approver was not enough; it was confirmed by that of others, also by that of Thugs in the gang who had turned approver. Systematically, the information was checked, the bodies exhumed and when possible identified, and bit by bit a mass of evidence built up to satisfy judges who were prone to refuse to convict on the slightest shortcomings. Sleeman's summary of evidence ran to some 40,000 words in this case. Early in June 1830 he sent it on to Francis Curwen Smith, the Governor-General's Agent in the Saugor and Narbada Territories, in which Jubbulpore was situated, with a formal request for trial and this supporting letter about the operations of the Thugs and present policy towards them:

> These common enemies of mankind, under the sanction of religious rites and ceremonies, have made every road between the Jumna and the Indus rivers from November to May a dreadful scene of lonely murder. . . . They are most numerous on roads between Saugor and Indore, leading through Bhopaul and Scindia's districts of Bhilsa, where Thugs seem to consider travellers as a kind of property they may seize and slay at their leisure.
>
> The chances against the life and property of ordinary citizens passing through it in any month between November and June have lately been as almost two to one. We must have more efficient police establishments distributed along the high roads . . . or we shall not be able to give the travellers that security of life and property which it is at once the interest and duty of government to give. This would do something to give security . . . but other measures will be required to root out entirely this growing evil which has been of late years, I fear, increasing under the sanction of religious rites and feelings. . . .
>
> It is to be hoped however that it will not be found a task of great difficulty to the Supreme Government of India to root out this evil whenever it shall be pleased to consider it a subject of sufficient interest, and to exert the legitimate authority with which it is invested . . . for this purpose.

The sting in the tail of this letter was not lost on Curwen Smith, for a few days later on 5 July 1830, this official wrote to Chief Secretary George Swinton—perhaps the most powerful man in the government after Bentinck—emphasising what Sleeman had already reported about the Thugs, and suggesting exceptional measures against them:

> . . . If they are to be brought to justice at all—than which nothing can be more desirable and imperative upon our government —it must be done by the aid of their confederates, and their arrest can only be effected by sudden and unforeseen measures.
>
> For the sake of the lives of all travellers thus miserably endangered, the liberty of the subject must bend to a temporary suspension as the least evil of the two; and therefore though the use of spies and general warrants will undoubtedly occasionally create evils and much distress to individuals, it must be submitted to. . . . Frequently Thugs arrested by British officials have been handed over to native local authorities, chieftains and others to deal with in the districts where they reside. His Lordship may rest assured that all Thugs thus made over to foreign jurisdiction will be made the subject of barter and trade, and will be set at liberty to levy their ransom upon travellers in all parts of India.

Sleeman's and Curwen Smith's letters at last bore fruit, for on 3 August 1830 that exalted official George Swinton composed a note of his own on the subject to the Governor-General.

He said in it that he had ordered extracts from Sleeman's proceedings against Thugs and his reports about the use of informers to track them down to be copied and sent for information to all other magistrates. Moreover, he suggested that convicted Thugs sentenced to imprisonment should be branded "like Cain, the first murderer". Regarding Thugs in the independent States, he wrote:

> As long as a profit is earned by local Indian chiefs in areas not subject to British jurisdiction, little hope can be entertained of any cordial cooperation on their part. Like the Pindaris, the Thugs must be hunted by British energy and British zeal and much, it is respectfully submitted, might be done in a few years if an officer like Captain Sleeman were especially appointed to this exclusive duty with authority to disburse certain sums on secret service, to correspond with the several local Agents,

> Residents and others and concert with them plans for the seizure of the gangs. . . .
>
> The evidence against them would not be difficult of attainment. We have now so many approvers in the person of pardoned Thugs, who are intimately acquainted with the principal leaders, that the parties apprehended would doubtless be recognised by some of them. . . . The very circumstances of association with a gang would be presumptive evidence. Some of the gangs, as has already happened, can be expected to turn informers to save their own lives and the leaders might in time be apprehended. . . . The spirit of animosity which the Sepoys are said to cherish against the Thugs, by whose hands so many of their comrades have perished would make the proposed Thug hunt a popular service.

At last, after nearly ten years a plan was taking shape. Before the Governor-General was the proposal that Thugs should be hunted down—and that Sleeman should be asked to do it. But the prudent Bentinck had yet to agree, and this he was slow to do. Writing through Swinton to Curwen Smith, he displayed much indignation over the Thugs, but even more caution about starting a full-scale campaign. The letter, dated 7 August 1830, seems to be playing for time—Bentinck was deciding what he should do, for the information he sought in this letter had been sent months earlier:

> With regard to the organised bands of inhuman wretches whose profession and livelihood is cold-blooded murder, the Governor-General in Council deems it of the greatest importance to break up if possible the whole system by the apprehension of the principal leaders, who must be known. You are accordingly required to consult with Captain Sleeman and other local functionaries who have the best means of obtaining information and to report the measures that you recommend most likely to effect so desirable an object.
>
> By the secret employment under due precautions of some of the witnesses and approvers, stimulated by the promise of a liberal reward on the conviction of the leaders in question, such a knowledge might be acquired of the place for their next annual excursion as might greatly facilitate their apprehension.

Bentinck also agreed that their names and the words "convicted Thug" in the appropriate Indian tongue should be stamped on the back and shoulders of all Thugs sentenced to seven years imprisonment and upwards, "a deviation from the Regulations fully warranted by the crime of Thuggism, which justly places those who practise it beyond the pale of social law".

Apart from recognition of the importance of breaking up the Thug gangs this letter made possible the completion of a master plan which might be put forward as a basis for operations. Francis Curwen Smith asked Sleeman to prepare the outlines of the plan, and Sleeman sent one forward based on methods he had already used. But harassed as he was by the preparation of Thug trials and his daily work of overseeing the day-to-day work of other magistrates, Curwen Smith made slow progress in approving it and forwarding it to Calcutta.

Sleeman must at this time have become desperate with impatience in the belief that action would never be taken; and perhaps have been urged by his determined wife into the uncharacteristic move he now made. He decided with a bold stroke—one that would have ruined him today—to try so to shock the feelings of educated opinion in India that swift and decisive anti-Thug action must follow. He wrote an anonymous letter, five or six thousand words long, revealing the whole shocking story of Thuggee and sent it, rather like Sherwood, to the Calcutta Literary Gazette, *Journal of Belles Lettres, Science and the Arts*. It appeared in issue number 40, on Sunday, 3 October 1830. Referring to the recent hanging of a number of convicted Thugs at Jubbulpore, he disclosed publicly for the first time his newest findings about Thug beliefs, rites, ceremonies and the great extent of their strangling expeditions throughout India. In particular he wrote:

> Kali's temple at Bindachul, a few miles west of Mirzapore on the Ganges, is constantly filled with murderers from every quarter of India between the rivers Narbada, Ganges and Indus, who go there to offer up in person a share of the booty they have acquired from their victims strangled in their annual excursions. . . . These pilgrimages to the temple are made generally at the latter end of the rainy season, and while on the road from their

homes to the temple, nothing can ever tempt them to commit a robbery. They are not however, so scrupulous on their way back, but they must be assured that a traveller has a good deal of property on him before they will strangle him. The priests of this temple know perfectly well the source from which they derive their offerings and the motives from which they are made, and they possibly console themselves with the conclusion that if they do not condescend to take them the priests of other temples will. . . . They suggest expeditions and promise the murderers in the name of their mistress immunity and wealth, provided a due share be offered up to their shrine, and none of the rites and ceremonies be neglected. If they die by the sword in the execution of these murderous duties by her assigned or sanctioned, she promises them paradise in its most exquisite delights, but if they are taken and executed . . . it must arise from her displeasure, incurred by some neglect of the duties they owe to her, and they must, as disturbed spirits inhabit mid-air until her wrath be appeased.

They attribute their ill-success at the present to their neglect of certain religious ceremonies and processions which formerly used to be performed by bodies of two or three hundred and with great pomp and splendour, but which cannot be so now without attracting the attention of the British authorities. They now make their pilgrimage to their Diana in small parties without pomp and noise and that is not always pleasing to her. To pull down her temple at Bundachul and hang her priests would no doubt be the wish of every honest Christian, but it would answer no useful purpose. Others would soon be found to answer the same purposes and probably the attention drawn to this temple by this communication will be sufficient of itself to deprive the priests of the offerings which they have been accustomed to receive from Thugs. After they have propitiated the goddess by offering up a share of the booty of the preceeding year and received the priests' suggestions on the subject, they prepare for the following year.

Under the sanction of religious rites and promises the pest is spreading . . . and becoming in my opinion an evil of greater magnitude than the Pindari system. It is an organised system of religious and civil polity prepared to receive converts from all religions and sects and to urge them to the murder of their fellow creatures under the assurance of high rewards in this world and the next. Sad experience teaches us how prone mankind has been in all ages and nations to prey upon the lives and property of each other under such assurances or under any sanction of law, human or divine, which they deem sufficient....

If these people are led by the priests to expect great rewards in this world and the next we must oppose to it a greater dread of immediate punishment and if our present establishments are not suitable for the purpose we should employ others that are, till the evil be removed, for it is the imperious duty of the Supreme Government of this country to put an end in some way or other to this dreadful system of murder, by which thousands of human beings are now annually sacrificed upon every great road throughout India.

In the territories of the native chiefs of Bundelcund, as of Scindia and Holkia, a Thug feels just as independent and free as an Englishman in his tavern and will probably begin to feel themselves so in those of Nagpur now that European superintendency has been withdrawn. But they are not confined to the territories of these native chiefs; they are becoming numerous in our own. And as hares are often found to choose their formes in the immediate vicinity of the kennels so may these men be found often most securely established in the very seats of our principal judicial establishments; and of late years they are known to have formed some settlements to the east of the Ganges in parts that they used merely to visit in the course of their annual excursions.

Here were hard facts. Public opinion must have been shocked and no doubt not a little amazed that the author, whoever he was, by letting the cat out of the bag had in effect at once publicly reproached the Government for allowing organised secret murder and challenged it not to hesitate any longer about suppressing it. The Governor-General was stung into writing to Curwen Smith through George Swinton, Chief Secretary, a deceptive letter which implied that operations against Thugs were already in effect and that the present was a fitting opportunity "to seize the leaders still at large", when, of course, they all were. The letter went on:

> With this in view you will be pleased . . . to endeavour to ascertain the writer of the letter, who appears to possess extensive knowledge of the character and habits of the Thugs and to have acquired his information from those individuals who have been employed as approvers. You will request him to communicate to you such further particulars as may . . . promote the object in view of apprehending the Thugs . . . whether by the offer of rewards, the employment of spies near the temple at which they are said to make their offerings, or such other mode as may appear to seem the most advisable, and report your sentiments for the consideration of Government.

Sleeman had achieved his object. He at once turned the situation to advantage by applying for authority to engage what he had long needed—a body of fifty mounted irregular troops to back up the arrest of suspected Thugs with armed force. He also admitted that he was the writer of the letter—it could of course have been written by no one else. Curwen Smith on 19 November 1830 reported to George Swinton:

> Captain Sleeman had authorised me to state that the account of the Thugs lately published in the newspapers was written by him, with a view to drawing attention to a subject daily becoming more interesting and which in his opinion would soon if not timely checked equal in atrocity and injury to India the Pindari system.

With nothing more than this brusque statement, he went on to submit a *Plan for the Eventual Destruction of the Associations of the Thugs*, which, he said, Sleeman "has seen and examined and the measures recommended are generally approved by him". It was, in fact, Sleeman's plan.

It provided for a Superintendent for the Suppression of Thugs, whose special duty it would be to seize suspects throughout a wide area of north and central India, including the independent princes' states, and commit them for trial by Curwen Smith in Saugor or Jubbulpore, without reference to the place of murder. Directly he was appointed, the Superintendent should send a list of all suspected persons and the evidence for it to British officials within the range of his duties. Rewards up to 1000 rupees (£100) should be offered for information leading to the capture of Thug leaders. The Superintendent should have a company of nujeebs (mounted irregular troops), a detachment of sepoys and a police establishment to help him in his work.

Heavy penalties should be inflicted upon the heads of villages convicted of harbouring Thugs. When a reward had been proclaimed for information leading to the arrest of a Thug leader, the Superintendent should be authorised to detain his wife and children until he was seized: "They being usually the only ties by whose misfortunes he can be affected. Thugs are generally hereditary; there could be no injustice therefore in chaining the lion's whelps until the lion himself is disposed of." A particular place at Saugor should be walled in for the safe residence of approvers, and for pardoned Thugs subjected to life imprisonment.

Thugs usually returned to their homes at the start of the rainy season. The British Residents in territories ruled by Indian princes —Hyderabad, Nagpore, Indore, Jodhpur, Jaipur and Gwalior— should therefore be directed to cause the arrest of all known or suspected Thugs and should be instructed to procure the rulers' sanction to all such persons being brought to trial before them, the proceedings being submitted to the Supreme Court for final decision. Curwen Smith concluded:

> Captain Sleeman is undoubtedly in my opinion . . . the most proper person to be selected for the situation of Superintendent. The appointment he at present holds at Saugor is admirably suited for his headquarters, being situated in a central position in the centre of the scenes of the usual operations of the gangs, and will form a screen whereby his peculiar duty will be masked and from which he will be able to plan and execute his schemes in secrecy. . . . He should be authorised to follow and seize these people in every direction north of the Narbada and where ever he might meet resistance he should make known the accused to the head zemindar or chieftain of the village in which the accused was found, who should be responsible for the safe custody of the person thus entrusted to his charge. He should also immediately apply to the nearest British Political Agent for aid. The lives of approvers . . . should no doubt as a measure of

> policy be spared, but they should never recover their unrestricted liberty, for numerous proofs exist of the utter impossibility of reclaiming them. Like tigers, their taste for blood is indelible, not to be eradicated while life exists. The case of Kurae is an example. As a boy he had a hand cut off in a native state for belonging to a Thug association. He witnessed the appalling exhibition of his confederates being blown away from guns but so far from abandoning his profession he is now in his old age condemned to death for the same description of crime for which he was punished in his youth.

The heart of this plan was twofold. First, to try to find out the names of all Thugs by offering convicted ones their lives and blood-money for the names of all others they knew in this close-knit fraternity. Secondly, to transfer judicial power over Thugs from the judges to Curwen Smith—who, in effect, became a special commissioner for Thug trials—and to British Residents in the independent states, subject of course to the Governor-General's confirmation of findings.

Were suspected Thugs under this plan put outside the pale of law, deprived of their civil rights and outlawed? For a verdict on this it will be best to see the arrangement in operation in the future, with all the conflicts it caused. Sleeman was now leading Curwen Smith and the Governor-General in the direction he wanted, having put forward his own plan in the certainty that it would be accepted and that he would be chosen to head it. So certain was he, indeed, that even before he had been appointed he had begun detailed planning of the campaign. Complaining that he had no maps of any use in his office, he asked for

> a skeleton map of ten or twelve feet square comprising the countries north and south from Madras to Delhi and east and west from Calcutta to Bombay; and containing all the principal rulers and lands and roads and principal stages at which travellers halt, and all the ferries at which they cross the rivers, together with all the seats of our own courts and military establishments within this range of territory. Jurisdiction should be marked, with the residences of the authorities, whether European or native. Such a map might soon be prepared to enable me to direct the operations with much more efficiency . . . than I could

> otherwise do, for I shall often be liable to direct them upon a wrong road and to lose time by doubts and mistakes as to the jurisdiction of the public officers with whom I have to communicate.

Such a request caused no little surprise—it is doubtful whether a map of this kind, with the recently acquired territories included, existed then in India. Letters went back and forth from Bentinck to the Surveyor-General, George Everest, who eventually set his men to work on this task. Bentinck, after reflecting a week or two, gave Sleeman the appointment, ordering him at the same time to carry out the details of the proposed plan of campaign under his Agent, Francis Curwen Smith. Everest obliged with the "map of a peculiar construction". At last freed from the frustrations and hindrances which had made progress almost impossible during the last few years Sleeman, not without, one may assume, a sense of triumph, set to work to destroy the Thug secret societies, root and branch.

8

The Plan

The task Sleeman had sought for so long was now his, but with characteristic reticence neither in his letters nor his books does he say anything of his reactions, his hopes or fears now that this day had come. Facts, organisation, evidence; other men's thoughts and feelings rather than his own interested him; and results most of all.

The task was formidable. His authority at the outset of the anti-Thug campaign in 1830 covered an area of central India almost twice as large as England, Scotland and Wales. But to seize Thug gangs estimated to total four or five thousand there he had a force of fifty nujeebs and a detachment of forty sepoys under Subahdar-major Rustum Khan—troops who certainly showed great zeal in the man-hunts that were to come. A plan of action with definite objectives so as to use this small force with effect was essential; mere haphazard searching for these wily killers would end in failure and exhaustion. Sleeman therefore devised one that should reveal the Thugs' entire system of favourite murder and burial places in central India, for this, he knew, existed. If the plan were to prove effective his operations should be cut by years, for there the gangs would be found.

Utilising the Governor-General's order that magistrates should give him all possible aid, he sent to every one of them two maps of the district over which they had jurisdiction, together with the request that any Thug informers or suspects in their charge should be ordered to mark on them the wayside groves used locally for murder and burial. One of these marked maps should then be kept in the magistrates' offices and the other returned to him.

The magistrates cooperated and returned the marked maps. Sleeman then marked in red ink the groves, known as *beles*, on his own master-map, and soon a vivid pattern told its own awful story. In one twenty-mile-stretch of road alone there were eventually marked eighteen such groves. Sleeman tested this information by ordering his approvers to name the most noted *beles* on roads between certain towns and villages. In almost every case he found that those marked on his master-map were the same ones that they mentioned. Finally, he sent small detachments of nujeebs and sepoys together with two approvers to search out and seize named Thugs.

Realising that the method could lend itself easily to abuse and lead to the arrest of innocent people, Sleeman issued strict orders as to procedure to the sepoys in charge of Thug-hunting detachments. They were: first, to obey the orders of the magistrate of the district; secondly, to seize no man who was not named in the list with which they were supplied, and to act then in consultation with local authorities; thirdly, to release no man once seized until he had been taken before the magistrate or other local authority for examination; fourthly, to leave it entirely to such local authority to retain, release or make over to them for escort to Saugor the prisoner seized; and lastly, not to allow any approver out of their sight and if it were necessary secretly to watch the movements of Thugs to send sepoys or nujeebs in disguise in small numbers.

These safeguards were also designed to satisfy the British Residents in the princely states that there was no wish to undermine the ruler's authority. But to let loose these Thug-hunting parties on the land invited conflict, which was to come later.

Meantime Sleeman interrogated the remaining approvers on every detail of every expedition in which they had taken part, so that bit by bit he built up a picture of every Thug safari in central India in the years they could remember. Each Thug jemadar's name and those of his followers were recorded in a file, together with details of all their murders. But, as Sleeman reported, the task needed enormous patience:

> The task of . . . conducting all those preliminary inquiries which enable us to fix the dates of the particular cases of murder that are tried at the sessions; to place them in their proper position,

and to connect them with those that have gone before, and those which have followed in the same expeditions, is one of very great difficulty.

An approver may be strictly correct in describing all the circumstances of a particular murder; and four approvers examined at the same time in different parts of the country may agree in all the principal points; and yet they may all differ as to the expedition in which it took place.

In the narrative of every one it may form one of a totally different series of murders. One believes it to have taken place on their advance; and places it as a link in the chain of murders perpetrated as they were going to Bombay—another believes it to have taken place on their return, and links it with the murders perpetrated on their way back—a third places it in the expedition in which they got the camel load of Spanish dollars; and a fourth declares that it was in that which took place the year after, and which gave them the doubloons, and the only way to settle the point is to bring them all four together. . . .

They will often describe with wonderful accuracy a murder perpetrated many years ago, which made a strong impression on their minds—the place of the murder and burial—the age, character, appearance and names of the people murdered—their place of residence, the place whence they came, the friends to which they were going . . . and yet they will be found to have placed this murder, so admirably described, in an expedition that really took place two years before or two years after that murder.

A hindrance to the assembly of evidence was this mental confusion, but Sleeman relied also upon the grim exhumations at the *beles* for the evidence he needed. In the heat of day, or in the moonlight, troops and police exhumed bodies wherever approvers said they were to be found, while chiefs from nearby villagers were ordered to attend as witnesses. At the magistrate's court, the chiefs' evidence corroborated statements made by approvers about the numbers of victims in each attack and, by inference, the Thugs whom they said had taken part in it. Articles Thugs had left on the bodies were removed and used as additional aids to identification.

For the news of Sleeman's war against the Thugs and of his

disclosure that it was a nationwide criminal conspiracy, no less than a religion, had spread far and wide; and with it among the ordinary villagers a wave of shock. People who had lost relatives and friends on the roads flocked to his Jubbulpore headquarters—or to magistrates' headquarters elsewhere in central India, and to police stations near the opened graves. When decomposition was too advanced for identification, relatives were asked to describe articles the victims carried, or their clothing. In this macabre fashion the complete story of which Thugs murdered what people where was reconstructed.

The legal task was formidable. Sleeman and Curwen Smith made it a rule that no suspected Thug should be held for eventual trial unless the evidence was so telling that conviction was as certain as could be. Persuading witnesses to agree to attend the courts remained another problem, about which Sleeman wrote:

> We often find it extremely difficult to verify, by a reference to the friends of the deceased, a murder that has been correctly described . . . and we are very often obliged to authorize the local authorities to give a pledge, that they shall *not* be summoned to give evidence in a court of justice, before we can induce the relatives to acknowledge that the deceased actually disappeared, and answered the descriptions given of them by the murderers.
>
> No less often have we been obliged to give a similar pledge to bankers, whose money had been taken from murdered treasure-bearers, before they could be prevailed upon to acknowledge that their money had been lost, or allow a reference to be made to their books. They all know that they shall not be able to recover any of the lost property, they feel no resentment against the murderers, whom they all consider as instruments in the hands of God—and they have no desire to make the sacrifice required to promote the ends of justice—"If similar losses are predestined, they will take place in spite of all sacrifices, and if not predestined, no sacrifices are required to prevent them."

Despite such problems, which sheer persistence enabled Sleeman to overcome, preparations for the trials went forward. More Thugs were convicted, more approvers added to the list. Slowly, steadily, Sleeman built up dossiers of gangs in extraordinary detail. Sent to magistrates throughout central India, these lists of named Thugs led one by one to more arrests and new approvers. These, in their turn, led to new details of other expeditions, names of new victims, of villages where Thugs were said to reside. The day would come, Sleeman foresaw, when, if he were given free rein, the present slow rate of progress would snowball.

He was inevitably hindered by doubts in the minds of government officials near to Bentinck about the chances of Thuggee ever being crushed. George Swinton, Chief Secretary, had put on record in 1830 that he feared success must be considered "altogether unobtainable", for he had "been given to understand by those who appeared to be well-informed on the subject, that the evil had taken deep root in all parts of India and extended itself to almost every village community".

Sleeman must have wondered who these well-informed people were. His own knowledge of Thuggee was far greater than that of any other Englishman in India. He knew well enough that there were few districts without Thug gangs—he had said so over and over again in reports to the Government. Yet he had never doubted Thuggee could be stamped out and now less than ever. He clearly refused to be discouraged by this defeatism.

Thug approvers were meantime out with troops, patrolling the roads and tracks and *beles* where Thugs were said to kill, to try to catch them red-handed. Early in 1830 two of them, Dhun Sing, and Doulut, were on patrol with a party of sepoys commanded by Lieutenant James Sleeman, aged twenty, William Sleeman's nephew. They saw camp fires flickering in the darkness one evening in a small grove near the village of Sewagunge, on the road to Mirzapore. Four sepoys, easily distinguishable in their red coats with white cross-belt, white collars and cuffs, were sent ahead to reconnoitre. In the grove were a party of about twenty-five men, many of them armed, and about the same number of ponies. It was a chilly night and the sepoys walked up to the fire and sat down rubbing their hands on the pretext of getting warm.

They pretended to be from an advance party of Native Infantry marching from Jubbulpore. Soon, they made their farewells and returned to their detachment, reporting that the party could possibly be Thugs. Lieutenant Sleeman next sent the two informers, Doulut and Dhun Sing, also dressed as sepoys, to observe and report. Trying not to look scared, for Thugs were known always to be able to recognise each other, and the two approvers feared they might be detected and killed, they too entered the grove and sat down by the fire just as the men were leaving in twos and threes.

They were a gang of Thugs commanded by Sheik Inaent and his brother Sheik Chund. The news that there were troops with English officers in the neighbourhood had alarmed them—earlier in the day they had strangled a group of travellers, two shopkeepers, two blacksmiths and a trooper. They still had the loot with them, including especially a tunic, a badge and a stick belonging to the trooper. When the four sepoys had gone they had thrown these things on to the fire. The experienced eyes of the two approvers spotted the articles immediately. Doulut is reported to have said softly to Dhun Sing: "That stick and those clothes on the fire must have belonged to a murdered sepoy and these men must without doubt be some of our old friends."

Both sat hunched up, staring terrified into the flames, according to their report, expecting at any moment to feel the *rumals* stopping their breath. Soon, all but the two leading Thugs had ridden off. The troops entered the grove just as Sheik Chund had mounted, and his brother Sheik Inaent had his foot in the stirrup. The two approvers flung themselves at the Thugs. Sheik Chund leapt from his horse. When his stirrup was seized, he attacked with his sword and made his escape on foot. But before Sheik Inaent could draw, the approvers had overpowered him. The troops rushed up and Dhun Sing pointed out the murdered sepoy's belongings on the fire. The troops drew their bayonets and would have cut Inaent to ribbons there and then, but for the command to fall back. The regimental badge and tunic were retrieved from the fire, yet even when confronted with them, Inaent denied being a Thug. But before Captain Sleeman in the dusty courthouse at Jubbulpore, when the chance of becoming an approver was dangled before him, he gave in, confessed his name and revealed that he was a Thug Jemadar. He is on record as saying:

> Had your approvers shouted "Thugs!" the sepoys might have captured most of our gang, but they seemed panic-stricken and unable to speak. When some of the trooper's clothes were found on the fire it was hard for the English officer to prevent them

from bayonetting me on the spot. I put a bold front on it and told them that they ought to be ashamed of themselves to allow a native gentleman to be thus insulted and maltreated on the high road, and that nothing but the dread of the same ruffianly treatment had made my friends run off and leave me.

William Sleeman's interrogation of Sheik Inaent produced valuable information—such details as the main routes Thugs followed when looking for victims, and the names of more of their leaders, the jemadars and sirdars. Inaent confirmed that among many other murders, he had commanded a gang which in 1816 had strangled twenty-five men and women simultaneously. Sleeman asked him for a full account of this gruesomely efficient attack. Inaent's story of these murders, known as the Shikapore Affair, as taken from Sleeman's records, sheds much light on Thug methods:

Our gang consisted of 125 Thugs. . . . Other jemadars and myself were encamped in the grove near the town of Sehora, in this, the Jubbulpore district in March 1816, when the Resident of Nagpore (Major Close) passed on his way to Bundelcund. We had heard of his approach with a large escort and determined to join his party in the hope of picking up some travellers, as in the time of the Pindaris, travellers of respectability generally took advantage of such opportunities to travel with greater security. Our gang separated into small parties, who mixed themselves up with the Resident's parties at different places along the road, without appearing to know anything of each other, and pretended to be like others, glad of the occasion to travel securely.

When the Resident reached Belehree some of our parties stated that, as the Resident was going by the western road, by Rewah, they had better go the northern by Powae, as there was no longer any danger from Pindaris and, by separating from so large an escort they should get provisions much cheaper, and that water was now becoming scarce on the western road, and was always made dirty by elephants and camels. Other parties pretended to argue against this, but at last to yield to the strong reasons assigned.

We had by this time become very intimate with a party of

travellers from Nagpore, consisting of eighteen men, seven women and two boys. They heard our discussions and declared in favour of the plan of separating from the Resident's party and going the northern road through Shikapore and Powae. On reaching Shikapore . . . we sent on Kunhey and Mutholee to select a place for the murder, and they chose one on the bank of the river in an extensive jungle that lay between us and Powae. We contrived to make the party move off about midnight, persuading them that it was near morning; and on reaching the place they were advised to sit down and rest themselves.

All our parties pretended to be as much deceived as themselves with regard to the time; but not more than half of the travellers could be persuaded to sit down and rest in such solitude.

The signal was given and all, except the two boys, were seized and strangled by the Thugs who had been appointed for the purpose and were at their posts ready for action. The boys were taken by Jowahir and Kehree, who intended to adopt them as their sons. The bodies of the twenty-five persons were all thrown into a ditch and covered over with earth and bushes.

On seeing the bodies thrown into the ditch, Jowahir's boy began to cry bitterly, and finding it impossible to pacify him or to keep him quiet, Jowahir took him by the legs, dashed out his brains against a stone, and left him lying on the ground, while the rest were busily occupied in collecting the booty. . . .

A fisherman going to the river to fish soon after we had left the scene, found the body of the boy lying by the stone against which his head had been beaten. He gave information to the Thakur (chief) of Powae, who went to the place with some of his followers and discovered all the other bodies. He collected all the men he could, and following our traces, came up with us as we were washing in a stream within the boundaries of the village of Tigura.

We formed ourselves into a compact body and retired upon the village. The Thakur repeatedly charged in upon us, and seeing Hyput Jemadar pierced through the chest with a spear, and Bhugwan receive a sabre cut in the face, we dispersed and made for the village of Tigura in the best way we could. The villagers all came to our support and defended us. . . . Tempted by the promise of part of our booty they protected us all that day and night, and in the morning escorted us to Simareea, where a promise of all the booty that we had left secured us a safe retreat till the pursuit was over, in spite of all that the Thakur could say or do.

The Thakur took all his prisoners to the Governor-General's Agent, Mr Wauchope, before whom Bahadera confessed . . . but being afterwards told that it was the practice of the English to hang all who confessed, and to release all who denied, he soon denied stoutly all that he had said, and pretended to know nothing at all about the murders; and being made over to the Magistrate they were all released for want of evidence. Ram Buksh Tumbullee came from Nagpore to the Agent, Mr Wauchope, in the hope of recovering his child, who was the boy that was killed by Jowahir.

Inaent was sent out with a small detachment of troops to watch the roads for Thugs and after a few weeks he recognised a gang of fourteen in a wayside grove. When accused, every one of them angrily denied it and tried to escape, but the troops fixed bayonets, surrounded them and one by one Inaent named them. This exposure by a Thug leader so demoralised them that they all confessed and were marched back to Jubbulpore. One of them, named Rumzam, a jemadar, became an approver. He was a revenue collector for the Raja Surat of Dunowlee—employment for which a readiness to use torture was then helpful.

Rumzam, who had authority over five of the Raja's villages, had been a Thug for twenty-one years and claimed to have murdered 604 people—an achievement, he argued, that placed him among those at the very top of the profession. "I could summon the people of these villages to my presence and make them stand or sit," he boasted. "I dressed well, rode my pony and had two sepoys, a scribe and a village guard to attend me.

"During these years I used to pay each village a monthly visit yet no one ever suspected that I was a Thug. The chief men used to wait on me to transact business and as I passed along old and young made their salaam to me."

Later, when still a Thug, Rumzam had been promoted by the Raja on account of his zeal in tax collecting. He had a military guard of fifteen men and authority to call out an army of 2000. "I was fully armed with a sword, shield, pistols, a matchlock musket and a flintlock gun. I was fond of being thus arrayed and feared not though forty men stood before me." Like most Thugs he showed no concern at sending comrades to their deaths. Here is his description, later given to Sleeman, of betraying a fellow Thug:

> I was asked if I could point out Buhram Jemadar, a notorious leader of Thugs, for whose seizure a reward of 100 rupees had been offered by the British government. I said yes, and that very night led forth an English guard of eight sepoys to the village of Sohanee. I went to the house where Buhram slept. Often has he led our gangs.
>
> I awoke him—he knew me well—and he came outside to see me. It was a cold night, so, under the pretence of getting us warm, but really to have light for his seizure by the guard, I lit some straw and made a blaze.
>
> As Buhram and I were warming ourselves, the guard drew around us. I said to them, "This is Buhram!" And he was seized, just as a cat seizes a mouse. Buhram confessed at once, saying: "I am a Thug, my father and grandfather were Thugs, and I have Thugged with many. Let the government employ me and I will do its work."

Still more good fortune followed. Rumzam named another noted strangler—Futty Khan, then on an expedition somewhere in a region of central India the size of Wales. Futty Khan and his gang had last murdered three entire families—husbands, wives and children. Sleeman acted ruthlessly upon this knowledge and ordered Futty Khan's own wife and three children to be seized and held. This move to snare him was successful, for Futty Khan gave himself up. He confessed later:

> I heard that my wife and three children had been seized by the guards of the British Government, so I returned home and in about a month after this, my last murder, I delivered myself up, confessing my crime. I at once turned King's evidence, and within three days pointed out to the guard two Thugs, Maigal and Ameer, who are now in gaol here. When I went to catch Maigal he was at his own house and readily came at my call: but when he saw irons on my legs great was his consternation! He

knew that I had come as an approver to seize him. The lamentation which he and his wife made soon filled the whole village with the news of his capture. He is a well-known Thug. He confessed on reaching Lucknow. Besides him, I had led to the capture of nine other Thugs by tracing them to their haunts.

Sleeman's methods were slowly proving their worth. The knowledge that their own brethren were turning against them and—"that ever at the stirrup of one of the Thug-hunting Englishmen went one or more apostate members of their own murderous guild, struck terror into the hearts of the fraternity".

The sanctity of the oath of secrecy had been violated. The belief that they could murder in safety was shattered. This once staunch, inviolable brotherhood was now in danger of becoming a treacherous association of murderers rent by the fear that any one might at any time send the others to the gallows.

Apart from betraying fellow Thugs, they informed on rajas, zemindars, police, and minor government officials who shielded and accommodated them. Sleeman was especially interested in the confessions of the Thug jemadars, most of whom mentioned the name of a leader named Feringeea with much respect—Rumzam and Buhram both revealed that for years past he had directed Thug expeditions in central India. At the beginning of the dry season Feringeea presided over talks with other jemadars about areas in which each gang would kill, so as to avoid overlapping. He negotiated agreements with other leaders about the size of Thug gangs, warned them to listen for and obey the omens, to carry out the rituals and to return some of their loot to the priests as thanksgiving to Kali. All this must have given Sleeman a sense of satisfaction, the feeling that at last he was nearing the heart of the Thug conspiracy.

He questioned convicted Thugs and their leaders day by day until he had built up a fairly complete picture of this leader who was both esteemed and hated. On the basis of what he had learned he wrote a note on Feringeea's background for the information of magistrates and his own staff. He told them how shortly before Feringeea's birth his mother, who was of the Brahmin caste, was staying at the house of a relative named Rai Sing, who owed 1800 rupees in taxes, which he refused to pay. A regiment of sepoys with English officers was sent to seize him. Rai Sing, refusing to surrender, organised his tenants and the local peasantry to defend his house. The troops assaulted, seized and set fire to the house, and in the middle of the shooting and the arson, Feringeea's mother prematurely gave birth to a son. She gave him his name in memory of the Europeans, or Feringhees, of the attacking force.

Sleeman went on to point out that Feringeea was well educated, about twenty-five years old, intelligent, and handsome. It was unlikely, he said, that Feringeea was forced through material need to become a Thug, but, he stressed, his influence among the fraternity was great. His capture would strike Thuggee in central India a heavy blow and this was the Thug above all others approvers should hunt and seize. Sleeman exposed himself and his wife to the full fury of the Thug gangs in ordering this man-hunt for Feringeea, but he was as well guarded as possible, and, moreover, Thugs had shown themselves to be superstitiously opposed to strangling Europeans—John Maunsell was the sole exception to this.

Yet William Sleeman so obviously spear-headed the anti-Thug campaign and it would so clearly have faltered and slowed to a standstill without him, that it is hard to believe that at this time no attempt was made to kill him—hard to believe that the Thug leaders did not employ professional assassins, swordsmen, or the poisoners of India, to gain employment in the Sleeman household and murder him without casting any suspicion upon themselves. Did he or his wife never wonder what would be the reaction of any of their scores of servants to the threat of death were they to refuse to leave open a door or a window upon a certain night? Would their loyalty have lasted longer than the flicker of an eyelid? Despite these personal risks, by October 1830, when the rainy weather ended and the season's Thug safaris began, Sleeman launched the hunt for Feringeea.

9

Prince of Thugs

Feringeea, prince of Thugs, lived with his family at this time in a white house at Gorha, near Jhansi, in the then independent state of Gwalior in north-west India. Sleeman describes him as tall and well built, with the powerful arms and shoulders and the long legs of the hereditary Thug. In October 1830 he had assembled a gang about fifty strong to take the auspices before setting out on a seasonal murder expedition. Two other jemadars, Zolfukar Khan and Muhammed Buksh assisted him, while Khurhora, described as an elderly Thug with a thin agile body, who was noted for his understanding of omens, came as augurer.

Here is a description of what happened, taken from the confessions of Feringeea and other Thugs. They gathered in a ground-floor room, with Feringeea, the two jemadars and two or three noted stranglers sitting on a carpet before a shallow pit dug in the earthen floor, ready for the sacrifice of goats to Kali. From the start, the omens were doubtful. The first goat, for Muslim Thugs, was properly sacrificed. The knife opened the animal's throat, its blood spurted, it stumbled and fell. A Hindu Thug seized the second goat by the haunches, the axe was swung to behead it at a blow, according to the law, but at the last moment the animal moved and the axe struck its cheekbone. This was a bad omen—everyone present later confessed to feeling its import. But the axe was swung again and this time the animal's head was severed. Feringeea and the leaders ate the two sacrificial goats. More were slaughtered, butchered and cooked quickly on charcoal fires, the smoke mingling with the smell of aromatic herbs and incense. The rank-and-file

Thugs ate, washed hands and faces over the pit, threw in the goats' skins, bones and offal, stamped the earth down so that nothing remained for outsiders to see.

Khurhora shouted the time-honoured words: "Great Goddess, Universal Mother! If this our meditated expedition be fitting in thy sight vouchsafe us a sign of approbation!" After some three minutes came the shrill cry of a crane outside, and almost at once the reply. It was a favourable omen, no doubt reassuring to those downcast by the failure to behead the goat at first blow. The gang set out in search of victims. A week later, they had killed no one. All, according to their later confessions, felt Kali's displeasure, seen in her refusal of the sacrifice. Mohammed Buksh, one of the jemadars, said when captured:

> It was a very unfortunate expedition. At Biseynee we fell in with some travellers, and should have secured them, but when Zolfukar came up, Bhola, who is always talking, could not help saying, half in Ramasee, half in Hindi—"After all, we shall not go home without something to please our wives and children." The travellers heard, suspected our designs, left our encampment on the bank of the tank [a small reservoir], and went into the village. This was our first *banij* (merchandise), and to lose it thus was a bad omen. . . .
>
> Then came the murder of the women at Manora, and to crown the whole, the foaling of Zolfukar's mare, which brought us all under the *itak*, all contaminated alike. We separated, to return home. Everything seemed to go wrong with us that season; and I often proposed to return home, and open the expedition anew; but I was unhappily overruled.

Sleeman, directing the big hunt for Feringeea in central India, had sent more than thirty approvers out on the roads and into the villages as spies, some—the trusted ones—alone; others with small parties of *nujeebs*.

Early one morning in December 1830, Dhun Sing, a young approver who worked by himself, raced into Sleeman's headquarters with the news that Feringeea and a party of Thugs were then on the road to Murdhee, in Bhilsa, some thirty miles away. He also told Sleeman where Feringeea's present home was. Within minutes one party of troops and police were galloping hard to the place by the river where Dhun Sing believed the gang would be found resting. Later in the day another party set out for his home, 200 miles north, with orders to bring back Feringeea or his wife and family. Sleeman restrained his impulse to take part in the hunt himself—it might have been a false alarm, spread intentionally to put him off the scent. He decided to remain at the centre of things where he could control the hunt most effectively. Feringeea, he was clearly determined, should not escape.

By the shallow, swift-flowing river at Murdea, a few miles from Bhilsa, Feringeea and his gang rested under the tall trees, shaded from the midday sun. Most of the Thugs lay asleep. That morning they had murdered a party of two women, a girl and a man. Feringeea heard a low and melancholy chirping in the branches directly above his head. It was the *chireya*, the cry of the small owlet and one of the worst of omens. Khurhora joined him. "It is bad—very bad. We must go quickly—back to the Sunj Basoda road at once," he was afterwards reported to have said.

Feringeea had a hard job persuading the gang not to return to their homes there and then, but to continue towards Saugor instead, for implicitly though he believed in the omens, Feringeea thought that prudence rather than panic was called for. After riding a mile, he stopped the gang at the village of Murdhee, a group of thatched, white-walled mud houses nestling under a layer of wood smoke. Leaving them waiting on the outskirts he dismounted and went on foot to ask the headman, who sympathised with Thugs, whether he had seen any police in the neighbourhood.

It was then that the approver Dhun Sing, and the leader of Sleeman's party of *nujeebs*, from their hiding place in a clump of bamboo, saw the gang waiting for Feringeea just outside the village. With drawn staves the *nujeebs* charged. Some of the Thugs leapt on their ponies and escaped, others ran for the safety of the bamboo jungle, but twenty-eight of them out of forty were knocked down and trussed hand and foot.

Feringeea heard the sudden uproar while still talking to the headman, and sprinted for his horse, which he had left tethered to a tree nearby, but the horse was gone. Frightened by the yelling and shouting, it had pulled loose, but a few minutes later he found it peacefully grazing. Feringeea decided to ride to his own home then move on at once with his wife and family to the north-west, where

Sleeman's arm was not so strong. His 175-mile-journey north took him along the valley of the Betwa river, which flowed as far as Jhansi before turning north-east to join the Jumna. He rode all day and much of the night, living on fruit and milk bought from villagers.

During the afternoon of the third day he led his exhausted horse up the grassy slope to his home. After a long hard ride it must have seemed a sanctuary, but he dared not stay, for he knew Sleeman would soon find out where he lived from captured members of his gang. He intended to take his family next day on the first stage of a long journey to Rajputana, 500 miles to the north-west, where he had friends. He could not leave them to be arrested and interrogated.

The party of *nujeebs* under a police sergeant, riding into the district that same night, were seen by Feringeea's servants. Feringeea escaped from the house only minutes before the police sergeant and the *nujeebs* pummelled on the door and burst in. They searched the house, found Feringeea's bed still warm and a pair of loaded pistols and a blunderbuss on a bedside table. The sergeant ordered that Feringeea's wife, mother and child should be ready to come with him next morning. A few days later, the sergeant and his men, accompanied by two palanquins, but no Feringeea, greeted Sleeman at Saugor.

Sleeman speaks of regret at this first failure, mingled with consolation over the capture of Feringeea's family. Among Thugs he knew family love to be the sole normal human feeling and he guessed that as long as his family were prisoners Feringeea would not leave the region. Sure enough, his spies reported a week or two later that Feringeea was still in the neighbourhood of his home, spending the nights successively in five different villages, where there were friends or relations of Thug prisoners in Saugor gaol, who might manage to bring him news of his wife and family. He never slept two successive nights in the same village.

Sleeman ordered a small party of sepoys with the approver Dhun Sing, to search in one and the same night all the houses where Feringeea stayed. He also offered a reward of 500 rupees (£50) for him. Dhun Sing and the troops set out on their raids, burst into the house in the first of the five villages, rudely awoke the householder and his family and searched the five rooms without success. In case Feringeea arrived later, they bound the householder, a Thug sympathiser, hand and foot, and left three soldiers on guard.

At the next village, two miles off, they also drew a blank, but again tied up the householder and left another three sentries. Two hours after midnight, they arrived at the third village, Jomum Sagura, which was eight miles distant, with only two men. Here again they were out of luck, but feeling they needed reinforcements, they seized the owner, a man named Soghur, and ordered him to assist them in searching the two remaining villages. They then trudged on through the night to Kisrae, the fourth village, reaching it just before dawn. This was their last hope, for if Feringeea was in the fifth village they would be too late. He would already have been warned.

So as not to cause alarm, the two remaining sepoys were left on the village outskirts, while Dhun Sing and Soghur crept in silently past the white-painted hovels, the reclining cows and the chickens. Soghur knew the house. They pounded at the door and persuaded the householder that they had a message for Feringeea. Inside, dejected and lonely, Feringeea heard the conversation and, he confessed later, guessed they were approvers who had come for him, but fearing a strong party of sepoys were within call, he made no resistance when the youths rushed in. He let himself be bound hand and foot though he could have strangled them with his bare hands. A week later, after marching in captivity along the very roads and tracks in which he had been accustomed to kill whomever he fancied, Feringeea, on 30 December 1830, was locked up in the Thug prison at Saugor.

This capture of so influential and knowledgeable a Thug as Feringeea was the second big milestone in Sleeman's struggle after the intervention of Bentinck on his behalf. Feringeea was brought to his court-house in irons. Sleeman saw him as his approvers had described him—"a tall and handsome young man, stoutly built and about twenty-five". From the start he talked freely, frankly admitting that his family, though Brahmins, the priestly caste, had been Thugs for generations. He himself, brought up to it as a boy, had given it up in his teens and joined the service of Sir David Ochterlony, then Agent for the Governor-General in Bundelcund. He became chief of Ochterlony's group of

Indian intelligence agents in due course, but when a relative named Bowanee Sing, whom Feringeea had recommended for employment there, was caught in the General's daughter's rooms making love to one of her maid-servants, Feringeea fled the General's vengeance. For a season he joined the Thug gang of his cousin Aman Subahdar. Next year, he formed his own gang.

> "From that time till I was taken, about ten years, I was always out with my gang except in the season of the rain—and for several even of these seasons we were out in Rajputana, where the rains offer little impediment."
>
> "Did your wife know you were a Thug?" [asked Sleeman].
>
> "Neither she nor her family knew it until you seized her and brought her here, where she found poor Jhurhoo and the other members of my gang taken at Bhilsa. Her family are of the aristocracy of Jhansi and Suntur, as you may know."
>
> To the question: "How did you allow yourself to be taken?" Feringeea answered: "Having lived among the clans of Rajputana and Telingana together for years, I should have gone off to some of them, but you had secured my mother, wife and child. I could not forsake them—was always enquiring after them, and affording my pursuers the means of tracing me. I knew not what indignities my wife and mother might suffer. Could I have felt secure that they would suffer none, I should not have been taken."

Though outstanding as a Thug leader, in one other respect Feringeea was no different from the rank-and-file. He was only too ready to betray the fraternity if his life was spared. Sleeman recalls how Feringeea quickly offered, as the price of his life, to secure the arrest of several large gangs who were in February to rendezvous at Jypore, and proceed into Gujerat and Candeish, and, says Sleeman:

> Seeing me disposed to doubt his authority upon a point of so much importance, he requested me to put him to the proof—to take him through the village of Selohda, which lay two stages from Saugor on the road to Seronge, and through which I was about to pass in my tour of the district, of which I had received the civil charge, and he would show me his ability and

> inclination to give me correct information. I did so, and my tents were pitched, where tents usually are, in the small mango grove.

Not even on this grim occasion did Sleeman's wife Amélie stay at home. They set out together, followed by a long train of horses, bullock carts and *nujeebs*, and camped in the grove that evening. When Sleeman got up soon after dawn, Feringeea shocked him by pointing out three places in the very grove in which they had slept, where he and his gang had buried at different intervals the bodies of three parties of travellers:

> A Pandit and six attendants murdered in 1818, lay among the ropes of my sleeping tent, a Havildar and four Sepoys murdered in 1824, lay under my horses, and four Brahman carriers of Ganges water and a woman, murdered soon after the Pandit, lay within my sleeping tent. The sward had grown over the whole, and not the slightest sign of its ever having been broken was to be seen. The thing seemed to me incredible, but after examining attentively a small brick terrace close by, and the different trees around, he declared himself prepared to stake his life upon the accuracy of his information. My wife was still sleeping over the grave of the water-carriers, unconscious of what was doing or to be done. (She has often since declared that she never had a night of such horrid dreams, and that while asleep her soul must have become conscious of the dreadful crimes that had been there perpetrated.)
>
> I assembled the people of the surrounding villages, and the Thanadar and his police, who resided in the village of Korae close by, and put the people to work over the grave of the Havildar. They dug down five feet without perceiving the slightest signs of the bodies or of a grave. All the people assembled seemed delighted to think that I was become weary like themselves, and satisfied that the man was deranged. But there was a calm and quiet confidence about him that made me insist upon their going on, and at last we came upon the bodies of the whole five laid out precisely as he had described.
>
> My wife, still unconscious of our object in digging, had repaired to the breakfast tent, which was pitched at some distance from the grove, and I now had the ropes of the tent removed, and the bodies of the Pandit and his six companions in

> a much greater state of decay, exhumed from about the same depth, and from the exact spot pointed out. The water carriers were afterwards disinterred, and he offered to point out others in the neighbouring groves, but I was sick of the horrid work, and satisfied with what he had already done.

Amélie's accompanying her husband on these expeditions is memorable. It was unconventional—not many wives then faced the rigours and privations of camping out in a tropical jungle unless they had to—and it was dangerous, for Sleeman was the Thug society's arch enemy.

She endured the discomforts for the pleasure of being with him. Nowhere in his writings does William Sleeman mention her reactions to camp life, so it is worth while hearing the words of another woman, Emily Eden, sister of Lord Auckland, the next Governor-General:

> Everybody kept saying, "What a magnificent camp!" and I thought I had never seen such squalid, melancholy discomfort. . . . The canvas flops about and it was very chilly in the night.

And again:

> It was so dreadfully hot yesterday . . . and everybody was lying panting in their tents. . . . They say I have no notion of what the hot winds are on these plains, and I have still six weeks to live in these horrid tents.

She complained of other discomforts:

> We drove down to the river-side through a dense cloud of dust. I asked one of our servants to dust me gently with my pocket-handkerchief and without any exaggeration, a thick cloud came out of my cape.

Emily Eden was obliged to accompany her brother and face the grim conditions of this official tour, but Sleeman's wife went voluntarily year after year. The campaign against the Thugs was waged by a man and a woman together.

Sleeman decided that Feringeea had exercised so much influence over the gangs and could be of such help in seizing them that he would recommend that his life should be spared.

> He has already [he reported to the Government] given me abundant proof of his disposition to be of assistance. . . . I feel assured that he will give us all the aid in his power under the promise of his life—though he should have no hope of release from gaol—provided his wife, mother and child have their subsistence allowed them.

Curwen Smith, on behalf of Bentinck, believing that the known treachery of Feringeea would lower the morale of the gangs and impress them with their impending break-up, authorised Sleeman in a letter of 18 January 1831 to spare him, provided that:

> (1) He shall make before witnesses a full and unreserved disclosure of every murder in which he has been involved, together with the name, caste and residence of all the Thugs engaged. (2) He shall through the means of his followers and with all his might assist in arresting and bringing to condign punishment all persons guilty of Thuggee. (3) Should he fail in any of these conditions or conceal any Thuggee expedition or murder in which he aided, his conditional pardon will be null and void. On his fulfilling these conditions you may promise that his life shall be spared and a small maintenance may be paid to his wife and child, who must for some time be kept under surveillance.

Feringeea agreed to the terms, remarking to Sleeman:

> My family have been Thugs for eleven generations. My grandfather, Tula, was a great chief among them. He had eight sons, of whom my father, Purasrah, was the youngest, and hung for murder at Gwalior. I am the last of Tula's descendants. Turah and Bowanee were seized by you at Bhilsa when I fled and they have been hanged. Maharaj and Gunesh you have taken and have in custody. Me you have purchased for 500 rupees and I will serve you freely and faithfully and no one knows so much of Thugs as I do.

Sleeman cross-questioned Feringeea and several other Thugs who had been members of his gang as to why they murdered women when it had been expressly forbidden by Kali. Feringeea replied:

"To that we owe much misfortune. It began some years ago with the murder of a woman of rank, the Kalee Beebee. My father was one of the ringleaders; Ghasee Subadhar was another and within a few years both suffered misfortune. Look at our families now—all that survive are in prison."

"But you still went on killing women although you believed that your misfortunes arose from it?"

"It was our fate to do so," said Dorgha.

"You murder handsome young women as well as the old and ugly?"

Feringeea said: "Not always. I and my cousin Aman Subahdar were with a gang of 150 Thugs on an expedition through Rajpootana about thirteen years ago when we met a handmaid of one of the nobility, on her way from Poona to Cawnpore. We intended to kill her and her followers, but we found her very beautiful. After having her and her party three days in our grasp—and knowing that they had £15,000 worth of jewels with them—we let her go. We had talked to her and felt love towards her."

"How came you to kill the Moghulanee? She also is said to have been very beautiful?"

"We none of us (Hindu Thugs) ventured near her palanquin" [Feringeea said]. "The Muslims were the only ones who approached her before her murder. Madar Buksh, who is an approver, strangled her."

"We met her and her party at Lalson," Dorgha said. "She had an old female servant with her mounted upon a pony, as well as one manservant and six bearers for her palanquin. We sent on men to select a place for the murder, and set out with her before daylight. But we lost the road in the dark and were trying to find it when the young woman became alarmed and began to reproach us for taking her into the jungle in the dark. We asked Feringeea to come up and quieten her, but dreading that some of the party might run off, the signal was given and they were all strangled. We got 600 rupees (£60) of property from them."

"And this was enough to tempt so large a gang to murder a beautiful young woman?"

"We were very averse to it. We often said that we should not get two rupees apiece and that she ought to be let go. But Feringeea insisted upon taking her."

"How came you to advise the murder of this young woman?"

"It was her fate to die by our hands," Feringeea said. "I had several times tried to shake her off before we met the Muslims. I told her to go on, as I had met some friends and would be delayed. She then told me that I must go home with her to Agra, or she would get me into trouble. Being a Brahman while she was a Muslim, I was afraid that I should be accused of improper intercourse and turned out of caste."

"Why didn't you go on another road?"

"We had already said we were going to Ateer, near Agra," said Dorgha.

"Had intercourse taken place between her and Feringeea?"

"No—or we could never have killed her. But he had much talk with her and she seemed to have fallen for him. She was fair and beautiful and we would never have killed her had he not urged us to do so. We either had to kill her or let Feringeea go home with her. He wouldn't go with her so we had to kill her."

"Who strangled her?"

"Madar Buksh," answered Dorgha, "while Khoda Buksh held her down and Feringeea helped to pull her from her palanquin."

"He knows this is not true," Feringeea interrupted. "I was not in sight at the time."

"Who strangled her?"

Madar Buksh said: "I did."

"Did Feringeea help?"

"No."

"You were a young man and she was a beautiful young woman. Had you no pity?"

"I had, but I had undertaken the duty and we must all have food. I have never known any other means of gaining it."

Feringeea then said in a revealing confession:

"We all feel pity sometimes, but the *goor* (sugar) of the *tuponee* (sacrifice to Kali) changes our nature. Let any man once taste of that *goor* and he will be a Thug, though he knows all the trades and has all the wealth in the world. I never wanted food. My mother's family was very rich, her relations in high office. I have been in high office myself and became so great a favourite wherever I went that I was sure of promotion. Yet I always was miserable when away from my gang and obliged to return to Thuggee. My father made me taste of that fatal *goor* when I was yet a mere boy, and, if I were to live a thousand years, I should never be able to follow any other trade."

"And you think that killing women has been one of the chief causes of your misfortune?"

"Yes," Feringeea finally admitted.

Turning to Moradun, a Thug from Behar, north-eastern India, Sleeman demanded:

"Do you Behar Thugs ever murder women?"

"Never! We should not murder a woman if she had a lakh of rupees (£10,000) on her," Moradun said.

"But, you Bundelcund men murdered women in abundance."

"Yes," Zolfukar admitted. "And was not the greater part of Feringeea's and my gang seized after we had murdered the two women and the little girl at Manora? And were we not ourselves both seized soon after? How could we survive things like that? Our ancestors never did such things."

Feringeea added: "We had no sooner buried their bodies than I heard the *chireya* and on leaving the ground we saw the *lohurburheya* (a pair of jackals crossing the road). These were signs that Kali was displeased and we gave ourselves up for lost."

Sleeman asked Lalmun, a Thug aged ninety, if he thought that much misfortune had arisen from the murder of women.

"We all knew that misfortune would come upon us one day for this and other great sins," Lalmun said. "We were often admonished but we did not take warning and we deserve our fates."

"What for—committing murder?"

"No, but for murdering women and those classes of people whom our ancestors never murdered."

Feringeea's arrest so pleased the hard-pressed Curwen Smith, occupied as he was then with all the legal problems of Thug trials, as well as with the weight of his normal duties as the Governor-General's Agent, that he wrote to the Governor-General paying Sleeman a generous tribute. Referring to his zeal and ability he said:

> The field in which he has to act . . . divided into many principalities, distracted by civil feuds and infested by rebellious chiefs, requires no ordinary share of sagacity and intelligence and it affords a matter of great congratulation that at this particular period I should have had so competent an officer at my disposal. Much has already been done, but we take the well-known aphorism as our motto, that while anything remains to be done, nothing has been effected. We must continue . . . as vigilant, as active and as enterprising as ever.

These words were the keynotes of Sleeman's Thug hunt early in 1831. Every possible approver was sent out with a supporting party of *nujeebs* or of sepoys on the track of gangs who Feringeea had sworn were on the roads. Sleeman felt confident now of capturing them.

10

The Hunt

While informers and troops hunted Thug gangs on the road, Feringeea and two helpers were put to work to identify those in prison. As each Thug suspect was brought forward, they said in turn whether they knew him and if so, which village he came from, who were his relations, and which Thug expeditions, if any, he had shared in. "Ormea took part in the murder of sixty on the road to Indore four years ago. During this expedition he himself strangled seven men and a woman." Or, "I know this man's father to be a Thug, but I don't know whether he follows the trade or not." Among the prisoners was a woman. Feringeea and Motee both identified her as Hollna, a Thug, of the village of Kishnae. Feringeea said: "I know her. She carries intelligence for Thugs." Motee said: "She Thugs and obtains information for Thugs." Ananda swore that Hollna regularly assisted Thugs. Sleeman had known only one other case of a woman involved in Thugee expeditions—a mother who led a gang of twenty-five Thugs, assisted by her three sons. No others came to light.

It became a grim routine for these testimonies to be tested by exhumations of victims at the places of burial and their identity proved by articles found on their bodies, as identified by friends and relatives. "Often," reported Sleeman, "I have seen incredulous visitors at my court-house come to seek information about missing relatives burst into uncontrolled tears at the sight of some small possession, which had been taken from the corpse and which they instantly recognised."

Acting on Feringeea's information, Sleeman compiled a dossier of Thug leaders still at liberty and on 11 March 1831 sent it to Curwen Smith with a letter about the extraordinary inner conflicts and hatreds he had discovered in the Thug fraternity:

> This list is made up from the depositions of the principal leaders of the main Thug gangs, who have already a deadly hatred for each other without any motive . . . to amuse any but professional murderers. The list may be relied upon, I believe. Feringeea is the head of the Brahman Thugs and animated by a deadly spirit of hatred against Kaleean Singh, the head of all the Lodhie (lower caste) class of Thugs and Doab Khan, once leader of the Musselman Thugs, in consequence of their having been instrumental in the conviction and execution of Jurha and Rada Kishan, his nearest relations. . . . Kalean Singh and Kara Khan are united in hatred against Feringeea and his class but deadly opposed to each other, having been each instrumental in bringing relations of the other to punishment. Beyond their own family and class these people have neither love nor hatred. We may be sure that they have each denounced those that are dear to the others, while none would be dear to them after years of maturity, but such as follow the same trade of murder.
>
> I could add a list of murders in which each of the men contained in the list are said to have been engaged, but this I have deferred to.

Sleeman's list included names, caste, village, district and state to which the Thug belonged with remarks as to gangs with whom he thugged and, where possible, relations' names. It was sent to magistrates and Residents throughout central India with instructions to seize those named wherever possible and send them for trial to Saugor. Almost to a man they were then out strangling on the highways and byways, but on their return they would fall into a trap.

Sleeman was now seriously handicapped by the small size of his force, all members of which were seriously overworked. Curwen Smith took the bit between his teeth and gave Sleeman authority to select and train another 500 *nujeebs*, the mounted irregular troops, and with this force at his command, Sleeman set on foot a vigorous extension of his campaign.

Meantime, he continued his interrogation of Feringeea. At

different times during his confession the former leader mentioned his foster-brother Rada Kishan and his nephew, two of eleven Thugs hung in 1830 at Jubbulpore; and, says Sleeman, "every time, the tears came to his eyes and ran down his cheeks. And yet this is the monster who could take me to a single grove thirty miles from Saugor and point out the bodies of twenty-five unhappy travellers at whose murders he had at different intervals been present."

Feringeea, however, showed feeling for his relatives only—feeling perhaps stronger even than that of the normal man linked with others by mutual regard and goodwill. Towards society he had the typical Thug attitude of implacable enmity. He was ready at sight, as one of his confessions indicates, to murder a sick man as soon as a fit one:

> About ten years ago in the month of Magh (January) I was with a gang of nearly one hundred Thugs at Lakheree, in the Boodee territory, lodged in some deserted houses outside the town to the east, when Akbar Khan Subahdar came up with eight companions, six being bearers, one a sepoy, and one a servant. . . . He was very ill, and carried by the six bearers in a *dooley* (stretcher). . . . He said he was going from the cantonments at Neemuch to his home in Ferruckabad, in consequence of a protracted pain in the head. He asked us to go on with him to Indergur, and after he had gone on, Khuluk, Bichoo, Aman and Chotee went after him with forty of our Thugs and reached Indergur. I with sixty remained at Lakheree, with five travellers on their way from Kotah to Cawnpore, a Rajput, two Brahmans and two Kaets. These men we killed that evening at Lakheree and went on to Indergur with the booty after midnight. . . .
>
> At Indergur we lodged at the Tukeea of a Fukeer, near a bhyi tree, with those who had gone on before. In the morning we left Indegur and lodged at the village of Pachoola in Jypore, and the following morning we reached Sherepore with the Subahdar and his party. Having determined to kill them on leaving this place we in the afternoon sent on Khomna and Junguleea to choose a *bele*, and they chose one on the road to Herowtee on a hill. In the morning we set out before daylight and on reaching the spot chosen, Aman gave the *jhirnee* (signal) and they were all

> killed and their bodies buried in the hill. The stranglers were Man Khan and Bhowanee, who have been seized; Gunesh and Mandhata, who are still at large; Bhowanee the second, now in jail, Lal Khan, approver, who lately died in jail and Soorjun and Peera who are still at large.
>
> Three months after, while we were encamped at Madhooraj-pore, two men, relations of the Subahdar, came and asked us whether we had heard anything of the Subahdar, and told us all they knew about him. We had an iron grey pony that we got in the booty from the Subahdar, and we threw a cloth over him lest they should recognise it.

Feringeea and his gang stayed with the Subahdar for two days and nights, showing him feigned consideration and sympathy, and when the moment came to consummate their treachery, put him and his escort to death with pleasure.

Such crimes explain a little why Sleeman, with his love for the ordinary people of India, was prepared to devote his entire career to crushing the fraternity. Yet directing a man-hunt he found an unattractive role. He was far from being a policeman by nature—sympathy rather than suspicion governed his relations with other people. There is evidence in his writings that he would have preferred happier more constructive work than that into which fate had led him. In a revealing letter to the magistrate George Stock-well, who had done much to support his campaign, Sleeman wrote:

> My part in the work I consider as an episode in my life. It is a duty to which I have devoted willingly and zealously all the little ability that God has given me, but it is one to which none of us would be led from taste or inclination. It is one requiring the finest abilities, but one to which fine abilities would not from choice be directed. If the protection of life and property be the first duty of Government, never did any object more imperatively call for the application of all energies than this.

Its idealism, its emphasis upon duty give this letter a nineteenth-century tone, for Sleeman was in many ways a man of that age, though born in the late eighteenth century. The concept of the greatest good of the greatest number seems largely to have motivated him, like many of the best of the young Englishmen who were to spend their lives at this time governing India. Yet he could be ruthless when opposed.

In June 1831 his efforts to seize a Thug gang were flatly defied by a chief in the territory of Ram Chund, the Raja of Jhansi, who had given loyal support to the campaign. The chief had throughout his life received a good income from Thugs. His home, a strong castle, was on a hill, defended with two cannon and at call by a thousand men. Ordered to surrender the Thugs, he replied that the Raja might have their skins and flesh, but he would never have the Thugs. Sleeman wasted no more time. He sought the services of the army and a vigorous attack by artillery and infantry was launched on this stronghold. The chief and many of his men were killed, and though when the smoke and dust cleared the Thugs had vanished, one more of their sanctuaries was destroyed.

Meantime, approvers and sepoys out on the roads were bringing in suspected Thugs by the score. In June, Sleeman reported that his operations had increased the number of prisoners in Saugor gaol by 266—from 180 to 346—and a further increase was anticipated. One apparently minor detail helped in seizing the gangs. Thugs always left signs for other Thugs in the wayside groves where they murdered and cooked food, indicating the direction they were taking. This co-operation enabled other gangs to trace them so that they could concentrate their forces on great occasions. These signs were well known to Sleeman's spies, so they were able to pursue the gangs with rapidity and certainty.

The presence of Feringeea in Sleeman's headquarters, ready at will to answer any question, ceaselessly pouring out information also helped him to get results in the first six months of 1831. On 11 July he sent to Curwen Smith a list of some 300 Thugs seized in this period, with the usual details of parentage, caste, nearest relatives, residence, in what murders they were implicated and the loot they had acquired. In a long supporting letter he said:

> The list comprises the greater part of those Thugs who were involved in the Lucknadown murders, for which twenty-seven were lately hung at Jubbulpore. These made their escape while crossing the valley of the Narbada river and they have been engaged in murder since. They are amongst the most hardened and notorious. . . .

Others are those who made their escape from Feringeea's gang at Bhilsa, after having been engaged in the murders for which 11 men were executed at Jubbulpore last year. These have also been engaged in other murders since. Several of the list are of the gang that rendezvoused at Lalsant in the Jypore territories in January last and perpetrated the murders on the roads in that district which have already been described by Doab—one of the gang which I forwarded on 11 April last. Buduloo and his followers were employed between Indore and Bombay last season and the greater part of them have been intercepted and taken since their return home by my parties posted in the vicinity.

These men all had Spanish dollars upon them, as the remittances from Surat on that road are made chiefly in this coin; and nothing has so much contributed to augment this system of murder as the temptation to make remittances in money and jewels from Surat and Bombay to central India arising partly from the increased growth and export of opium.

In several of the cases for which these men will have to stand trial before you, money and jewels to the value of twenty, thirty and forty thousand rupees (£4000) were taken at a time, and scattered over the jagheers of Bundelcund, giving irresistible motives of self-interest to all classes, from the prime to the silversmith, to be part of the general system, and to promote to the utmost of their respective abilities the success of these murderous expeditions.

There is not a rajah or chief of any kind in Bundelcund who might not be convicted of having received jewels as presents, or who does not purchase them at half price from murderers whom they have protected, knowing them to have been obtained by murder. Of course, the profits upon the remittances depend upon the cheapness of the conveyance and these remittances were sent under escort entirely inadequate, and to dispose of them was an enterprise of little trouble and less danger to the Thugs. In the Dhoreea Malagow affair they took 35,000 (£3,500) rupees after strangling the whole party of seven. In the Dhoree Kote affair, 24,000 rupees and had only to dispose of four men. In Dhunraj Seth's affair they got about 50,000 and strangled eight escorts and one traveller. In the Dhoreea affair nine men

1. *Major General Sir William Sleeman: he penetrated the Thug secret society and called it 'the most dreadful and extraordinary recorded in the history of the human race'. From a painting by George Duncan Beechey, 1851.*

2. *The goddess Kali dancing (Balinese bronze, 17th c.).*

3. Devi, Hindu goddess believed by the Thugs to be one of their protectors (bronze from Madras, 14th c.). 'People commit crimes and shed blood in her name.'

4. *Thugs with tattooed eyelids (drawing from Paton's papers).*

5. 'Thugs *about to* strangle *a Traveller*! *These* infamous Assassins *in order that the* Neck *of their unsuspecting victims may be the more exposed for their Satanic purpose, pretending to see something extraordinary, direct his attention to the stars or skies! and when he lifts up his head* strangle *him.*' (*Paton's papers.*)

6. *'Thugs strangling a Traveller. This sketch was shown by me [Paton] to three Thug assassins . . . leaders who all declared it to be a very faithful delineation.'* (*Paton's papers.*)

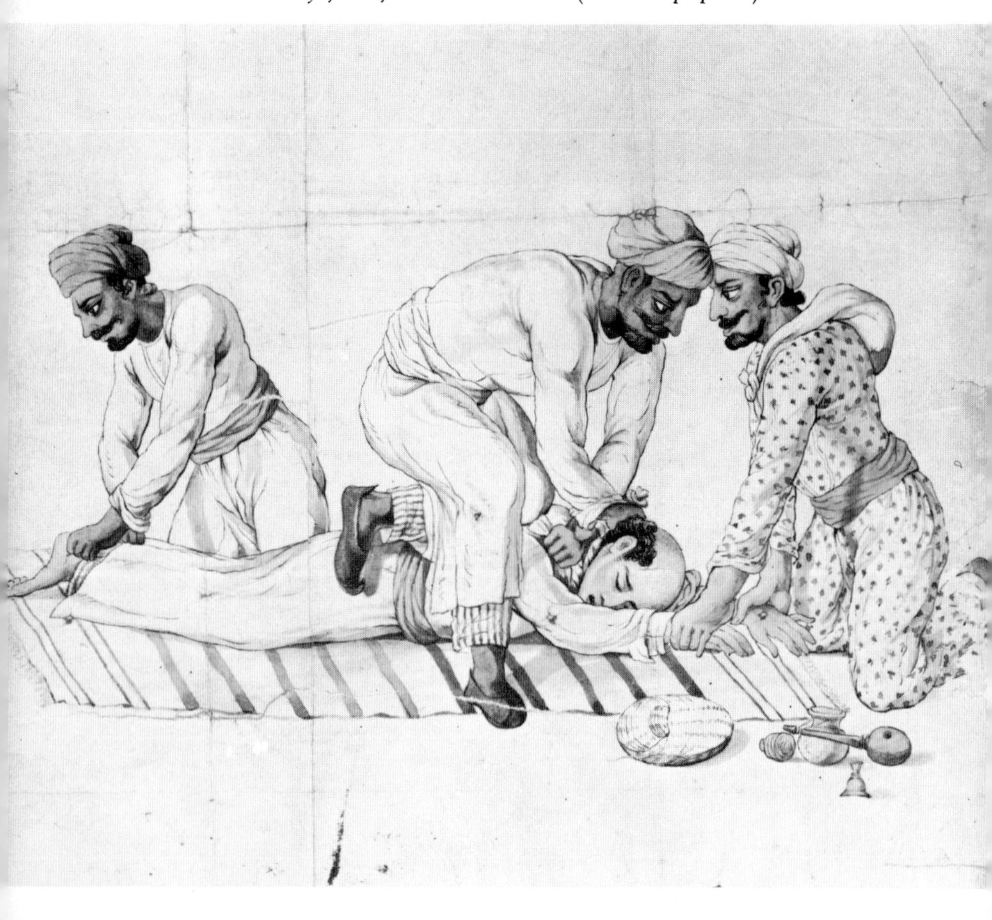

7. *'Thugs strangling a Traveller on Horseback.'* (Paton's papers.)

8. *'Thugs stabbing the Eyes and Bodies of the Travellers whom they have strangled, preparatory to throwing them into a Well.'* (*Paton's papers.*)

> were escorting about 100,000 rupees worth of pearls. Eight of them were strangled, though one escaped and led to the immediate recovery of the greater part of the property and the seizure and execution of the gang.
>
> Far more has been done this season than I could have hoped from the means placed at my disposal. Many Thugs have been taken who will I expect, be convicted on the clearest evidence of particular murders and these convictions, together with those which have already taken place at Jubbulpore and Indore, will have taken the greater part of the numbers of every Thug family of note, while they will have given us the means of knowing the occupation of all the remaining members and the residence of almost every other family of Thugs and individual Thugs north of the Narbada; and it would hardly be too much to hope that if pursued with equal zeal another season, scarcely one of them would remain at large.

Most of the Thugs mentioned in the list had been captured and brought in by the party of regular sepoys under the command of Rustum Khan Subhadar, stationed at Jhansi, aided by the Rajah, Ram Chund. Feringeea had headed most of these gangs and in his new role as prince of traitors he willingly revealed the names and places of residence of all Thugs involved. Troops raided their homes in search of hidden loot. The finds were stupendous. Gold, precious stones, jewellery, silver, coins and bales of silk were recovered, and the lists, in faded copperplate writing on yellowing paper, glitter like an inventory of the treasure of an Aladdin's cave. In one Thug leader's house were found 715 huge pearls and 1108 medium and smaller ones; 65 big diamonds, 20 smaller diamonds; a large chest crammed with Spanish dollars and doubloons; many heavy gold bangles, hundreds of gold rings, bracelets, necklaces and ear-rings. This hoard was fairly typical for a Thug leader; probably it represented the harvest of generations.

Sleeman, with scrupulous honesty and attention to detail compiled a careful inventory with a total value of hundreds of thousands of pounds. Of this treasure he remarked in prosaic manner:

> Some of this will probably be recognised by the proprietors, another portion has been sold by the Thugs . . . but after these

deductions enough will remain to cover all expenses incurred by the Government in the pursuit of these enemies of mankind and to offer rewards to those men whose services I have found most successful, that is, the sepoys.

He was determined that the sepoys should be rewarded. Again and again he reminded the Governor-General of the worth of these ordinary private soldiers. Regretting their impending departure, he stressed that he could not place the same confidence in the *nujeebs*, for though good men, they had not the same character or capacity to oppose attempts to bribe them; nor had they the same weight and influence over the Indian chiefs whose co-operation was sought.

As the 71st Regiment is to leave Saugor for Meerut after the rains I should neglect my duty to Rustum Khan and his party were I not to request you to solicit for them some mark of the Right Honourable the Governor-General's favourable consideration. A thousand or fifteen hundred rupees distributed among them in dresses might be sufficient. . . .

Throughout 1831 the hunt for Thugs went on relentlessly, parties of *nujeebs* and approvers ranging over areas of India several hundred miles in extent, arresting entire gangs, whose downcast members, their faith in Kali badly shaken, were marched past the wayside groves where they had strangled so many victims, back to Saugor and eventual trial.

In a report on 27 September 1831, Sleeman revealed that more than 610 Thugs were then packed in a gaol built to accommodate only 200. He had to request the Governor-General's authority to build another which, he said, could be done with the help of the prisoners themselves. He showed anxiety about the discomfort of the prisoners in these conditions. "I feel anxious to commence upon the third building as soon as possible," he wrote, "to relieve the prisoners of sickness that might be the consequence of these conditions."

By October Sleeman's parties were chasing Thug gangs west across India into the territory of the Bombay Government. Bentinck sent orders that magistrates and local authorities should give these parties the fullest assistance in their power, but Curwen

Smith sometimes regretted Sleeman's habit of ordering parties hundreds of miles in pursuit of them.

Though Sleeman would if he could, force the hand of the authoritarian regime in Calcutta, or, if there was the slightest chance of succeeding, avoid referring questions to the Governor-General at all, Curwen Smith, this functionary of whom we hear so much yet know so little, was almost devout in his subservience to authority. Once in all seriousness, he wrote an official letter, replete with all the trimmings, complaining that the Venetian windows in his office were broken during a gale of wind and requesting authority for their repair.

Inevitably, he received the sharp answer that the matter was not one which should have been addressed to the Supreme Government. Francis Curwen Smith, though a very thorough and hard worker, seems at times to have been something of a ninny. Mostly his reports to the Governor-General were outright copies of Sleeman's, sent as if initiated by himself, and complaining at times of the demands made upon him. Sleeman, despite an obvious lack of reverence for the Government, was at the same time meticulous in recording and reporting his work. The result is that today, despite the careless indexing later of these records by the East India Company clerks, we have, once it can be found, an exact record in page after page, of every Thug ever arrested, with even his family background and list of murders, all testifying to Sleeman's capacity for detailed but tedious routine.

Towards the end of 1831 marked differences in the psychological attitude of arrested Thugs were first noticed. In the summer those captured had denied their guilt in the face of the most clear and definite proof of guilt. But by November numbers of them were willing to make full confessions in the hope of saving their lives. Thug morale was at its lowest, the former staunch faith in the fraternity which had survived for centuries was fading. "There is no fear now," a Thug named Morlee told Sleeman.

"Thugs are everywhere seized and punished with impunity. There is no resisting your *iqbal* [good fortune]."

"The Company's *iqbal*," Dorgha, another Thug said, "is such that before the sound of your drums sorcerers, witches and demons take flight. How can Thuggee stand?"

"Thuggee? Why, it is gone," broke in another. "There are not fifty Aseel [hereditary] Thugs left between Ganges and Jumna."

Sleeman was encouraged by this wavering morale. And at the end of 1831 he had evidence of a distinct improvement in safety on the roads. Together with a list of fifty-three Thugs arrested during the last month he reported this improvement in a report on 7 November:

> Three great results have already been produced by these extensive seizures. First, the roads have been secured from Thug depredations and from those of the numbers who have been by the dread of a similar fate deterred from going this year on their annual expedition. Secondly, their confidence in each other has been so entirely destroyed that in the smallest parties seized there are some found ready to disclose the murders committed and to point out the bodies of the murdered; and I may venture to assert, that from Delhi to Bombay, Bombay to Hyderabad and Hyderabad to Cawnpore there are hardly ten miles of road in which the bodies of travellers murdered within the last eight years might not be found in masses if we had parties sufficient to escort the men who were present at their murder and who would point them out to the local authorities. Thirdly, there is hardly a family of these wretches north of the Narbada of which we have not some of the members in prison, and thereby the means of learning what members are still at large, with increasing facilities of seizing them and convicting them when seized.

This report, with its astonishing picture of the virulence of Thug murders, yet gives an optimistic and slightly exaggerated impression of actual progress. It is possible, of course, that Sleeman was referring to his own particular district, Jubbulpore, because his claim that in 1831 the roads were "secure from Thug depredations" was hardly true elsewhere in India. Weakened by malaria and anxious to see his task over so that he could undertake happier work in a healthier region, he had probably let his feelings and maybe those of his wife colour his thinking.

Only between six and seven hundred Thugs had then been arrested out of an estimated 4000. And the records show that in the three months from October to December 1831, one gang 125-strong alone in northern India had murdered 108 people and robbed them of 25,000 rupees (£2500), several horses, a dozen bullocks, 30 guns and pistols and a champion fighting ram. And a gang 60-strong in central India, operating from January to May and from October to December 1831, strangled 201 people, robbing them of 19,000 rupees (£1900), three camels, seven ponies, 12 horses and a quantity of arms and ammunition.

But it is true that by the autumn of 1831 Thugs could no longer patrol the roads in disguise, secretly seeking victims with the freedom they had enjoyed a year ago. Sleeman's parties were everywhere hunting them down, both with warrants naming individual Thugs and sometimes the notorious general warrants that empowered them to arrest any suspected persons.

Whenever the chances seemed favourable Thugs fought for their freedom. In the spring of 1832 a party of five *nujeebs* commanded by Poorun Sing and led by an approver named Bhooree were searching for a gang of six Thugs led by Feyz Khan, near Delhi. Remnant of a bigger gang, the Thugs had been on the roads since October and had murdered more than 100 men and women, but, says Sleeman's official report:

> On leaving Bahadergur, the Thugs that morning heard the *putora*, a bad omen, and dreaded evil. Saadut proposed returning, and avoiding the city, but Badam opposed it, and he was over-ruled. On reaching the *serai* (inn) of Chetaram, they saw the guard (*of nujeebs*) coming towards them in blue uniforms, and mistook it for one of the Begum Sonbre's (a local ruler).
>
> Feyz Khan was in advance, mounted upon one of the ponies, and he was seized by Maherban Sing, a *nujeeb*, while Bhooree held the bridle. He got off and unable to shake off the *nujeeb*, drew his dagger and stabbed him to the heart. The *nujeeb* fell dead, but Bhooree, the approver, seized his sword as he fell and with one cut severed Feyz Khan's head from his shoulders, it merely hung by the skin; and he fell dead upon the body of the *nujeeb*. Each of the other *nujeebs* seized his man, while the trooper galloped off for assistance from the police, and the whole were secured. Five of the six were mounted, four upon ponies and the other upon the mare when the guard came up;

and it is probable that some of them would have escaped had they not been deterred from attempting it by the sight of the trooper. They were all taken to the magistrate of the city, before whom they confessed their crimes and were sent to Saugor.

Although between five and six hundred Thugs were held at Saugor by the end of 1831 few had been tried since Bentinck set the campaign in motion because too few members of each gang had at first been seized to justify summoning witnesses, usually from afar, to testify as to the victims' identities. But by early 1832 enough were held and on the basis of the evidence gathered by Sleeman, Curwen Smith went ahead with final preparations.

One of the less desirable results of waiting until as many as possible of a gang had been seized before sending them for trial was the possible imprisonment of innocent suspects for months and months. Sleeman defended this practice with the argument:

> It is no doubt better that ten guilty men should escape the *punishment of death*, and all the eternal consequences which may result from it, than that one innocent man should suffer that punishment; but it is not better that ten assassins by profession should escape, and be left freely and impudently to follow everywhere their murderous trade, than that one innocent man should suffer the inconvenience of temporary restraint.

Sleeman is saying that the means is justified by the end, because he believed that India was under attack—that the foundation of human society there was in danger of being destroyed by a sect far more cruel and subtle than were the Pindaris, to crush whom the Marquis of Hastings had to field a powerful army. Sleeman's knowledge of the extent of Thuggee made him wise to this danger, when few others were. He recognised Thugs as instruments of the ultimate evil in their day, of that which as an end in itself takes human life indiscriminately. He was inspired with the belief that Thuggee must be destroyed, and, because no one else with equally strong convictions had come forward, destroyed by him—though he was too modest and sensible to see himself playing the role of a destroyer.

By April 1832 Curwen Smith had finished his preparations and the trials were announced. Much depended on their outcome.

11

The Trials

Before the trials started, the Governor-General confirmed an order issued three years earlier, in 1829. George Swinton, Chief Secretary to the Government, had stated, in somewhat florid language then:

> The hand of these inhuman monsters being against every one, and there being no country within the range of their annual excursions from Bundelcund to Guzerat in which they have not committed murder, it appears to His Lordship in Council, that they may be considered like pirates, to be placed without the pale of social law, and be subjected to condign punishment by whatever authority they may be seized and convicted.

This order authorised British Residents to try Thugs in the Indian states, with the agreement of their rulers—which of course, it would have been unwise for them to have withheld; and Francis Curwen Smith to try all Thugs seized in territories ruled by the Company, at Saugor. Sentences were subject to the revision and final orders or the Calcutta Government. Thus Thug trials were transferred from the hands of the High Court judges to those of the Government, which, tired of what it saw as the frustrating legal niceties of the judiciary, boldly took over judicial power where Thuggee was concerned.

Until the end of 1831 one of the rules of evidence in India had also opposed the destruction of Thuggee—"the testimony of any number of confessing prisoners shall not be considered a sufficient ground to authorise the detention of their associates". And were the confessing prisoners set free—too often they had been—the fraternity speedily murdered them.

Therefore, Sleeman argued, to suppress a sect like the Thugs in a society like that of India

> . . . a departure from rules like these, however suitable to ordinary times and circumstances, and to a more advanced and rational system of society, becomes indispensably necessary; and as they have matured their system to deprive all governments of every other kind of direct evidence to their guilt but the testimony of their associates, it behoves all Governments (in India) . . . to mature another by which their testimonies shall be rendered effectual for their conviction without endangering the safety of the innocent. This I hope, has now been done.

When the rule that guilt should not be based on the evidence of associates was in December 1831 suspended for Thug cases, the fraternity's last line of defence was removed. It was now in mortal danger, for Sleeman's system of approvers could eventually net every hereditary Thug in India.

Usually Thug suspects were tried for one particular case of murder, done on one expedition, in which all the gang took part and in which the evidence was the most complete. On an average more than ten Thug attacks were found to have occurred on every expedition and every Thug had on an average been on more than ten expeditions. The murders for which they were tried were not therefore usually more than a hundredth of those they had done during their active association with the sect.

During 1832 a total of 349 suspect Thugs committed by Sleeman were tried at Saugor by Curwen Smith; and forty others, committed for trial in Indore, tried by Martin and Wellesley, British Residents there. Two only of these 389 were acquitted. The other 387 could therefore be assumed on the above basis to have taken part in the murder of 38,700 people, a sum of death that marks Thuggee's fevered virulence.

Nowhere in the records of the trials is there mention of anyone acting in defence of the accused. They were brought before the magistrate, the evidence was heard, the accused were asked what they had to say, and sentence, subject to confirmation, was passed. The magistrate was no doubt scrupulously fair in assessing the evidence, but no barrister was at hand to question the witnesses for the prosecution—there were normally none for the defence. A case could well be built up against the accused therefore which only the magistrate, or judge, who also filled the role of jury, could test.

For judges to play also the role of jury was customary at this time in India—it had indeed been authorised by Parliament. Only when the judges themselves were replaced in Thug cases by the Governor-General's nominees, generally men who were less qualified and experienced, do the scales of justice seem to have been potentially weighted against the Thugs. Rough justice this no doubt was—it reflected the condition of India and British rule then.

By the end of the first sessions in 1832 Curwen Smith had passed sentence of death on more than 100 convicted Thugs. At last the fraternity faced destruction, but Curwen Smith found the experience almost as much as he could bear, for in a letter to Lord William Bentinck in July he wrote:

> In all my experience in the judicial line for upwards of twenty years I have never heard of such atrocities or presided over such trials, such cold-blooded murder, such heart-rending scenes of distress and misery, such base ingratitude, such total abandonment of every principle which binds man to man, which softens the heart and elevates mankind above the brute creation. Mercy to such wretches would be the extreme of cruelty to mankind and they must be paid in their own wages by rigid adherence to the law of *lex talionis*.

Through the inflated, high-sounding prose one senses his horror at the words he had to listen to—and to pronounce—week after week in the dusty sweltering court. "I have had the ordeal of passing sentence of death upon 110 of my fellow creatures," he groaned to a fellow official. *Lex talionis*—blood for blood—haunted and oppressed him, applied as it was without distinction to those who had taken part in one or two murders and to hardened Thugs who had spent their whole lives killing.

Although he carried out the law scrupulously, Curwen Smith seems to have seized any chance excuse for mercy. Once when the Governor-General questioned seeming leniency he argued that the two Thugs in question had been convicted in only one trial of one murder; and considering also that the bodies of the victims had not been found he thought it appropriate to pass a reduced sentence upon them.

Sleeman, during these first trials, seems to have been not so much worried about the death sentences as about the question of guilt, often stating his opinion, perhaps to reassure himself and other people, that no one who saw the swaggering, unrepentant manner of Thugs on the scaffold could for one moment doubt their guilt. Referring to this bravado, in what seems an attempt to rationalise his misgivings, he reported:

> Spectators are impressed with the conviction that men who can yield up their own lives with such daring impudence must have been long accustomed to assisting in taking those of others and must have some notions regarding the future state of rewards and punishments.

In support of this remark he quotes the answers of Thugs asked in court whether, having murdered people who had done them no injury, they did not feel compunction or pity. Came the answer:

> "Is it not our trade? And does any man feel compunction in the execution of his vocation?"
>
> "How many men at a rough guess have you strangled with your own hands?"
>
> "None."
>
> "Have you yourself not confessed to many?"
>
> "Yes, but they were not killed by me. Does any man die by the hand of man? Is it not by the hand of God?"

Logic was powerless against such fatalism.

Curwen Smith contended that all the cases had been proved by "collateral and circumstantial evidence", not by the approvers, who were Thugs and accomplices in the murders in question. The exhumation of victims, the recognition of plundered property found on prisoners, their confessions and other evidence of a similar kind *had left no doubt that the murders had been committed.* But, he argued, "to prove the guilt of individuals, the evidence of their accomplices in guilt could alone be procured. The secrecy with which the Thugs act and their precaution of never robbing an individual until they first kill renders the attainment of any other evidence impossible."

On the face of it, the approvers were chosen with care and sent out under guard to point out at their homes or on the roads the Thugs whom they had already denounced. The guards were ordered strictly to seize no man whose name was not on the list given them. And to avoid at the trials any combination of approvers against accused persons, the prisoners in each case were first identified in court by number only and the approver was then directed to name them.

It was believed that there was little chance of innocent people being injured by what Curwen Smith called "such cautious proceedings", and that were any innocent individuals brought to Saugor "their innocence at the trial could hardly fail to be made manifest".

Herein lay the possible defect of the system, for once arrested on the word of the approvers and taken to Saugor for trial, for which he could wait in grim conditions for months, it would seem that the chances of a suspect's release were small indeed. The system was geared mainly to make convictions rather than to examine impartially evidence both for and against the accused, according to the accepted axiom that a man is innocent until proved guilty.

Upon Sleeman alone really rested the whole weight and worth of it. He backed his own judgment, his own insight into the character of the peoples with whom he was dealing in choosing approvers upon whom he could rely and he then tried to make doubly sure by making their lives dependent upon never failing to tell the whole truth. The approvers were mainly chosen from hereditary Thug families of different castes who knew each other and each other's disciples well. They had led to the arrest of each other's dearest friends and relatives so often that the deadliest hatred existed between them and it was believed they could keep no event secret from Sleeman and his staff, let alone deceive them by joining in evidence against anyone.

Referring to the abilities of Thug leaders who became approvers, in a letter to the Government dated 11 June 1832, defending the system, Sleeman said:

It was only about two months ago that a party of mine pointed out a notorious Thug, a non-commissioned officer, who was superintending the drill of soldiers in the very courtyard of His Highness the Holkar [an Indian ruler], to the great astonishment of the court. He was secured and soon after acknowledged that during the whole twenty years that he had been a sepoy in the service of the Honourable Company, or that of different native chiefs, he had been himself a Thug or in league with the gang that passed annually up and down the country; and that there was not a Thug of any note in the Hyderabad territories and those of Scindia, Holkar and the Bundelcund states with whom he had not in that time become personally acquainted....

Others who are now here and who have been convicted upon most unquestionable evidence and their own confessions of leading gangs of Thugs . . . were found reading the scriptures to admiring villagers, and pointed out as murderers to the astonished local officers, who indignantly declared that they were the most pious and amiable of men and had been known never to leave hcme except to pay their devotions once a year to distant shrines and holy places.

The notorious Heera, jemadar and one of the murderers in the Indore gang, for whose apprehension government offered in October 1829 a reward of 1000 rupees, was by a party of mine found only a few days ago innocently employed in the pursuit of agriculture in the name of Kalee Khan . . . and given up by the local authorities. Even he thought it idle any longer to conceal his real name and character seeing his old associates around him and knowing that his two brothers and almost all his relations were in custody at Saugor.

To win the confidence, favour and affection of men is the business of Thugs from infancy to old age; and they frequently enter the service of native chiefs and rise high in office to secure their indecision in time of need and to collect *purwanahs* [official passes] and other valuable documents to carry with them and lend to their friends in their distant expeditions. Indeed, there are few leaders among them that have not been at some time in their lives in the service of great men, Europeans or native, and it is a fact worth recording that one of the leaders about to suffer death at Saugor was admitted an approver by the late

> Mr Molony. He remained in orderly attendance for some time upon the office in charge of the Jubbulpore district, went on an expedition to Baroda at the head of a gang during a short leave of absence to visit his family and perpetrated the murders for which he has now been sentenced.

Entirely upon these willing, but treacherous informers—or approvers, to give them their official euphemism—rested the anti-Thug campaign. A dubious method of destroying Thuggee it may have been, but it is hard to see how else it could have been accomplished. A risk that Thugs would try to work off old scores against innocent people there was, but in comparison with their murders it was negligible. When sentences were submitted to the Governor-General for final approval, excessive harshness, undue leniency and a lack of conformity in sentences, if they occurred, were quickly challenged. In the Bheelpore case twenty-one Thugs were accused of having murdered numerous travellers at seven different places between December 1830 and March 1831. One of them, Jafir, confessed and became an approver. The others pleaded not guilty.

In a supporting letter to the Governor-General, Curwen Smith, who tried them, said that the names of several of the persons slain had been obtained, the bodies of the strangled twelve persons had been exhumed, part of the property taken had been produced in court and altogether the evidence against the prisoners appeared to be of a most conclusive nature, and therefore he begged to recommend that the sentences be confirmed. A fairly typical Thug trial, it opened with Jafir swearing on the Koran and describing the expedition's mindless murders thus:

> We stopped at Udipore and there fell in with two travellers, whom we took to a place about five miles away towards Baroda. We halted under a bhyr tree and murdered them in the evening, but got nothing out of them. We buried their bodies close by in a nullah. Noor Khan and Jooghar strangled them and Phoomin and Perrum Suk held their hands. Several others helped . . . [*he named them*]. We then went on to Baroda and having remained there three or four days returned to Bheelpore and fell in with four men in blue coats who said they were going to Jubbulpore. We halted with them under a mango tree on the

bank of a river and strangled them in the evening, and got 300 rupees from them. We buried them under the mango tree—it was the only one in the place. Jooghar, Doorga and Keema strangled them while Gurrhi, Bhodi and Burrun held them. Each of us got two rupees, the remainder was spent in offerings to Kali.

Next morning four persons came up, one of whom was a writer of English with a pock-marked face, mounted on a bay horse and carrying a book bound in red leather. He was wearing some English clothes, had a servant with him and sat down with us about 12 o'clock under the mango tree. In the evening we murdered all four and buried them under the mango tree about a foot and a half from the spot where we had buried the other four. We burnt the writer's clothes and buried him naked with his boots and his book. Lal Khan strangled the writer, Noor Khan, Keema and Jooghar strangled the three others. We got 20 gold coins and 40 rupees from them as well as the horse.

We continued another four or five miles and halted at a tank situated near Bahurdapore. Two men on horse-back had joined us and we prepared a lavish dinner for them. While we were doing this a woman and three more horsemen and a servant joined us. We offered them dinner as well, but they would not take anything at our hands. That evening we murdered all seven and buried them all in one hole near the tank. A thousand rupees worth of property was taken, including a carpet, a turban, a piece of red silk and a tent, which I now see here before me. Jooghar, Noor Khan, Keema, Poorun, Deroo, Lal Khan and Bhodi strangled them. Bahadur Khan assisted in holding hands. We then returned home.

The accused Thugs were marched one by one before Jafir, who stated their names and the part they had played thus: "This is Bahadur Khan. He was present in all these affairs which I have related. He held hands in murder number seven and looked out for a good place to bury the murdered persons."

Three others of the gang, including Noor Khan, subsequently confessed, became approvers and confirmed this evidence. The prisoners were asked what they had to say in their own defence. Some of them claimed that they had been unjustly accused and were in fact honest tillers of the soil. One said the approvers had caused him to be arrested unjustly. Bahadur Khan answered with dignity that he had no excuse whatsoever, and several others followed his lead. Said by the approvers to have held the hands of victims while they were strangled, Bahadur was found Guilty of having taken part in the murder of five people and sentenced to death with several others. The remainder, also found Guilty, were transported for life. And so, no longer in the over-scrupulous hands of the judges the trials went forward, eliminating Thuggee by passing for the most part sentences of death, or transportation overseas for life—a punishment involving travel over the ocean that then meant loss of caste for Hindus.

In June 1832 fifty-three Thugs who took part in the notorious Burwaha Ghat murders and the seizure of 15,000 gold dollars four years earlier were tried. The money had belonged to a banker named Dunraj Seth, who was sending this money from Bombay to Indore for payments to those concerned in the East India Company's opium monopoly. When Dhunraj Seth, a very influential person, heard of the robbery, he immediately wrote to the British Residents in Indore and Gwalior requesting troops to aid in seizing the Thugs and recovering his money. With their help and that of an agent of Seth's named Bearee Lal, who occasionally employed Thugs for his own purposes, several of the main leaders in the affair were arrested.

The British Residents—in 1828, that is, when Thugs were tolerated—turned them over to the Indian local authorities, who let them go. Most of them were re-arrested in 1830 and '31. Moklal, Jonooa and a few others confessed, and fifty-three of the gang Sleeman committed for trial. The report, based on Sleeman's official record, is of special interest for three reasons: it shows how the Thugs worked, how they hung grimly on to an evasive quarry, and most important, how the sect was linked with people of influence in India.

12

The Bankers

The second day of the expedition brought two victims. The gang, led by Roshun, Zolfukar Khan and Maharaj Pattuck, crossed the Narbada river in the later afternoon, camped for the night near the village of Cheepaneere, and early next morning rode over low hills and through thick jungle until at midday they stopped by a small river to eat and smoke.

A pony carrying two armed men approached. Roshun greeted them and enticed them to sit down in the shade. A junior Thug put rice and fruit before them. The travellers, both Muslims, gave thanks, and with their matchlocks beside them, confided that they were going to Aurungabad, some 200 miles south, in Hyderabad. Roshun had heard all that he needed to know—the two had been on the road for some days already and were not known locally, so would not be missed. They were perfect victims. For their part the two Muslims were so pleased at meeting these honest people that they willingly agreed to travel on the same road and camp with them overnight.

Roshun's gang secretly made preparations and in the evening, after they had ridden some miles, two of them signalled the lonely spot chosen for the murder—a small glade near a river, where already some of the gang had unrolled carpets and were resting. A fire was lit and dinner eaten. A cool breeze fanned the weary travellers and a Thug apprentice stood up and twanged an appealing melody on the sitar. The travellers were entranced, and asked the young man to sing the tune. The boy's voice rose up and down the scale, soft and seductive in the dark night. The travellers sat with eyes closed, swaying with delight, while the chosen Thugs moved silently into position behind them. Both victims raised their heads, baring their throats, and began to sing as well. Roshun quietly spoke the signal: "Bring tobacco!" The *rumals* flashed round the victims' necks and their song ended, they fell and lay still.

In the dense undergrowth beside the rivulet a small shallow grave was ready and here the victims' bodies were pillaged and stripped. In the usual way sharp stakes were driven into them, their joints were broken, earth was heaped on them and stamped down, the top of the grave was smoothed over and handfuls of dry earth scattered over it. Roshun turned away and followed by the other Thugs concerned strode back to the camp fire. The glade in which music had sounded so sweetly must have seemed strangely quiet, but Thugs were insensitive to such things. They celebrated a sacrifice to their goddess—the ceremony of the *tuponee*, the sacrifice of *goor* in which all joined after a killing and which the fraternity regarded as a communion with the goddess that it was dangerous to neglect. Afterwards, the loot—150 rupees (£15)—was shared; the proceeds from the sale of the two matchlocks and the pony would be divided later.

The Thugs lay down on their blankets, undisturbed by conscience or their memories of the two men whom they had befriended—who had trusted them, shared their food and music, and who were then lying mutilated in an unknown grave in the jungle, awaited by wives and children who would never see them again. Fears of retribution the Thugs had none. They knew the danger of their being apprehended was slight in the extreme. Even if the bodies were found, which was unlikely, no one would link them with the killing. They slept soundly by the dying embers of the fire.

Thugs had in the course of ages perfected their trade with many smooth confidence tricks and these two particular murders were based on a cunning adaptation of one they named the *gan kurna*—to feign sickness to bring the travellers into a situation and condition favourable for strangling. The *ganoo*, or sick person, fell down and pretended to be taken violently ill. Some of his fellow Thugs raised and supported him, others brought water, some felt his pulse. At last one pretended that a charm would restore him. The victims were asked to sit down around the pot of water, take off their waistbands, uncover their necks then look up and count a number of stars. While they were thus engaged in trying to restore the sick Thug to health, *rumals* were thrown round their exposed necks and they were strangled. Roshun's gang had with devilish subterfuge got the sitting victims to look up at the standing figure of the musician and expose their throats by singing.

Late in the afternoon of the next day the gang arrived on the outskirts of a town named Edulabad and Roshun sent two Thugs disguised as sepoys to seek out likely victims around the brothels and bazaars. Informants told the scouts that a party of treasure-bearers and matchlock-men carrying a large sum of money and jewels from Bombay to Indore had arrived there and that they would leave the following day.

Back at the Thug camp, the news sent the gang into a high pitch of excitement. Roshun ordered spies back to the bazaar to see which road the treasure-bearers took. The spies waited until nearly midday before discovering that their quarry had somehow quietly slipped off and taken the road to Borhanpore. Roshun sent a dozen scouts after them, but not until late that night did the scouts return and report failure—the treasure-bearers were neither in Borhanpore nor had they passed along the road to it.

Roshun sent off more scouts, offering a joint reward of 100 rupees over and above their share of the treasure. He received the news next day that the quarry were on the road to Asseer, several miles to the north-west, and he pushed the gang hard in pursuit. On the outskirts of Asseer, the scouts reported that the party were held up at the customs. Roshun led the gang on the road to Boregow, the next village, hoping to intercept them in a jungle. He left two scouts to keep him in touch. But the treasure-bearers matched the Thugs in craftiness. Fearful of robbers they had deliberately laid a false trail. A scout from Asseer rode up to tell Roshun that, after all, the quarry would not pass that way, having turned off for Punchpuhar, on a different road.

Roshun returned through the jungle to Asseer and rode on to Punchpuhar, only to find no trace of the quarry here either. It was now late, so they camped beneath some trees outside the village. Early next morning a crane called twice in the distance. It was a good omen for success and Roshun sent six of his best

Thugs in different directions—two back to Asseer, two to Boregow and two to Sherepore, while the main body waited at Punchpuhar.

Just before sunset two scouts returned from Sherepore with the news that the treasure-bearers had lodged there last night and had set out for Indore that morning, intending to stay at a small village about thirty miles ahead. Said Moklal, the Thug who first confessed to these murders:

> On learning this, although we were all much tired, we at once set out for that village. . . . We arrived there at midnight and encamped outside the village under a large peepul tree. The next morning when the treasure-bearers set out we followed, but about two miles from the village we were detained by the village customs men. We paid them one rupee and four annas, but meantime the treasure-bearers had gone on ahead and crossed the Narbada river at Burwaha ghat and gone on to the village and put up at a serai there.
>
> We followed, crossed the Narbada at the same ghat and encamped outside the village under a bhyr tree near the small reservoir. The next morning the chief of this village customs station held up the treasure-bearers to settle duties on their treasure and we were held up too, but we decided not to pay until the treasure-bearers had settled, so that we could follow them. The customs demanded a very high rate of duty from the treasure-bearers and a great row broke out between them. It went on through the morning and the afternoon until finally Marharaj Patuck went to the chief official and reproved him, asking why he did not settle and let the bearers go on, as, in the event of any loss to their treasure if they moved at a late hour, he would be responsible for it. The chief became alarmed at this and took from them what they offered.
>
> It was now late, and the treasure party decided not to go on that night. We paid our customs dues and went on to a garden a few miles on, where we cooked, ate our dinner and passed the night. While we were preparing to move next morning, we saw the camels and the treasure-bearers coming, and we at once rode on quickly ahead to a nullah in a bamboo jungle, where there was an uninhabited village. After cutting some large bamboo rods, we all sat down, thinking it was a suitable place for the murder.

While we were smoking, a man on horseback who had been the companion of the treasure-bearers since the night before came up and sat down with us to smoke. Soon after, the treasure-bearers arrived. The six matchlock-men sat down to rest and talk, but the camel-men stayed in their saddles. We surrounded them from every side and seized and strangled the six matchlock-men and the horseman. The camel-men we tumbled out of their saddles as they tried to ride off and strangled them as well. We buried the bodies in the nullah . . . and took the camels through a by-road through the jungle. . . . A few miles from where we had committed the murder we sat down and took the loads off the camels, put them on our ponies and turned the camels loose in the jungle.

Here we left the Indore road and took another towards the east. In three days we reached Sundalpore and encamped on the banks of a tank. We cut the treasure bags with knives and swords, finding 15,000 Spanish dollars, 100 rupees worth of silver bullion and a small sealed brass box. We found in it four diamond rings set with jewels, eight pearls and a pair of gold bangles, all of which amounted to 1000 Spanish dollars in value.

From this booty Zalim took a handful of Spanish dollars as an offering to Devi (*Kali*), which we intended to give to the priests of Bundachul. . . . We had about 150 Spanish dollars each. We passed that night at Sundulpore and afterwards returned to our homes by regular stages.

This particular crime was soon detected. The camels were found wandering in the jungle, the bodies were discovered and the news was reported to the owner of the stolen treasure, Dhunraj Seth, the banker.

What happened next was typical of the morally lax administration and disregard for human life that enabled Thuggee to flourish. Seth discovered through his spies the identity of the Thugs responsible and sent his agent, Bearee Lal, who frequently arranged protection for Thugs, with the names of some of those involved to the British Resident in Bundelcund, north of Sleeman's district. This official had those Thugs whom Seth named arrested and turned over to the Indian rulers in whose jurisdiction they resided, with orders that the stolen money should be returned to Seth. The Indian authorities ordered the Thugs to give three-quarters of the money to the owners and the rest to them. Said Moklal:

> We agreed and were let go. Some paid out of the fruits of former expeditions; others borrowed in anticipation of future success; and those who had neither money nor credit, pledged themselves to pay part of their future earnings. To this, Bearee Lal agreed, and sent them on expeditions, retaining Choti, Bukhut and other jemadars of great influence about his person. He also got a good deal of money at this time by procuring the release of all the noted Thugs then in confinement at different places.
>
> He got 9000 rupees (£900) for the release of Dhurum Khan Jemadar from Gwalior, on the pretence that he was engaged in the affair, when he had been in prison long before. Dhurum had got a great prize of jewels from some men killed near Kotah, and his family could afford to pay.
>
> Such was Dhunraj Seth's influence that he could get a gang released from prison in any part of India; and for some time his agent Bearee Lal had always half a dozen of the principal Thug leaders about his person. He used to attend all our marriages and festivals. What his master got we know not; but he got a great deal of money.

Later Sleeman found out that this rich and powerful banker was making strenuous efforts to become the main financial backer of the Thug gangs. In a warning letter to the Government about this sinister development on 12 April 1832, he wrote:

> It is essentially necessary for the success of this or any other plan for the suppression of Thuggee that we should prevent Dhunraj Seth, the great banker of Omrautee, or any of his partners or numerous agents from having communication with the Thugs seized; or any attempts to indemnify themselves, to profit by their murders, to effect their release by bribery, corruption, intrigue or solicitation from all the native chiefs in whose dominions they have found them imprisoned; and to send them again upon the roads with advances of money or subsistence till fresh murders have brought them fresh treasure for division.
>
> Had their attempts not been providentially checked by our

operations I declare before God that I believe that this House would have become the great capitalists and patrons of murder from Lahore to Cape Cormorin; and that the price of blood would have flowed into their coffers from every road throughout this enormous empire.

Wherever a few Thugs are to be found they have their agents employed and I have been repeatedly urged since I came to Saugor to permit a branch of this House to be established in this town, where they have had an agent ever since I began operations against the Thugs. But I have always refused with the open declaration that I believe the sole object of such an establishment would be the prospect of a profit from the extensive employment of murderers.

I am every day . . . hearing young men acknowledge that they follow this trade of murder in the service of the very wretches who they know murdered their parents while they were yet infants. . . . I asked how they could do so after they had discovered that their fathers and mothers were put to death by them. Their only answer has been invariably that their habits had been formed before the discovery was made and that it is difficult to change one's occupations and associates in life.

So it is with this great banking establishment. They began with an attempt to recover lost property and they will go on to speculate in the trade of murder from habit if not prevented by our continued watchfulness.

It was a bold charge, yet based on sound evidence, and it is tempting to wonder to what extent the Thug secret societies were dependent on a central financial source for their working funds. Then, as now, bankers worked in concert. It is possible therefore that Dhunraj Seth sought to get a bigger share of the Thug profits. But it came to nought. Bearee Lal was arrested, tried and imprisoned for conniving with Thugs. Dhunraj Seth turned his attention to a safer field—financing the opium trade which the Company was so industriously developing with the unfortunate Chinese.

Meantime, having forced the Thugs in central India to stay at home or go into hiding rather than risk seizure at their favourite roadside haunts, Sleeman turned his attention to the independent states of the Indian rulers, where so many Thugs still received sanctuary. He sent Thug-hunting detachments to Hyderabad, Gwalior, Nagpur and Rajputana, especially along roads frequented by sepoys going home on leave from Madras and Bombay—they were mostly Rajputs, and favourite victims of Thugs. Reporting this in April 1832 he wrote:

> These detachments are now provided with approvers well acquainted with the usual movements of all the principal Thugs who have hitherto considered the annual leave period as a legitimate kind of harvest, so we have a good chance of securing some of their gangs. At all events we will prevent their depredations along the roads from Madras, Bombay and Central India to the Gangetic provinces.
>
> Thugs have often told me that the reason why they choose the native officers and sepoys of our armies in preference to other travellers is that they commonly carry more money and other valuable articles about them and are from their arms, their strength, self-confidence and haughty bearing more easily deceived by the vain humility and respect of the Thugs, and led off the high roads into jungly and solitary situations . . . where they are more easily murdered and their bodies disposed of.

By July 1832 the detachments had swept the roads in a circle through Baroda and Nagpur in the south, Bundelcund in the north-west and Jodhpur in the west. Scores of alleged Thugs had been seized and hundreds of lives were presumed to have been saved. Sleeman had also sent Major Stewart, Resident at the court of the Nizam of Hyderabad, a list of 150 Thug jemadars. Stewart organised his own detachments and soon Sleeman received reports of arrests of known Thugs. A list of 464 jemadars leading gangs in the upper provinces of India, north of Delhi, he sent to magistrates there, with the comment that because they invariably used so many different aliases it was hard to find them without the aid of their one-time colleagues the approvers.

The detachments were now hunting down Thugs over an area three or four times as big as Britain, and Bentinck had at last recognised Sleeman's urgent need for help. In May 1832 Captain Reynolds was appointed to superintend in the low-lying plains south of the Narbada river, but excluding Hyderabad. In September, a junior magistrate named Wilson took over in the

Doab, the delta between the Ganges and the Jumna rivers, aided by a force of forty sepoys and twenty *nujeebs*, the mounted irregulars. Later, Captain Paton was to be appointed in the Lucknow district of Oude and Lieutenant Elwall sent south with 100 *nujeebs* to help Captain Reynolds.

Sleeman was now aided by several officers and between seven and eight hundred *nujeebs* and sepoys, a useful force but still absurdly small for hunting thousands of wily Thugs, natives of the country whose entire lives had been spent in learning the arts of deception.

He ordered these slender forces to seek out and seize not only the jemadars, so as to destroy the society leadership and obtain its secrets, but the *gurus* too, elderly and infirm Thugs upon whom apprentices depended for instruction in Thug lore in their rise to the much revered rank of strangler. In this way he hoped to prevent the teaching being passed on to the younger generation, and thus to strangle Thuggee itself. By the end of July 1832 many of both were in prison awaiting trial.

But the remaining jemadars outside central India went into hiding, or into military service with the princes, who, Curwen Smith remarked pompously, "they know to be averse, from a besotted and ignorant point of honour which knows not how to discriminate, to give up even a known murderer". In central India all the jemadars of note except four had been arrested. Sleeman reported:

> We have at least twenty jemadars in captivity who could, if released, at any time collect 1000 followers at short notice. Once a Thug always a Thug is their motto and their creed. Nothing can reform or deter them. . . .

In the second half of 1832 Sleeman's targets were still the Hyderabad, Nagpore, Jypore, Rajputana, Baroda, Gujerat and Gwalior gangs. Curwen Smith meantime informed British Residents in Indian states throughout these regions that the Thug-hunting detachments would enter their rulers' jurisdiction. In pursuance of the Governor-General's policy their zealous aid was requested. A more extensive campaign was about to be launched, but obstruction and non-cooperation by British Residents at the courts of the Indian rulers now became a barrier to progress.

13

Cavendish Opposes

Sleeman's detachments, commanded by Indian non-commissioned officers and accompanied by two or three approvers each, sallied into the independent states to seize named Thugs. Sometimes they were driven by their zeal to disobey orders and avoid consulting with the local authorities, many of whom were known to be Thug supporters. Indian rulers raised an outcry at this, both owing to sensitivity about their remaining independence and because some of them wished to protect these murderers who contributed so generously to their annual revenue. Sleeman believed the vizier of the Raja of Tehree to be a member of the fraternity, so ardently did he try to prevent the detachments from entering the Raja's dominions.

Outstanding among apparently non-cooperating British Residents was Richard Cavendish, at Gwalior. Frequently the detachments were stopped at the state frontiers; once when they were let in they were subsequently attacked by the ruler's troops and a sepoy was killed. Word spread among Thugs there that Cavendish had given the ruler free reign to shelter them if he so wished and Gwalior remained a sanctuary to which, after a glut of murder elsewhere they returned, as Sleeman put it, with as much safety as an Englishman to his inn.

The Gwalior state even levied a tax of 24 rupees on each of 318 houses inhabited by Thugs in the Sindhouse region. Sleeman estimated that there were three men who went on Thuggee in each of these 318 houses and that there were accordingly some 954 Sindhouse Thugs in Gwalior. Later, this was revised to include another 122 families not on the list although the zemindars levied the tax on them. The estimated total of Thugs in this region alone was therefore 1320, based on three Thugs for every house.

Cavendish's seeming toleration of an evil it was part of his duty to urge the ruler to suppress held up progress. Sleeman protested, and in turn Curwen Smith complained in a report to the Governor-General, giving Cavendish a chance to mend his ways by saying that his attitude seemed to have been caused by misunderstanding about how the parties assigned to arrest Thugs in Gwalior were controlled. He added:

> Should, unfortunately, the gentleman still adhere to his former opinion and way of proceeding the government may rest assured not only that we shall be seriously checked and affected thereby . . . but that the Gwalior territory will become an asylum for all Thugs still at large and the source from which Thuggee will again spread all over the country, and the system will arise with renewed strength. . . . The snake will have been scotched, not killed.

It was a grave setback. Then R. T. Lushington, Resident in Bhurtpore [Bharatpore], saw the power of the Thug-hunters to enter his Raja's dominions at will as an infringement of independence and protested vigorously to the Governor-General about a Thug-hunting party arresting three people without permission from him or the Raja. One of these was a sepoy serving in the Raja's personal guard, the other a Brahmin.

None of the three were named on the list of wanted Thugs and upon inquiry Lushington found that the only "evidence" this party had for the arrests was that of a prostitute, who said she had heard from her keeper, a man named Meer Khan, then in prison, that the accused used to accompany him on his Thug expeditions: "And on this mere hearsay respected members of the community are apprehended as murderers and to be sent in chains to Saugor. I beg to ask whether it is consistent with justice to capture persons on such a charge and evidence and this too, without allowing the prisoners to say a word in their own defence . . .?" he wrote indignantly to the Governor-General.

Lushington raised other important issues, arguing that Thug approvers were not separated and that they could therefore with perfect ease agree among themselves to bring charges against any persons whatsoever:

> It follows that even if their statements agreed together they are not entitled to credence. The agreement if it existed would prove nothing. But in the case of the Brahman they arrested there was not even one of them who attested to the Brahman's criminality but the prostitute, who when questioned kindly volunteered her hearsay evidence and on this hearsay the man was arrested.

Innocent people of substance arrested without any hearing of their defence, Lushington said, could perhaps obtain their liberty or avoid going in chains to Saugor by bribing the approvers or *nujeebs*. He requested that Thug-hunting parties be prohibited in the future from seizing any person except through the constituted authorities and that a full record of the evidence of the approvers and what the accused had to say in their defence should be taken.

He added as a footnote that he had just received information that the inhabitants of the city of Bhurtpore had not unnaturally been thrown into a state of great alarm and dread owing to the approvers persisting in searching persons without informing the authorities, or asking their aid.

> I have written to them . . . and have also summoned their leader before me and have not scrupled to assure them that if they continue to act in this manner a guard of sepoys shall be placed over them, nor shall they be released until they have learnt to conduct themselves with propriety.

Reasonable and fair, though forceful, Lushington's protest appears to have been taken by the Governor-General as a challenge to continued operations in Bhurtpore by Thug-hunting parties. It brought an answer by William Macnaghten, his personal secretary, an intensely ambitious specialist in Hindu and Muslim law and a linguist who nevertheless seems to have lacked understanding of practical affairs. (Macnaghten was ten years later to be assassinated in Kabul by Akbar Khan, son of the deposed ruler Dost Mahommed.) His letter was a masterpiece of evasion.

> Your observations [he wrote], are doubtless just in the abstract, but to check the dreadful evil of Thuggee extraordinary

> measures are necessary. This is sufficiently apparent from your own judicious remarks on the subject. The natives of your city, strange as it may appear, do not cooperate heartily . . . and the very *moonshees* (secretaries or interpreters) who read official letters to the Raja on the subject have it in their power to thwart the objects in view by communicating the approach of the police party, thereby enabling the Thugs to keep out of the way.

Defending the plan of operations, he accused Lushington of believing that

> the assertions of the approvers constitute the sum total of evidence against the persons apprehended. The evidence by which those individuals are indicated is unquestionably meagre and wholly insufficient for a conviction, but this usually is the case at the start of every criminal investigation and was especially to be expected on an occasion like the present, where the pursuit is surrounded by too many difficulties.

No British officer, he went on, begging the question to the end, would convict accused persons on this very slender evidence, nor would approvers have reason to point out people as Thugs without proof of guilt.

Meantime, in Gwalior, Richard Cavendish too had responded little to requests to assist Thug-hunting parties. Cavendish had an aristocratic regard for his status and his powers as Resident at the Gwalior court of the Regent, the Baiza Bai, a formidable and some times a violent woman, widow of the former ruler, Daulat Rao Sindhia.

Cavendish maintained a stable of elephants as well as horses and rode out with them in procession to impress the people with his splendour. He kept a herd of cattle, lived in lavish style, importing fine furniture, glassware, linen, silver, works of art, wines and brandies on a scale far exceeding the financial entitlement of a Resident, and charged much of it to his contingent expenses. But the Regent, he complained to the Governor-General, lacked a proper respect for his status. On ceremonial occasions she made him stand on her left, minus his shoes, among those of lesser rank, instead of on her right among princes and others entitled to wear their shoes.

Now, on the grounds that this woman was despotic and unmanageable, Cavendish failed to persuade her to cooperate with the Thug-hunting parties. When these were totally frustrated Sleeman protested again and Macnaghten, writing to Cavendish on behalf of Bentinck, pointed out that local authorities alone could do little to crush Thuggee and only a well-planned system centrally directed could succeed. He went on to say that the mass of evidence Sleeman had collected had supplied him with the names and enabled him to convict nearly all the professional Thugs in upper India. He could moreover act with a degree of certainty and efficiency which, if properly supported by local authorities, promised a speedy end of Thuggee. "I have been directed to furnish you with this brief outline . . . with a view to impress upon you in the most serious manner the necessity which exists of your . . . assisting in these efforts with all the means at your command," he ended.

It was a sharp rebuke, but a man of Cavendish's temper was not easily moved. Curwen Smith was soon complaining again about him:

> The territory of Gwalior is so situated that Cavendish has if he chooses the means of entirely frustrating our exertions. . . . It is a true though melancholy fact that the officers of these native states will, if they can, screen the Thugs. It is not many years since each government openly protected the Thugs of their own country or of their allies.

In an effort to persuade Cavendish to obtain free movement for Sleeman's Thug-hunters, Curwen Smith then reminded him of the strict regulations ruling those in charge of detachments, and continued:

> I am assured you will in future grant us your cordial assistance . . . more so that you cannot but be of the opinion that the temporary confinement of a few innocent individuals until they can be tried and acquitted at Saugor cannot be put in competition with the paramount necessity of rooting out and exterminating the Thugs.

Here was the essence of the dispute: the belief by Sleeman and Curwen Smith that the means justified the end; and the insistence by Cavendish and Lushington upon correct judicial procedure to safeguard the rights of the rulers and their subjects. There is also little doubt that Cavendish had great difficulty in getting a hearing at the court of the Regent. But Bentinck had committed the government to the present plan as the only one able to end Thuggee. He had no intention of being sidetracked by protests about human rights and justice by British representatives in Indian states acknowledged to be grinding military despotisms, in which everybody's rights but the rulers' were laughed to scorn.

Sleeman apologised to Lushington for the breach of regulations at Bhurtpore. In the absence of his trusted helper Rustum Khan, he said, the *moonshee* had assumed unjustified authority over the detachment. Orders were that they should arrest only a gang of Thugs known to be in the region and make them over at once to the local authority. Cavendish then wrote to the young Maharajah and the Regent, his mother, urging compliance with the policy of the Supreme Government regarding Thugs. The Maharajah answered through the Regent that he had the matter at heart and that he had given orders to this effect. But there was no improvement; and Curwen Smith let the issue grow into one of personalities between Cavendish and him. He wrote an angry letter:

> So long as the people under your superintendence right or wrong believe you to be opposed to the special duty entrusted to me and Captain Sleeman, so long will it be futile, nay dangerous, to send detachments in search of Thugs into the Gwalior territory and I have therefore sanctioned Captain Sleeman's proposal to refrain in future until we can rely upon your support —not a cold dubious support, but your warm and cordial co-operation. . . . But the responsibility for this must rest on you. The success of your measures has been indeed complete, for not one Thug can now be touched in the Gwalior territory.

It would appear that Richard Cavendish was unduly touchy about his status and tried to disregard the social parity which existed on the whole among British officials in India then. There is support for this view in a letter Sleeman wrote to Curwen Smith:

> I have been favoured with the perusal of the Honourable

Mr Cavendish's letter to you of 28 July and I regret to see he thinks the style of my letters to him has not been sufficiently respectful and conciliatory. I have written several private letters to him since I entered upon this delicate and arduous duty and every sentence has been with the most sincere and best wish to be both respectful and conciliatory. First, because I consider it due to his exalted situation as the representative of the Governor-General at a foreign court. Second, because I thought it most calculated to promote the great end we all have in view and thirdly, because I am in the habit of doing so to all men and have no earthly reasons why I should do otherwise to him.

The anti-Thug campaign in Gwalior had been brought to a standstill. And Lushington, in Bhurtpore, smarting both from the humiliation done to the Raja by the Thug-hunters and by Macnaghten's justification of these methods, now counter-attacked with a reply in which he opposed its entire basis. His object, he said, had been to point out the wrongfulness of arresting people on mere hearsay. He wrote to Macnaghten, the Governor-General's personal secretary:

I now learn, I must confess with no little astonishment that however extraordinary the measures adopted may have been, still they were both just and necessary because Thuggee cannot otherwise be checked. In other words that the end justifies the means, a doctrine which I had erroneously supposed to have been long since exploded alike from morals and politics. . . . Nor is notice taken of the insult put upon the Bhurtpore Rajah in arresting one of his sepoys without his knowledge, or consent. The Government may be of opinion that humiliation of this sort is not felt by a native prince, but I can take upon me to assert that it was felt, and deeply too, and that it is not by such measures as these that the Bhurtpore or any other native authorities will be induced to co-operate heartily in the suppression of Thuggee.

Lushington, British representative at an obscure court, was boldly lecturing the Governor-General upon abstract justice. He was perhaps right; the policy was open to objection, but of the two evils Thuggee was infinitely worse, and it was a fact; whereas harm that could arise from the methods of seizing Thugs was only potential.

So Lushington's bold try at calling the tune was bound to fail and, for its tone, sure to land him in trouble. Macnaghten replied on behalf of Bentinck, not directly to Lushington, but to the Governor-General's Agent for the region, asking him to intimate the displeasure his Lordship felt at the improper style of Mr Lushington's letter. He was ordered to be more accurate in the substance and more sober in the style of his future comments and to understand that the measures, however extraordinary they might be, were considered by his Lordship to be just and necessary.

After this any ideas Lushington may have had about encouraging the Raja to oppose the entrance of Thug-hunters were nipped in the bud. Yet he had gained one point—the detachments would henceforward pay strict attention to their orders not to move without the knowledge and approval of the local authority, for Sleeman had taken them to task.

Macnaghten now tried to conciliate Cavendish. His Lordship, he wrote on 24 July, did not consider it necessary to make any further observations on the subject, feeling assured that the instructions which had already been issued to Mr Cavendish would have the effect of urging that gentleman to a more zealous co-operation.

But Cavendish then argued that it would be hard to overcome support for Thugs in Gwalior, pointing out again that the Regent was a violent woman who would not hesitate to go to war if hard-pressed by the Supreme Government on any issue she believed to be her own business. He wrote, on 1 August 1832:

> You will, I hope, do me the justice of attributing any immediate failures to the real or true causes and I will hold myself responsible to bring about the apprehension of all the gangs of Thugs and the suppression of Thuggee within six months. I need not, I hope, conclude by observing that I shall always be thankful for any and every information you can procure regarding the Thugs residing in this dominion.

Cavendish followed this letter—in effect a denial of entry for Sleeman's detachments—with another to Sleeman setting out the difficulties he faced in Gwalior. His own powers, he said, were purely diplomatic, whereas Sleeman's were political and judicial; in his judicial capacity he was supreme, his orders could not be disputed. He himself had to manage the most independent territory, apathetic and suspicious court possible, a court showing in every way personal disrespect towards British officers, who could not ride out a short distance from the Residency without a mounted and armed escort. In a remark that made clear his own weakness, he added: "I am not as you are, armed with *judicial* power. Whatever remonstrances are made, must be made in diplomatic language and not in *judicial* orders."

But Curwen Smith was not to be put off by excuses without action whatever the circumstances, and he now moved into the ring again and in sarcastic tone asked what actually was being done to co-operate:

> Sir, As your opposition to our measures to arrest Thugs in the Gwalior territory has I have no doubt originated from your good though mistaken motives, I flatter myself you will on the receipt of Mr Macnaghten's letter of the 24th be induced cordially to extend your countenance and assistance with all the means at your command to us, to enable operations to be again commenced upon. It was with unqualified regret that I felt compelled to suspend proceedings until I could be assured that our parties would be protected . . . and I shall therefore as soon as you communicate your intention of supporting us request Captain Sleeman to proceed as usual.

But no such assurances were given, for on 16 August Macnaghten wrote stiffly to him on behalf of the Governor-General:

> Sir, In reply to your letter dated the 3rd I am directed to observe that it does not appear what notice you have taken of Mr Smith's letter, a copy of which is enclosed. . . .

Cavendish replied with a blunt letter opposing Thug-hunting parties and informers being sent into Gwalior in any circumstances. He argued:

> These informers are themselves Thugs acknowledging murders innumerable. In my opinion no native or natives ought to be entrusted with such unlimited power and I beg leave to suggest

that a British officer or someone of great experience with regard to rights and independence of the native states should be deputed with such a party.

Cavendish then struck his strongest blow yet against the anti-Thug campaign—a request that there should be an immediate inquiry as to whether the employment of informers be considered absolutely necessary for the suppression of Thuggee. He suspected that oppression or corruption could lead to the detention of innocent people, who would be transported to Saugor in chains:

> Their apprehension, detention and confinement, if innocent, must be considered a great evil. The Gwalior territory has had several visits for this purpose since my arrival and having been a magistrate in former days I know of the difficulty of preventing extortion and oppression.

A deadlock had now arisen, for while Cavendish was clearly determined not to give way, Bentinck would certainly not allow him to stop the campaign in Gwalior indefinitely. Nor was it likely that he would agree to the suggestion that there should be an inquiry as to the need for informers when they had been proved to be so effective. Macnaghten, replying to Cavendish's letter on behalf of the Governor-General, dodged the issue by arguing that Cavendish was mistaken in thinking that parties of informers were sent from Saugor into all independent states to apprehend Thugs. They were sent merely for the purpose of pointing out individuals who had been practising Thuggee.

For a British officer to accompany each party, he said, was quite impossible; a trustworthy *subadar* was in command of each one, but if Cavendish felt that there was a danger of collusion he was at liberty to appoint any other officer in whom he had confidence to act as a check upon the proceedings. Macnaghten continued with a statement of Lord William Bentinck's attitude to the issue of arrest of possibly innocent people:

> Some of the people pointed out as Thugs and apprehended as such by the informers may be innocent, His Lordship is ready to admit. But he does not consider it at all probable that any incidents of this nature are liable to occur. Nor does His Lordship think we should suffer ourselves to be deterred by the

purposes of possible evil from the prosecution of a scheme which would alone appear calculated to protect the lives and property of the community.

The Governor-General had in one line of this letter admitted that it was likely that innocent people might be arrested, and in the next claimed that it was unlikely, thus showing his uncertainty about the system, despite his determination to continue with it. But just after he had made this avowal, he received a jolt that must have made him more uncertain than ever. In October 1832 Curwen Smith admitted in a letter to George Swinton, Chief Secretary, that among the detachments of nujeebs and informers bribery and corruption had in fact occurred. The need for effective supervision of them had, he said, "been written in letters of blood".

Cavendish's opposition was now seen to have been fully justified and on the face of it the anti-Thug campaign based on the use of informers was in jeopardy. Cavendish had become even more of a thorn in the Governor-General's flesh. But Bentinck could hardly remove him over such an issue—there could well have been political repercussions and a storm in Parliament at home. Cavendish had influential relatives.

Fortunately, there was another way at hand of bringing Cavendish to heel. It may have been pure coincidence, but at this time Swinton refused to authorise Cavendish's heavy expenses for the maintenance of his establishment—his elephants, his herd of cattle, his other numerous status symbols. Cavendish protested bitterly, complaining that he was being forced to live below the standard of an ordinary Indian merchant, but in vain. He was forced to discard all these trappings.

At the same time a concession was made to his point of view by the appointment of D. T. Macleod, a junior magistrate who had done much to forward the campaign, to superintend anti-Thug operations in Gwalior, Rajputana and Malwa. In obtaining sanction for this appointment, Curwen Smith, in a note to the Governor-General, claimed that it would conciliate the authorities of these states and that already such a measure had been proposed by Lushington and Cavendish—the latter had in fact asked for a British officer with each and every detachment. But Cavendish's brave opposition to the Governor-General came to an end at this point. A much chastened man, he eventually prevailed upon the Regent to allow the detachments to enter her state.

Were innocent men convicted upon the evidence of revengeful informers? Curwen Smith doubtless had evidence that they were when he spoke of "letters of blood". Those Thugs who were no longer free to strangle on the roads may have conspired together to send victims to the gallows instead, for by killing in this way they could at once show Kali their continued devotion and save their own lives. Thuggee may have been doomed, but it still lusted for death, using its destroyers to take its victims' lives and thus going to its end with a satanic laugh.

By the end of 1832 Sleeman and his assistants had arrested and sent for trial in that year 389 suspected Thugs—and possibly a few innocents. Of the total, 126 were hanged, 177 transported for life; 38 imprisoned for life; 10 imprisoned for shorter periods, 2 acquitted and 31 made approvers. The anti-Thug operations extended over three-quarters of India by the end of 1832 and the next year the seizures would be even greater. Fate now rewarded Sleeman with something nearer to his heart.

14

Thug Genealogy and Dialect

Sleeman began an official tour of the Saugor and Narbada Territories on New Year's Day, 1833. As a matter of course, he was accompanied by his wife—both were carried in the commonly used palanquin—Sleeman, who much preferred to ride a horse having temporarily given it up owing to rheumatism. He wore his gold-faced blue tunic and cocked hat with feathers, was preceded by a detachment of cavalry and an elephant, and followed by a party of sepoys in red tunics and white trousers with Brown Bess muskets at "shoulder arms". Behind came a long line of servants on foot and on ponies, with bullock carts and horsedrawn wagons piled high with camping equipment, food and baggage.

For Amélie it can have had few compensations, but the company of her husband. "I shall always respect marching," remarked Emily Eden of her own similar tour in these parts, "for making me . . . feel the advantage of a quiet room, with books and tables and chairs all clean and in the same place every day." Progress of this long untidy procession was necessarily slow, but it did not matter—Sleeman could observe the country and the people in more detail than if he was travelling faster. At villages of the usual white-washed mud and cow-dung hovels they passed en route he halted and, not far from the reclining cows and the chickens, heard as usual cases sent for trial by the local thanadar.

It was to have been just one of his routine tours on which he went once or twice a year, but fate, or the joltings Amélie—who was heavily pregnant—suffered on the journey, decided otherwise, for on the sixth day she was suddenly seized with the pains of childbirth. There was nothing for it but to stop in the next grove. Sleeman knew it to be a Thug *bele*—hardly an ideal place for their first child to be born in, yet symbolic of the intertwining of Sleeman's life with the fraternity. (For Thugs, the birth of a child in a grove where they had been accustomed to kill would contaminate it for generations ahead.) Indian servants pitched and furnished the tents, Sleeman helped his wife from her palanquin to one of them, and her own servants then took over.

Sleeman had sent two horsemen at the gallop to Saugor with a note to a doctor, but long before he could arrive, there, in the *bele* beneath whose lime and peepul trees generations of unsuspecting victims had been strangled, their first child, a boy, was born. They called him Henry. The boy would have three sisters in six years' time, and three years later, a fourth, but never again would Sleeman risk Amélie taking to the roads while she was in an advanced state of pregnancy.

Sleeman was now heartened to hear that Richard Cavendish, who for so many months had given no support to the campaign in Gwalior, in early 1833 had persuaded the Regent to send a company of sepoys and two field guns against a zemindar who refused to give up a gang of Thugs sheltering in one of his villages. When this well-armed force appeared the zemindar sent the women under guard secretly into the jungle and opened a hail of matchlock fire upon the troops. The fighting lasted from daybreak until darkness, when the zemindar signalled that the Thugs had fled during the afternoon. One of them said later when arrested:

> We heard that the troops were in pursuit and we hid ourselves at Biraji, but we were finally caught. Our hands were tied behind our backs and we were taken to prison. They took away all our clothes and would not let us call in any of our friends to bring us more. We remained four days in prison and were finally sent to . . . Saugor.

In the spring of 1833 while the Thug-hunting parties were out on the roads all over India and Curwen Smith was assembling the witnesses for that year's trials, Sleeman himself worked on two projects which, he believed, could prevent Thuggee ever rising again in its former virulence.

The close family links of hereditary Thugs gave him the brilliant idea of drawing up a series of family trees to cover the entire fraternity, root and branch, and early in 1833, he began work on them. From every hereditary Thug in captivity he obtained names of all the families of Thugs of opposing factions, their places of birth, their ancestors' names and their present home. This huge mass of information he carefully checked with local revenue lists (the most reliable registry). Slowly, bit by bit, he compiled family trees of the entire fraternity. When finished, this genealogical achievement would be ready for use at any time, a blue-print, as it were, of everyone, Muslim and Hindu, linked with Thuggee by blood.

Caste jealousy was the key to this operation. Try though they might to save relatives and friends, the approvers who supplied Sleeman with such information were themselves then betrayed by approvers of other castes. Wholesale betrayal was helping to destroy the Thug fraternity.

The other important project, which Sleeman tried now to finish, was the complete vocabulary of the Thug secret dialect *ramasee* which ran to several hundred words and offered important clues to their beliefs. It provided a weapon with which to hunt them down, for the knowledge that their long-secret dialect was in part known to their hunters greatly demoralised them. In addition, Sleeman thought it essential that a permanent record should be made of it for future students of the cult.

Curwen Smith tried another 203 suspect Thugs during the first four months of 1833. All were found Guilty; 40 of them were hanged, 156 sentenced to transportation for life and to be branded; five were given short sentences and two died after trial while awaiting sentence. These Thugs were tried for the murder of 112 people, fifty-six of whose bodies were exhumed. The money and valuables stolen from the victims amounted to 71,722 rupees (about £7,100), but owing to their having been arrested mostly at their homes and not on expeditions, almost none of it was recovered, the Thugs having hidden or disposed of it. Sleeman notes that he had forbidden his *nujeebs* to search for stolen property in and around Thug homes because both bribery and the finding of treasure put too much temptation in their way.

More Thugs were now being arrested at home than on the roads, for the Thug-hunting detachments were discouraging more and more from venturing on expeditions. Arrest on the roads made for easier conviction; Thugs had to account for the loot found on them and give reasons for being perhaps three hundred miles from home for several weeks. To invent reasons sound enough to convince experienced cross-examiners like Sleeman, Macleod and Wilson was hard indeed. Therefore much more at this time depended on the approvers, who led the sepoys and *nujeebs* to Thug homes.

Meantime, Curwen Smith's admission of conspiracy and corruption among approvers and *nujeebs* and the possible conviction of innocent people, had made the Government grow a little apprehensive and it had asked for more details about safeguards. Sleeman at the same time in 1833 had to apply new and rigorous checks against such conspiracy. Captured suspects were at once paraded before groups of mutually hostile approvers. He reported:

> Until I came to Saugor our approvers were almost all of the Lodhee (small landowner) caste and they exerted themselves so effectively to screen their relations that very few were arrested, while almost every great road in India was infested by them. Soon after my arrival here a few of the leading characters of the Brahman, Musselman, Buneea (merchant) and other castes of Thug were induced to come forward, and with their aid we have been able to secure the greater part of the Lodhee Thugs who resided in Bundelcund and a great many of those who lived in the Dooab, and to establish at once a stimulus and a check without which our proceedings must have been much less satisfactory.

He went on to say that some of these approvers felt obliged to mention the share that they and their own relations had in various expeditions, in order to establish a good character in their new vocation and in the hope that these friends and relations would be induced to deliver themselves up. Were they not to expose them, they believed, their enemies the approvers of other castes would observe their attempt at concealment and try to lead to the inference that their testimony could be of little value in general.

The approvers were better fed and were kept apart from other

Thugs in prison, since otherwise they would be poisoned, or murdered in some other way. Sleeman reported:

> I shall never venture to recommend that any man who has taken a prominent part in these dreadful expeditions be let loose again upon society. He would sooner or later return to his old trade of murder. But I shall hereafter recommend that a great many of those whom we now employ have a decent subsistence for life with such employment as it may be safe and advantageous to give them.

These hints Sleeman from time to time dropped were his method of preparing the Governor-General for a scheme that he was maturing, for giving profitable work to convicted Thugs. He went on to say that when there were sufficient grounds from the approvers' testimonies to believe the men named to be Thugs, they were entered in the general lists furnished to the officers whose aid he required in their arrest:

> The evidence for and against them is taken and weighed by these officers and by other local authorities when they are arrested, and they never send them to Saugor unless they feel satisfied that the grounds are good. Immediately on their arrival at Saugor they are examined by me; and the approvers, their old associates, are never suffered to see them until they are confronted one after the other with them in court and required to state what they know of their name, family, character and proceedings. The approver examined is not suffered to remain in court while the next approver is under examination, nor to return to those unexamined till the examination is closed, so that nothing can be concerted between them, and unless the grounds are so strong as to leave scarcely any doubt that the prisoner is by trade a murderer he is immediately discharged.
>
> In the next place I examine in his presence the evidence against every individual in the case of the particular murders for which he is to take his trial. . . . Before he is sent for trial I bring him again before all the approvers who deposed to his identity on his first arrival, and the principal of every one of the factions assembled together and again question them confronted with each other, regarding his character and calling. Here they

> are again often confronted with their oldest friends and nearest relations, all anxious to see them escape, but still they are willing to give their enemies of other factions the advantage of a false declaration; and with the labour I take and the knowledge regarding these men and their proceedings that I have acquired and am acquiring, it is hardly possible that I should send for trial . . . a man who has not been engaged in these murderous expeditions, whatever share he may have had in the particular crime for which he is to be tried.

Curwen Smith, defending the practice of trying at Saugor Thugs taken anywhere in the Company's territories, argued that with so many approvers of different castes held there, they had a a better chance of being freed if innocent and were most likely to be convicted if guilty. Regarding methods used at the trials, he wrote:

> Besides the evidence of the approvers, each trial is furnished with collateral proof obtained by the exhumation of the bodies of the murdered. I consider the exhumation of these bodies is proof against every person concerned in their murder, not only against the approvers themselves, but the whole of their accomplices.
>
> But in order to make this proof tell against an individual it is necessary to prove by another description of evidence that he was present at the atrocious act; and that—in midnight murder, or in gang robberies where no witnesses save and except accomplices could possibly be present—can only be furnished by approvers. Where the best description of evidence is unattainable, the rule to obtain the best procurable and to give it weight *quantum valeat*, must apply as well to Thug trials as to others. The credibility of the evidence of the approvers is doubtless increased by the exhumation of the bodies of the murdered at their suggestion, and by their pointing out the very graves in which they were buried: which, added to the precaution already adverted to, will make their evidences as credible as that of any other description of witness. The graves of the murdered have in one or two instances afforded, I may say, positive evidence. For instance, in case No. 22 of Sessions 1831/32 and No. 11 of Sessions 32/33 the witnesses, long before the graves were

> opened, deposed to the fact that several of the murdered persons were *smiths* and that their tools had been buried with the bodies. The murders were committed in 1819 and the graves opened in March 1832 and the tools were found as described.

The genealogical tables Sleeman had drawn up and which were attached to this document, also, Curwen Smith argued, helped to prevent innocent people being framed, and, he added:

> They show the connection of the families of the principal Thugs committed for trial since 1830 with the Sindhousee (hereditary) Thugs. The tables were revised by Captain Sleeman often in the presence of the members of the different families . . . and the tables of their respective families have been acknowledged by them to be correct, though framed from information derived from members of opposite parties.
>
> It is an extraordinary fact, illustrative of the strength of memory of the Thug leaders as well as of the extent of their information, that they are acquainted with the principal Thug leaders and Thugs all over India and can recognise them though they are not always familiar with their persons.

These explanations appear to have satisfied Lord Bentinck, for there was no subsequent criticism, but Sleeman later obtained sanction for less rigid application of death sentences—according to degree of guilt instead of rigid rules. Henceforward, a young Thug who had taken part only in one or two murders could receive a punishment less severe than the death sentence passed on an older Thug who had strangled two or three hundred people. Behind this decision was also the hope that less guilty Thugs would be encouraged to confess when arrested or even to surrender themselves. Sleeman seems to have been moving as far as possible now from the policy of retribution towards one of prevention.

Convicted Thugs sentenced to death were hanged in public at Saugor. At the request of the condemned Sleeman authorised the hangmen to allow them to put the rope round their own necks, thus to escape the horror of being touched and sent to death by a person of low caste. "They all walked up to the ladder, put the rope round their own necks, prayed that no man of low caste might be allowed to touch them and most of them threw themselves off before the signal was given."

Such was their touching faith in Brahmins that some of the local inhabitants at Saugor argued that despite their guilt they should have been spared; reverence for the priestly caste was not weakened by their being professional murderers. But there was another reason for this. Whatever their crime it was believed both wrong and dangerous to take the lives of Brahmins. Added to the execution of lower caste Thugs the hanging of Brahmins caused a wave of fear among the citizens of Saugor. The spirits of the Thugs, would, it was held, owing to the violent manner of their death, become *bhutas** who would haunt the town and do evil to the inhabitants.

Sleeman met a deputation of leading citizens. They told him of their fears and requested that an occult rite might be carried out upon the body of each Thug immediately after death. A slight incision just above the right ankle bone of each body would, they said, effectually prevent the spirits remaining in the sublunary world. Sleeman ignored a circular order of the High Court judges forbidding the incisions and reported officially that he had allowed them. It is a sign of the regard in which Sleeman was held that when Curwen Smith reported and defended this defiance of the order the Government neither reprimanded nor even criticised Sleeman. The rite was carried out upon all the Thugs executed at Saugor.

In a summary of the progress of the campaign up to the end of 1833 Curwen Smith joyfully reported to the Governor-General:

> It is impossible to form an accurate judgment on the number of lives saved since 1830 by our operations, but they must be immense. We have taken off the roads upwards of 1500 professional assassins who infested all parts of India, spreading ruin and death wherever they went. The roads are now in most places perfectly safe and in all except Oude, Benares and the lower provinces, comparatively speaking free from danger. The final extirpation of these enemies to mankind cannot be far

* A bhuta was believed to be the evil being that arose from the body of anyone who met with a violent death.

distant and will afford the noblest trophy to adorn His Lordship's return to his native country.

Yet the Benares and Bihar provinces were still infested on the left bank of the Ganges, for the river Thugs there were then only just beginning to feel the weight of Sleeman's attacks. Although Thuggee was not quite as near to death as Curwen Smith claimed in his efforts to light the flame of gratitude in Bentinck's heart, it was greatly weakened. An unaccustomed feeling of safety was growing among merchants and others on the roads. Substantiating this, George Stockwell, a fellow magistrate, wrote to Sleeman on 24 October 1833:

> I can hardly say more of it than that I have heard persons equally unknown to you and to me, but who have travelled through your districts, call down blessings on your head for the security to the lives and property of travellers which has been brought about by your exertions and penetration. This is the sort of praise which must come home to a man's breast.

For Sleeman the tide had truly turned now that men were praising instead of ridiculing him, yet he knew well enough that much remained to be done. His detachments in Bihar had reported to him that they had discovered another sect of Thugs who killed by striking their victims on the temple with a small stick loaded at the point. Then came rumours of still another sect, who specialised in seeking out poor families, strangling the parents and stealing the children for sale into prostitution.

In November 1833 the bodies of two women and three men were found trussed and strangled on the banks of the Jumna river at Delhi. A police detachment and a Thug informer were sent to the spot. But the informer at once hotly denied that his own fraternity could have done the deed. "It was altogether too clumsy," he protested, "and must have been done by men new to the trade and very awkward. The bodies would never have been left exposed and in such a position: the strangling cords would never have been left about the victims' necks nor such clumsy knots have been tied."

A detachment of sepoys was sent out in pursuit and late that night, only minutes after they had murdered again, the gang were seized—eight men and several women, together with six children recently taken from murdered parents. Some of the women had years ago been themselves stolen and kept as concubines. They were sent through to Saugor, where Sleeman recorded the replies of one of the women to his questions:

> "Where were your parents murdered?"
>
> "Near the village of Dunkari in the Bulandshahr district."
>
> "How many Thugs were present on this occasion?"
>
> "Between forty and fifty."
>
> "Did you witness the murder of your parents?"
>
> "No, they were murdered during the night and I and my two young brothers were entrusted to the charge of the female Thug, and we were offered for sale a few days afterwards to some gypsies, who would not give a sufficient sum for me, and I was subsequently adopted by Salga Jemadar, a relation of Khema."
>
> "Have you ever heard anything of your two brothers since the murder of your parents?"
>
> "No."
>
> "You have been in the habit of accompanying your adopted husband on Thuggee since you have been living with him?"
>
> "Yes. I have been on three or four expeditions with him."
>
> "A poor Faqirni woman was murdered in your house at Jonli eight or nine months ago. Did you feel no compunction in taking charge of her children during the time your husband was employed in strangling her?"
>
> "I was compelled by the orders of my husband, who directed me to prevent the children making a noise."

The Thug informer's denial that these assassins were members of his own fraternity was correct. Sleeman soon established that they were mere vagrants who had nothing in common with the antique sect against whom he had been fighting for so long. But the comparison threw into sharp emphasis the extraordinary, satanic nature of the true Thug fraternity—their formidable discipline, their blind devotion to Kali's blood-lust, the baffling contradictions in their collective mentality.

How could the sect attract at once Brahmins and merchants as well as sepoys and humble cultivators? How was it that the worship of Kali transcended both the Hindu and the Muslim religions?

How could Thugs be devoted husbands and fathers and yet go on killing other men's wives and families year after year without a qualm? Whence came their perfect manners and those magnetic powers which made other people trust and confide in them so easily?

Some of the answers to these contradictions had their roots in the structure of Indian society, which as much as anything had enabled an evil sect like Thuggee to thrive for so long, but these social cleavages could not be blamed entirely for the existence of Thuggee. At this time, when many Thug approvers were held at Saugor, Sleeman often assembled two or three dozen of them at a time, at first to help him complete the vocabulary of their dialect *ramasee*. He says of these occasions in the preface to *Ramaseeana* that he offers "the almost literal translation of some of the conversations I have had with the approvers in revising the vocabulary of their peculiar dialect* for the last time".

> These conversations were often carried on in the presence of different European gentlemen who happened to call in, and as they seemed to feel a good deal of interest in listening to them, I thought others might possibly feel the same in reading them if committed to paper; and from that time I, for several days, put down the conversations as they took place in the present form.

Sleeman was a good reporter. These frank talks with the Thugs represent, apart from his fight to destroy their society, an attempt to reveal as much of it as possible for posterity.

* See Appendix.

15

Thug Philosophy

The conversations, as Sleeman called them, took place in the sweltering court-room at Saugor, the Thugs, in turban and dhoti, cross-legged on the dusty floor facing Sleeman, at a table and chair in his dark-blue tunic with gold facings, much of his thick auburn hair now gone. On either side of him would sit the *moonshees*, busily recording for his subsequent translation confessions that seem nearer fantasy than the truth they had been proved to be.

The Thugs present represented a cross-section of the fraternity's castes and of the various interpretations of its rules and customs. They included Feringeea, Thukoree, Sheik Inaent, Dhorga and Zofulkar from various parts of central and northern India; Moradun and Shumshera from Bihar and Bengal; the Muslims Sahib Khan and Nasir from the south. To Sleeman's western logic all of them in turn opposed oriental topsy-turveydom and the rooted conviction that they were supernaturally influenced.

Many Thugs confessed to an extraordinary number of murders. A notorious Thug named Buhram claimed to have strangled 931 persons during forty years of Thuggee. Sleeman was incredulous:

"Nine hundred and thirty-one murders? Surely you can never have been guilty of such a number?"

"Sahib," replied this courtly Thug, "there were many more, but I was so intrigued in luring them to destruction that I ceased counting when certain of my thousand victims."

"Do you never feel remorse for murdering in cold blood and

after the pretence of friendship, those whom you have beguiled into a false sense of security?"

"Certainly not! Are you yourself not a *shikari* (big-game hunter) and do you not enjoy the thrill of stalking, pitting your cunning against that of an animal, and are you not pleased at seeing it dead at your feet? So with the Thug, who regards the stalking of men as a higher form of sport.

"For you, sahib, have but the instincts of the wild beasts to overcome, whereas the Thug has to subdue the suspicions and fears of intelligent men and women, often heavily armed and guarded, knowing that the roads are dangerous. In other words, game for our hunting is defended from all points save those of flattery and cunning.

"Can you not imagine the pleasure of overcoming such protection during days of travel in their company, the joy of seeing suspicion change to friendship, until that wonderful moment arrives when the *ruhmal* completes the *shikar*—this soft ruhmal, which has ended the life of hundreds. Remorse, sahib? Never! Joy and elation, often!"

After this admission, Sleeman sought some reassurance.

"What do you think, Sahib Khan, am I right in thinking that we shall suppress Thuggee . . .?"

"There have been several *gurdies* [inroads] upon Thuggee," this Thug replied, "but they have ended in nothing but the punishment of a few; and, as Nasir says, we have heard our fathers and sages predict these things as punishments for our transgression of prescribed rules; but none of them ever said that Thuggee would be done away with. This seems a greater and more general *gurdie* than any, and I know not what to think."

"But tell me freely; do you think we shall annihilate it?"

"How can the hand of man do away with the works of God?"

"You are a Musulman?"

"Yes, most of the Thugs of the south are Musulmans."

"And you still marry; inherit; pray; eat and drink according to the Koran; and your paradise is to be the paradise promised by Mahommud?"

"Yes, all, all."

"Has Bhowanee [Kali] been anywhere named in the Koran?"
"Nowhere."

(Here, Sleeman records, a Musulman Thug from Hindustan interposed, and said he thought Bhowanee and Fatima, the daughter of Mahommud, and wife of Alee, were one and the same person; and that it was Fatima who invented the use of the ruhmal to strangle the great demon Rukut-beej-dana; "which led to a discussion between him and some of my Musulman officers, who did not like to find the amiable Fatima made a goddess of Thuggee. . . . The Thug was a sturdy wrangler, and in the estimate of his associate Thugs had, I think, the best of the argument.")

"Then has Bhowanee anything to do with your paradise?"

"Nothing."

"She has no influence upon your future state?"

"None."

"Does Mahommud, your prophet, anywhere sanction crimes like yours; the murder in cold blood of your fellow creatures for the sake of their money?" Sleeman persisted.

"No."

"Does he not say that such crimes will be punished by God in the next world?"

"Yes."

"Then do you never feel any dread of punishment hereafter?"

"Never; we never murder unless the omens are favourable; we consider favourable omens as the mandates of the deity."

"What deity?"

"Bhowanee."

"But Bhowanee, you say, has no influence upon the welfare or otherwise of your soul hereafter?"

"None, we believe; but she influences our fates in this world and what she orders in this world, we believe that God will not punish in the next."

"Do your wives never reproach you with your deeds?"

"In the South we never tell our wives what we do lest they should disclose our secrets," Sahib Khan explained.

"And if you told them wouldn't they reproach you?"

"Some would, and some, like those of other Thugs who do tell them, would quietly acquiesce."

"And be as affectionate and dutiful as the wives of other men?"

"The fidelity of the wives of Thugs is proverbial throughout India."

"That is among Thugs?"

"Yes."

"And the fear of the ruhmal operates a little to produce this?"

"Perhaps a little, but there have been very few instances of women killed for infidelity among us," Sahib Khan claimed.

Sleeman then asked Feringeea: "Do you worship at Kali's temples?"

"Yes, of course, all men worship at her temple."

Sahib Khan interposed: "In the Deccan the greatest Nawabs and officers of state worship at her temples and prostrate themselves and their children before the image of the goddess when the smallpox or cholera rages. We have ourselves seen them do it often."

"And do they believe you Thugs to be under her special protection?"

"Some of them do, and though they often try to dissuade us from our trade, they are afraid to punish us. Bura Sahib Jemadar, of Madura, had several hundred followers, and used to make valuable presents to Nawab Dollee Khan, who knew how he got them, and offered him a high post with rent-free lands if he would leave off the trade. He would not."

"What became of him at last?"

"There was a great Dacoit leader of the same name who had been committing great ravages, and orders were sent by the Nawab to the local officers to blow him away from a gun as soon as they could seize him. They seized Sahib Khan Thug, and blew him away by mistake, before the Nawab got information of the arrest. In a few hours after his death a message came from the Nawab to say that he feared there might be a mistake, and when he heard that Sahib Khan Thug had been blown away, he was much grieved, but said that God must have ordained it, and the fault was not his."

Sleeman then asked:

"Above the Narbada, chiefs have never had the same dread of punishing Thugs as below it, have they?"

"They had formerly, and still have in many parts," Feringeea said.

"Why should they fear—have there been any instances of suffering from it?"

"A great many [Feringeea assured him]. Was not Nanha, the Raja of Jhalone, made leprous by Devi (Kali) for putting to death Bodhoo and his brother Khumolee, two of the most noted Thugs of their day? He had them trampled under the feet of elephants but the leprosy broke out upon his body the very next day."

"Did he believe that this punishment was inflicted by Devi for putting them to death?"

"He was quite sensible of it," said Dorgha, a Muslim Thug.

"Did he do anything to appease her?"

"Everything. Bodhoo had begun a well in Jalone; the Raja built it up in a magnificent style; he had a *chubootra* (tomb) raised to their name, fed Brahmans, and consecrated it, had worship instituted upon it, but all in vain: the disease was incurable, and the Rajah died a miserable death in a few months. The tomb and well are both kept up and visited by hundreds to this day, and no one doubts that the Raja was punished for putting these two Thugs to death."

"But Bodhoo had his nose and hands cut off before, and could have been no favourite of Devi's," [Sleeman reminded him].

"He was a Thug of great repute," Feringeea said. "For sagacity we have never seen his equal. People who had been robbed used to go to him as an oracle."

"But he had turned informer and was sent to Jalone by Mr Stockwell to arrest his associates."

"He went to Mr Stockwell in a passion," argued Dorgha. "His heart was not fully turned away from us then."

"Have you any other instances?"

"Hundreds!" exclaimed Sheik Inaent. "When Madhajee Scindheea caused seventy Thugs to be executed at Muthura, was he not warned in a dream by Devi that he should release them? And did he not the very day after their execution begin to spit blood? And did he not die within three months?"

Feringeea added: "When . . . the Kuchwaha Rajpoots arrested eighty of the Thugs who had settled at Nodha after the murder of Lieutenant Maunsell, they had many warnings to let them go; but they persisted and kept them till some thirty died. They collected 14,000 rupees (£1400) at the rate of 125 rupees from every Thug. What became of their families? Have they not all perished? They have not a child left. Rae Sing Havildar, the Gwalior Subah of Nodha, took the money, but that very day his only son and the best horse in his stable died, and he was himself taken ill and died a miserable death soon after."

"Ah," interrupted Nasir, "Devi took care of you then, and why? Was it not because you were more attentive to her orders?"

"Yes," Zolfukar said, "we had then some regard for *religion*. We have lost it since. All kinds of men have been made Thugs and all classes of people murdered without distinction, and little attention has been paid to omens. How after this could we expect to escape?"

"Be assured that Devi never forsook us till we neglected her," agreed Nasir.

"And do you think that the chiefs have still the same dread of punishing Thugs in all parts of India?"

"Certainly not in all parts," Sahib Khan said, "because in many they have been suffered to punish them with impunity on account of their neglect of rules and omens."

"Nasir and Sahib Khan think that it can never be suppressed in the Deccan."

"I think it never can," Nasir agreed.

"I do not say it never can," Sahib Khan said. "I say only that the country is very large; that in every one of the five districts there are hundreds of Aseel (hereditary) Thugs who are staunch to their oath, and attentive to their usages, that the country is everywhere intersected by the jurisdiction of native chiefs who cannot easily be persuaded to assist."

"Assist!" exclaimed Nasir. "Why, when we go into their districts after a Thug we are every instant in danger of our lives. I got nearly killed with all the guard lately when close upon the heels of a gang, and when I complained to Captain Reynolds, he told me that we must consent to bear these drubbings on account of the Company, or I could be of no use to him in such a country as that!"

"And you think that all these obstacles are not to be overcome?"

"I think not."

"That is, you think an institution formed by Devi, the goddess, cannot be suppressed by the hand of man?"

"Certainly, I think so."

"But you think that no man is killed by man's killing; that all who are strangled are strangled in effect by God."

"Certainly."

"Then by whose killing have all the Thugs who have been hanged at Saugor and Jubbulpore been killed?"

"God's of course."

"You think that we could never have caught and executed them but by the aid of God?"

"Certainly not."

"Then you think that so far we have been assisted by God in what we have done?"

"Yes."

"And you are satisfied that we should not have ventured to do what we have done unless we were assured that our God was working with us, or rather that we were the mere instruments in his hands?"

"Yes, I am."

"Then do you not think that we may go on with the same assurance till the work we have in hand is done; till, in short, the system of Thuggee is suppressed?"

"God is almighty," said Nasir humbly.

"And there is but one God?"

"One God above all gods."

"And if that God above all gods supports us we shall succeed?"

"Certainly."

"Then we are all satisfied that he is assisting us, and therefore hope to succeed even in the Deccan?"

"God only knows!" Nasir exclaimed at last.

"If God assists, you will succeed," Sahib Khan said, "but the country is large and favourable, and the gangs there are numerous and well organised."

"Do you not think that if we persevere, we shall be able to

do in the Deccan what we have done here, and in the Dooab?"

"It will be a work of greater difficulty. Half or three-quarters of these gangs were *Kaboolas* [tyro Thugs]. In the Deccan they are almost all composed entirely of *Borkas*—men well born, staunch and able; above all the men of Arcot."

"And the Hindu Thugs of Talghat upon the Krishna river," put in Feringeea.

"Yes, they are extraordinary men," said Sahib Khan.

"They have three painted lines on their foreheads extending up from a central point at the nose," said Feringeea. "I served with them once for two months."

"Yes, they have those lines," Sahib Khan recalled.

"But do not all the Hindus in that quarter wear the same marks?"

"All Hindus wear them occasionally," Sahib Khan agreed, "but they always wear them. They and the Arcot [South-east India] Thugs associate and act together; but they will never mix with us in Telingana."

"Have the Talghat men the same language and usage as you have?"

"They have the same omens and language, and observe the same rules; but we hear that they use the round instead of the oblong grave to bury their victims, the same as the Bihar men. They call it the *chukree*; the Bihar men and others call it the *Gobba*."

"What is commonly the proportion of Musulmans to Hindus?"

"In Oude," answered Feringeea, "nine-tenths are Musulmans. In the Dooab four-fifths were Hindus. South of the Narbada three-fourths Musulmans. In Bundlecund and Saugor one-half were Musulmans. In Rajpootana one-fourth Musulmans. In Bengal, Bihar, and Orissa about half and half. This is a rough guess, since we have no rule to ascertain them."

Later, Sleeman asked the approvers who sat before him:

"If Devi's displeasure visits all who punish Thugs, how is it that you all escape so well?"

"Devi's anger visited us when we were seized," answered

Moradun. "That was the effect of her resentment. She cast us off then and takes no notice of us now."

"And if you were to return to Thuggee, she would still guide and protect you?"

"Yes, but what gang would now receive us?"

"And you are not afraid to assist in suppressing Thuggee?"

"No; we see that God is assisting you, and that Devi has withdrawn her protection on account of our transgressions. We have sadly neglected her worship. God only knows how it will end."

"True, God only knows; but we hope it will end in the entire suppression of this wicked and foolish system; and in the conviction on your part that Devi has really nothing to do with it."

"That Devi instituted Thuggee, and supported it as long as we attended to her omens, and observed the rules framed by the wisdom of our ancestors, nothing in the world can ever make us doubt."

The conviction of the supernatural origin of the fraternity was strengthened in the minds of Thugs by the belief that its mysteries were depicted in stone bas relief carvings in the so-called caves of Ellora, in Hyderabad. These are in fact a series of underground temples that were hewn into the red granite base of the mountain in A.D. 800, and decorated with sculptures, and figures in relief. A huge figure of Kali, supported by a lotus, with on each side an elephant whose trunks form a canopy over her head, dominates the entrance to the main temple.

Sleeman said to Feringeea:

"You told Mr Johnstone, the traveller, that the operations of your trade were to be seen in the caves at Ellora."

"The operations of every trade in the world can be seen in those caves," Dorgha said.

Chotee, another Thug, said: "Whenever we passed near we used to visit the caves. Every man will find his trade pictured, however secret he thinks it. And they were all made in one night."

"Does anyone else besides you believe that any of these figures represent Thugs?"

"Nobody does," Feringeea said. "But all Thugs know that

they do. We never told anybody else what we thought about them. Everybody there can see the secret operations of his trade, but he doesn't tell others about them. And no other person can understand what they mean. They are the works of God. No human hands were employed upon them. That everybody admits."

"What particular Thug operations are shown?"

Sahib Khan said: "I have seen the inveigler sitting upon a carpet with a traveller in close conversation with him, just as we are when we are worming out their secrets. In another place the strangler has got his ruhmal over his neck and is strangling him, while someone else holds him by the legs."

"I have seen these, too," said Nasir. "The holder is pulling his legs *thus*, while the strangler tightens the ruhmal round his neck *thus*."

"Have you seen any others?"

Feringeea said: "I have seen these two and also the *Lughaes* carrying away the bodies to the grave and the sextons digging the grave with the sacred pickaxe. All is done just as if we had done it ourselves. Nothing could be more exact."

"Who do you think did this work?"

"It couldn't have been done by Thugs because they would never have given away our trade secrets. No other human being could have done it. It *must* be the work of the Gods. Human hands could never have performed it," Feringeea insisted.

"And supposing so, you go and worship it?"

"No," said Sahib Khan, "we go to gratify curiosity, and not to worship. We look upon it as a mausoleum—a collection of curious figures cut by some demons who knew all mankind's secrets and amused themselves here in describing them."

Sleeman asked a Thug named Thukoree Aheer: "You were, I believe, among the Thugs arrested after the murder of Lieutenant Maunsell towards the end of 1812?"

"I was, and the Indian authorities kept us in prison 13 months and maltreated us horribly."

"What made them maltreat you?"

"To get money from us."

"Then those who paid were well treated and released?"

"Not so. Those who could not pay were beaten in the hope

that their friends would in time pay. And those who paid were beaten in the hope that their friends would in time pay more."

"I understand that some 40 Thugs died from the beating and confinement."

"Not from the beatings. They were all killed by a great demon that visited our prison every night and killed or tortured someone."

All the Thugs cried out that they had heard the demon described many times by the survivors.

"I only saw him once myself," Thukoree admitted. "I was awake while all the rest were asleep. He came in at the door of our cell and seemed to swell as he came in until his head touched the roof—the roof was very high—and his bulk became enormous. I prostrated myself and told him that he was our great god and we poor helpless mortals depended entirely upon his will. This pleased him and he passed me by, but took such a grasp at a Thug named Mungulee, who slept by my side, that he was seized with spasms from the nape of the neck to the soles of his feet."

"Was this the way they all died?"

"Yes—and but few survived. They all died like Mungulee. They had rheumatic pains and spasms all over. The prison was for a long time visited by him every night."

"Was it in the cold and rainy season?"

"This demon came most often in the cold and rainy weather."

"Who seized you in the first place?"

"Local Zemindars, at the request of the Indian magistrate of Mynpore."

"Yes," Feringeea said, "and not a soul of their families is now left to pour the libation at the funeral obsequies!"

Thukoree agreed—"They were severely punished afterwards for giving us such annoyance."

"By whom?"

"By Kali."

"How many were you?"

"A hundred and thirty-three of us were seized, at the magistrate's request," Thukoree said. "He might have had all of us up before him, but he only wanted four, and four were sent to him. The only evidence against them was Aman's, and he became so frightened that he let the cup of Ganges water fall out of his hands before the magistrate who didn't believe him in consequence. All four were released, though they were all present at the murder of Lieutenant Maunsell. The other 129 were kept in prison until each of them was able to raise 129 rupees, altogether 16,601 rupees (£1,660). Fourteen thousand were paid to a nobleman, the Rae Singh. The very day the money was paid into his treasury, his son and a fine horse died and he himself was taken ill. He was advised to give all the money away to charity and release the survivors, because it had been acquired by secret murder and those who got it seemed to be under supernatural influence. He did so, but his sickness and misery continued and he died."

"Ah—Kali took care of us then—and why?" exclaimed Nasir. "Wasn't it because we were more attentive to her orders?"

Captain James Paton, assistant to Colonel Low, the British Resident in Oude, and responsible for catching Thugs there, also cross-examined them, often more searchingly than Sleeman. Their answers, as these excerpts from Paton's dialogues with them show, were often more revealing.

"Do Thugs look up to or think worse of those associates who have strangled many victims?" he asked a Thug strangler named Buhram.

"They respect the *Borka*, or expert Thug the most," Buhram said. "He has his attendants from amongst the *Kaboolas* (or tyros); several of them wait on him as servants, shampoo or press his limbs, carry his bundles. He often rides upon his horse! Whereas the tyro is held in no estimation amongst us."

"Do you set out upon your murderous expeditions with sorrow or pleasure?"

"With pleasure to be sure!" said Buhram. "Why should we have gone had it not been pleasure to us? What else?"

"We start with pleasure especially when the omens have been favourable," said Rambux, a Hindu Thug. "We are encouraged by Bhowanee, goddess of destruction, whom the Hindus universally worship."

"Do Thugs like to be told to perform the office of strangler? Or would they rather that others should perform the duty?"

"A 'kutchajee' or feeble-hearted Thug," answered Rambux, "shrinks from it and keeps behind, but a bold Thug prefers the office of strangler."

"Does it require great force to strangle your victim?"

"Yes, great strength, with both hands, it is soon over. If the timing is mismanaged it is a long business."

"Most men dislike handling dead bodies. Have Thugs no disagreeable feelings when handling the dead bodies of their victims?"

The Muslim Thug Futteh Khan replied: "If a man dies a natural death we fear to go near him; but when we murder, then we have no fear, and though many murdered bodies were there, we would sit down amongst them without fear. . . . Why should we fear the corpse we have ourselves murdered? It is our trade, we are gratified to see the body and to think we have got plenty of money from it."

"How are travellers dispatched by river Thugs?"

"The strangler sits down before him," answered Allayar, another Muslim, "and thus throttles him. . . . (Here Allayar showed energy as he went through the motion.) His back is then broken, thus, by bending the body backwards and striking the spine with the hand. The most tender parts of the body are destroyed, and the corpse is thrown into the water and devoured by the crocodiles which follow the boat."

"As a man fed today expects food tomorrow," added Futteh Khan, "so do the crocodiles follow the Thug boat."

"Have you no compassion for the victims?"

"What!" shouted Allayar. "Has the murderer any compassion?"

"Do Thugs ever become so much impressed with the kindness and manners of travellers, as to relinquish their idea of strangling them? Do not young inexperienced Thugs sometimes yield to emotions of kindness, and plead for the life of an intended victim?"

"We silence him (*who pleads to spare the travellers*)," Allayar said.

"But in time," Futteh Khan said, "the tyro, by getting

clothes and spoil gets a relish for the business and ceases to plead."

"If we always listened to pity, how would we get on?" pleaded the Hindu Thug Sheodeen.

"Who amongst you has been in the largest gang of Thugs?"

"Jean, in jail here, who has got the wound in his arm, was in a gang with 300 Thugs . . ."*

"Do men, being strangled, make any noise or is the voice stopped."

"There is no noise whatever," Futteh Khan said, "except when the business is mismanaged when there is a great outcry made."

"Once, when I was present," Sheodeen recalled, "when two men were to be strangled, by mistake Dhumna (hanged at Saugor) seized the throat of Bundeea, a fellow Thug! (since hanged at Saugor) and had nearly strangled him ere Ritchut Jemadar (hanged at Jubbulpore) exclaimed—'A Thug is being strangled!' when the noose was loosened, but the Thug's throat was a little swelled in consequence! The really intended victim was then seized and dispatched."

* This was too much for Paton, a deeply religious Scot. In one of many footnotes akin to a Presbyterian sermon he exclaimed: "What a sad but faithful picture of our ruined nature does this present! Three hundred sons of fallen Adam leaguing themselves together for purpose of *murder*! Are *we* by nature in the sight of God better than they? Certainly not. Was not the first man born in the world a *murderer*? Did not Cain murder his own brother! Are we by nature better than the sons of *Adam*? Were not the sons of Jacob guilty by intent of murdering their own brother Joseph when they decided on casting him into the well? Are we better than they? 'Wherefore,' saith Paul, 'as by one man sin entered into the world and death by sin; and so death passed upon all men for all have sinned.' We are all then, even you gentle reader—in the sight of God by nature as those 300 Thugs. 'As it is written, there is none righteous, no not *one*! There is none that understandeth—there is none that seeketh after God! They are all gone out of the way, they are together become unprofitable, there is none that doeth good, *no, not one*. Their throat is an open sepulchre—with their tongues they have used deceit—the poison of asps is under their lips—their mouths full of cursing and bitterness—their feet are swift to shed blood. There is no fear of God before their eyes. That every mouth may be stopped, that all the world may become guilty before God!' (Romans, 3rd.) Our only hope then of pardon and salvation is that we may be 'born again'—'created anew'."

"Does the cloth you use leave any mark upon the neck?"

"Yes, it leaves a red mark and the neck swells."

"Why do you stab the dead bodies?"

"That no life may remain."

"And that Bhowanee [i.e. Kali, Devi, Doorga] may have her blood, she delights in blood," Futteh Khan said.

"Who is Bhowanee and what is the extent of her powers? Do you suppose that she wards off evil or bestows good upon her worshippers?"

"Bhowanee is a spirit created by God," Futteh Khan explained. "She has no body."

"God is pleased with Bhowanee, otherwise he would not permit men to worship her," Rambux observed.

"Bhowanee is happy and more so," Sheodeen said, "in proportion to the blood that is shed."

"I saw with my own eyes at Bindachul, a place of worship," Dhoosoo said, "200 or 400 goats sacrificed to Bhowanee, and the blood was taken away from her, before whose image a crowd of about 50 Sukhees (men who dance in women's clothes) were dancing."

"Hundreds of prostitutes dance before this goddess Bhowanee at Bindachul," said Rambux.

"It is God who kills, but Bhowanee has the manner of it," remarked Sheodeen. "If Bhowanee had her will, she would kill every human being upon Earth in one day. Blood is her food . . . God has appointed blood her food, saying—'Feed thou upon blood!' "

"We love her because she patronises our trade of Thuggee and forgives us," Futteh Khan confessed reverently.

"This Bhowanee seems to have a large portion of Satan's spirit. How then do you venture to set her against God and worship her."

"What!" Futteh Khan exclaimed. "Is Bhowanee the enemy of God! If she were would she be tolerated? We have no fear in worshipping Bhowanee—we consider it to be God's order to worship her—I have no fear of her—I serve her in my trade of murder."

"If a man murders anyone," Dhoosoo said, "without reference to Bhowanee, he will be haunted by ghosts. But we who kill under the patronage of Bhowanee are not troubled in the least."

"Do Thugs alone worship Bhowanee?"

"All Thugs, thieves and robbers worship some god or other," answered Taija, a Hindu Thug. "They worship Devi (the same as Bhowanee or Kali) praying for success in the undertaking."

"Then Devi would appear to the patroness of crime, in spirit a very devil?"

"She is like a devil and people commit crimes and shed blood in her name."

"Then as you allow, she is like a devil, why do you worship her—is not this the same as the worship of Satan?"

"All the world worships Devi, because she prospers their undertakings. Satan and all evil accompany Devi."

"Devi then, appears opposed to God?"

"God is pleased with Devi—if it were not so how could she exist?"

"If God were not pleased with Satan how could he exist?" Futteh Khan argued. "All men committing theft venture not to do so without some supernatural protection."

"She and the Devil are the same," exclaimed Rambux. "She has all evil in her train."

"She is our shield from the wrath of God and man," Sheodeen concluded.

"Do Thugs help themselves to their neighbours' property?"

Six Thugs [present] at once shook their heads and exclaimed —"No, we do not steal!"

"If we got 1000 rupees we would not steal," Allayar protested.

"We never steal!" Futteh Khan exclaimed. "What God gives us He gives us in Thuggee. God is the giver, we never steal."

"There were many thieves in my village," Sheodeen said. "My father used to counsel me against them, saying—'do not join them, they take money without Thugging.'"

Buhram then exclaimed with great animation: "A thief is a contemptible being, but a Thug—rides his horse—wears his dagger—shows a front! Thieving? Never! Never! If a banker's treasure were before me, and entrusted to my care, tho' in hunger and dying I would spurn to steal. But let a banker go on a journey and I would certainly murder him."

"In how short a time do you dispatch and bury a band of travellers after reaching your ground?"

Rumzan answered: "Before the signal words are out of the mouth, quick, like the pulling of a trigger, every man is strangled —thus! (Here the assassin Rumzan, smiling, showed with what energy it was done.) Jhut! Instantaneously are the whole party murdered, though there would be twenty of them. It is all the work of an instant. You are long in writing it—but in reality it is instantaneous. Their bodies are with the same dispatch thrown across a pole and carried off and buried or thrown into a well. When the travellers are very powerful the leaders of our gangs offer five rupees more to the Thug who will strangle them."

"Do Thugs strangle each other?"

"Thugs will strangle approvers, but not each other."

"Are not Thugs brothers?" demanded Mugdooma.

"Have you known a Thug become rich and respectable and leave the trade?"

"Yes, but even though they get rich they do not leave the trade."

"How do you dispose of the dead bodies of the men you have murdered?"

Futteh Khan explained: "Where rocks oblige us to bury the bodies near the surface we cut them to pieces with knives and swords and cover them with earth—and then to disarm suspicion from the appearance of the grave, we cook and eat our food over the bodies and sleep there, leaving the fireplace."

"What! Cook your food and eat and sleep over the graves of the victims you have murdered?"

"We cook, eat and sleep there without concern and remain for a day or two with relish. But had the body died a natural death, we would not so eat and sleep over it for fear of the Devil."

Rumzan told Paton in a later statement:

"I have led gangs of thirty to forty men on the roads at various times. I have been a Thug from ten or twelve years of age and I am now about thirty-eight years old. I may have seen as many as eighty or ninety men strangled yearly." (This would give in his twenty-two years of Thuggee 1760 victims.)

"You could not have seen so many strangled?"

"I was at the work for nine years without returning to my home. . . . I was a great strangler. Near Punna in the hills, near the Sher Ghat, there was a secret bele called Baisuneedain, where no tidings of our victims transpired. Hundreds of travellers were strangled there. We hid their bodies under large stones there and tigers ate them. Travellers in this wild country used from fear to go in small parties through the Ghat, lest tigers or Thugs should fall upon them. Those who escaped the tigers fell into the hands of Thugs, and those who escaped the Thugs were sometimes devoured by the tigers."

While thus boasting of the prowess of the stranglers, Rumzan is also identifying them with tigers, whose characteristics of blood-lust and cruelty and strength Thugs so much admired.

But over and over again the Thugs also struck the same ringing note of a faith in Kali's or Devi's supernatural guidance so strong that it transcended their alleged attachment to the tenets of true religion.

For Kali, like Satan tempting Christ with riches on the high mountain, offered all the treasure in India to those of her followers ready to kill for her. In contrast to Christianity, Islam and Hinduism, she imposed no moral code, set down no limits to man's animal nature, made no call to his flickering spiritual being to burn with a flame so bright and hard that he would live in illumination. On the contrary, her creed amounted to defiance of all that true religion held sacred.

"Kill!" cried Kali. "And I will give you all. No one will harm you, for I will guide and protect you with my signs and omens. Obey them and remember me and you will never again have to work, for you will be rich and feared."

The promise of riches, the pull of the Black Mother, the thrill of imagined contact with the sinister occult force flowing from this goddess who commanded evil—these were the attractions of Thuggee. And so grew the rumour that members of this secret society were under supernatural guidance.

By the end of 1833 another 316 Thugs had been tried. All were found Guilty. Eighty were sentenced to death and hanged—a smaller proportion than before the introduction of the new regulations; 201 were transported for life, twenty given life imprisonment, seven under age released on security, two became approvers and six died in prison before sentence. All the evidence suggests that Sleeman was careful that prison conditions should be as little harmful as possible and that ill-treatment was prohibited. Some Thugs, bereft of their belief in Kali, lost their will to live in prison and died.

Sleeman's health was so undermined at this time that to carry on must have been an immense strain. Rheumatism in the alternately sodden and superheated climate of Saugor had struck him for years, on and off. As early as October 1822, advising Charles Fraser about a horse this friend wished to buy, he had written: "I have had an attack of rheumatism or otherwise I would ride the horse and tell you more about him; but my bones will not permit me now."

Sleeman was then only thirty-five. He was now forty-six; moreover, malaria, then termed "fever" and not then known to be injected by the anopheles mosquito, had attacked him when he first came to live in Saugor. By the middle of 1834 he realised that he could continue only at risk of shortening his life. He decided reluctantly that since Thuggee was in full retreat he should resign his leadership of the campaign and ask for suitable work in a healthier climate than that of central India. He wrote to Bentinck accordingly. The Governor-General paid him the rare compliment of a reply in his own hand, but offered worse:

> I have to acknowledge your letter of the 20th June, and I can inform you that no officer stands higher in my estimation than yourself, and I should be very glad to place you in another appointment, which might better suit your impaired health; but this is no easy matter: the political line is every day contracting, and the other districts where military men are employed, are liable to some objection on the score of climate. It is not impossible that the Arakan Commissionership may be disposable. . . . In respect to climate it may be different from Saugor, but in respect to healthiness I fear it is now election between the frying pan and the fire. Let me know what you think of this situation. . . . You will be a very great loss to the country, in the administration of which you have had so great a

> share, and I know not how you could be replaced in that work so important to humanity of the extirpation of the Thugs, which has been so successfully carried on towards its complete accomplishment under your especial direction. Believe me, with very great esteem and respect, Very truly yours, W. H. Bentinck.

Arakan, in Burma, was probably at that time the least healthy district in the whole of the two countries. Wisely, Sleeman decided against this offer. The idea that he might retire and go home to Cornwall occurred to him—he wrote at this time of his longing for "life at Falmouth with my family and my sister", for he was "growing weary, sadly weary with Indian customs". But he had a son to educate and dependent relatives to help. And his obsessive desire to be in at the death of Thuggee, stimulated by Bentinck's letter, reasserted itself. He wrote declining Arakan and agreed to remain at his post for the time being.

But Sleeman then began to feel in 1834 that both his status and the recognition of his central part in the anti-Thug campaign were being eroded. Leading members of his staff—Reynolds, Macleod and Wilson—had been given the title of "superintendent" in the areas under their control, even though the work was still directed from Sleeman's headquarters. Juniors, whom he had chosen and taught, were thus raised to Sleeman's level, whose will and vision over the years had generated the campaign. Sensitive now about pay, rank and status, in January 1835 Sleeman wrote to Curwen Smith, for transmission to the Governor-General:

> If I am right in concluding that it is your wish and that of government that I continue . . . to superintend . . . over the whole field of our operations as I have hitherto done, it would be much more satisfactory to me and would render my communication with the officers employed in different parts more regular and intelligible if an alteration can be made in the designation of my office. . . . I venture to suggest that my office be styled that of *General Superintendent of Proceedings for the Suppression of Thug Associations.*

Diffidence, however, would not let him press for his due rights without rather laboriously excusing himself:

> However important to society . . . this duty may be, no person can be better aware than yourself how odious and painful it often and indeed generally is, and I trust I shall not be thought anxious to covet a greater share of this duty and responsibility . . . in order to give full effect to the measures now adopted for the suppression of this, the most dreadful and extraordinary system recorded in the history of the human race.

"Odious and painful"—for the first and only time Sleeman overcomes his usual reticence and shows in these two words his true feelings about Thug-hunting—the endless pursuits, exhumations, trials and executions. He had gone on, year after year, despite this sense of disgust, sustained perhaps by the belief that for the sake of society it had to be done. Bentinck rewarded Sleeman's steadfastness and allayed his anxieties, appointing him General Superintendent, as he wished and in addition freeing him from his onerous duties as magistrate, which hitherto he had also been obliged to bear. It involved a move 120 miles south-east from Saugor back to Jubbulpore again for Sleeman and his family. Worried about his two-year-old son Henry's health, Sleeman looked for good from the move and wrote of it:

> At Saugor we had a large society, at Jubbulpore a small one, but Jubbulpore seemed to me more like my home than any other, and consequently I liked it better. Our boy had been very delicate at Saugor and I hoped the climate of Jubbulpore would agree with him. He was becoming more and more interesting every day and I more and more fond of him, but I had determined that if he were not stronger the next cold season than he had been, I should send him to England and confide him to the care of my sister Mary Furse. I learnt that Mary's eyes were failing as indeed were mine, so that I had to forego reading by candlelight and to play cards or chess of an evening.

These words signal Sleeman's twin worries at this time: concern for his young son in the overpowering heat and new fears for his own physical condition. But encouraged by his promotion, he pressed himself and his assistants, Macleod and Wilson especially, as hard as possible during the first months of 1835. Inevitably, his own health worsened, and in August his doctors told him he must take a year's leave or crack up completely. The ceaseless work in an unhealthy tropical climate that the destruction of Thuggee involved had taken its toll. Sleeman's *iqbal*, or good fortune, as the Thugs called it, seemed now to falter. But the Governor-General, pleased to know that he would not be losing the only man whose drive and resolution seemed able to match the cunning of the Thugs, willingly granted him a year's leave.

Before going, Sleeman encouraged his staff by the publication of a statement of the trials which had taken place since the anti-Thug campaign began in a feeble way in 1826. It showed that up to 14 October 1835 a total of 1562 Thugs had been sent for trial, that 382 of them had been executed, 909 transported for life, 77 imprisoned for life, 21 released on security, 71 given limited imprisonment, 21 acquitted, 11 had escaped, 31 died before sentence and 49 were made approvers.

A number of the total were gang leaders, hereditary Thugs who were able to attract new recruits and thus constantly regenerate the system; a few others were the *gurus* who transmitted Thug lore to tyros and newcomers. Hundreds of minor Thugs had gone to ground, but without leadership they were incapable of operating. So much of the system was now paralysed.

Accompanied by his wife and son, Sleeman left for Simla, about 175 miles north of Delhi and some 650 miles north of Jubbulpore, in November 1835. Up in the heights, seven thousand feet above sea level, he hoped to regain his old zest and vigour. He occupied himself writing letters to his sister Mary Furse in Cornwall. They were published in 1844 as a book named *Rambles and Recollections*. Though somewhat heavy in style it is given character and interest by the lively verbatim reports of Sleeman's talks with Indians from rajas to peasants. On 24 February 1836, while at Meerut en route to Simla, Sleeman's wife Amélie gave birth to their second child, a daughter.

During his leave Sleeman seems to have felt once more that for the sake of his health and his family, his painful and exhausting struggle against Thuggee over almost the whole of India was no longer worth while, especially for the relatively meagre pay of a Captain. For no extra reward was allowed by grasping John Company, either to Sleeman or his staff. He had without success pressed the Governor-General hard on this point and in

December 1835 had written of it to his friend Charles Fraser: "One thing I cannot get is the increase of pay with length of service for the officers of the Department—not one rupee can I squeeze out of the Governor-General for them."

Sleeman was concerned for his staff, but it applied no less to him. And though pay was by no means the only or the decisive factor, it was an important one. Accordingly, in October 1836, while still on leave Sleeman wrote again to the Governor-General asking, for the second time, to be allowed to resign his post and to return to the magistracy of Jubbulpore district.

The first reply to his request came in February, after he had returned from leave and had taken over the anti-Thug campaign once more. He was promoted to Major, so the pay issue was partly solved. The question of his resignation was referred to the Board of Control in London. The outcome was hardly what he had expected. The Board accepted his resignation and put on record that they "could not allow the occasion of Major Sleeman's relinquishment of the important trust in which he has rendered so eminent a service to India and to human nature itself, to pass without directing the Government to intimate to that Officer their warmest approbation of the manner in which that trust has been executed. . . ." So Sleeman returned to charge of the Jubbulpore district—only to find, ironically, that to run the Thuggee Department as well, was now part of the duties of this post. Thus, in its accustomed way, the Company had trapped him; his request had merely doubled his work. The Company knew how to flog a willing horse and soon was to double Sleeman's load.

Two hundred and two Thugs—159 Hindus, 43 Muslims—were tried in fifty-three separate cases in 1836 of the murder of 392 people during many past years, though hundreds more Thugs were involved. Inquests were held on 265 exhumed victims, leaving 127 unfound.

Sleeman's family life suffered the first blow to its happiness in the latter part of 1837. The climate of India so wore down the health of his young son Henry, that he and his wife decided that they had no choice but to send him home. One sees in this heartbreak situation one of the worst of the privations suffered by our nineteenth-century forebears in India and, in their staunch acceptance of it—which we would never tolerate—how far we of today are from them, for whom service came before ambition.

They saw the boy off at Calcutta. With him five-year-old Henry took seven cabin trunks with a list of contents written by his father. Apart from masses of clothing, it included 300 eggs, several boxes of sugar candy and barley sugar, enough bottled soda water to last the voyage, and, in case of shipwreck, a pocket water filter and a small sword. The ship sailed away over the horizon. Sleeman and his wife cannot but have wondered if they would ever see their son again; and home at Jubbulpore they must have asked themselves how soon it would be before their year-old daughter too would need to sail to England.

But William Sleeman had much to occupy him. It was at this time that it became necessary to tackle more energetically the river Thugs of Bengal, who of the entire fraternity had proved most resistant to the campaign.

16

River Thugs

The placid brown Ganges and its tributaries running through the lush green jungles of Bengal had for centuries been busy links between Calcutta and northern India. Merchants, traders and pilgrims who could afford to pay found the boats plying for hire there seemingly a safer and more comfortable way of travelling than the narrow dusty roads and humid jungle tracks. Sail was rarely used; men towed the boats, some 20 feet long, ventilated with a large porthole on either side of the cabin, up and down the shimmering tree-lined rivers from landing stage to landing stage.

Along the rivers, like their brothers in the forests and the plains, the river Thugs worked in gangs, each member with an allotted task, some as boatmen, others posing as merchants, or as devout pilgrims travelling up-river to the sacred shrines of Benares or Allahabad.

When Captain Lowis, Sleeman's deputy for Bengal, was appointed at the end of March 1836, nothing more than this was known of river Thuggee. And even this vague and scanty information had been gleaned from informers from central India gangs who either had or pretended to have practised with the river Thugs. But soon after his arrival Lowis speeded up the tempo of operations by the lucky capture of a small gang, some of whom became approvers and revealed names of fellow Thugs and their cruel murders on the quiet rivers.

Between the two types of Thug, there were certain differences in methods of killing. River Thugs slung the ruhmal from in front and pushed their victims' heads backwards, while those on land slung the ruhmal from behind and pushed forward. And unlike the land Thugs, they strictly observed Kali's *no* to the killing of women. Sleeman was quick to turn this to account by pointing out to those captured that the inroads he was making against them could not be put down to Kali's displeasure, because they had kept all her commands.

It could only be, he argued, that his own *iqbal* and that of the Government were stronger than Kali's. Kali could not protect them, but he could, in exchange for the information that he wanted. Some of them confessed, and in a preliminary report based on what he had found out in this way, Sleeman wrote:

> They are supposed to be between two and three hundred, and to employ about twenty boats, which pass up and down the Ganges during the months of November, December, January and February. Each boat is provided with a crew of about fourteen persons, all Thugs. Several boats belonging to the same Thug association follow each other at the distance of four to six miles, and when the travellers show any signs of disliking or distrusting the inveiglers of one, or any disinclination to embark at the ghat where his boat is to be found, the inveigler of the one in advance learns it by signs from the other, as he and the travellers overtake him.
>
> The new inveigler gets into conversation with the travellers, and pretends to dislike the appearance of the first, who, in his turn, pretends to be afraid of the new one, and lags behind, while the new man and the travellers congratulate each other on having shaken off so suspicious a character.
>
> They never keep any article that can lead to suspicion, as their boats are constantly liable to be searched by the custom-house officers. This class contains Muslims and Hindoos of all castes, and they go up the river Ganges as far as Benares, and sometimes even as far as Cawnpore, it is said. The Thugs who reside in Behar and Bengal are all acquainted with them, as the principal scene of their operations is along the banks of the Ganges and other large rivers into which they throw the bodies of their victims.
>
> Their resting places, or thapas, are almost always upon the banks of these rivers, where the large and most frequented roads

approach nearest to them. And there they remain for a long time together, destroying such travellers as they can. . . . When they fall in with boats, and see the chance of a good prize, some of the members of their gang go on board and assist in the murder; and the whole gang shares equally with the boatmen in the spoil.

The jemadar of a gang of river Thugs, well-dressed and with a servant carrying his baggage, would walk slowly along the road nearest to the landing stage where his boat was moored when on the look-out for possible victims. As wayfarers overtook him he greeted them cordially, began talking with them and when they said where they were going, told them that he was bound for the same place. When the sun grew hotter he would say he was tired of the road—that a boat on the cool river would be more agreeable and that he was acquainted with one or two of the boatmen and could possibly persuade one of them to lower the fare. Wayfarers could find this hard to resist. Together they would make for the nearest landing stage, where, in the cool breeze rising off the water the gang waited in a spick-and-span boat—none were better kept or more inviting than those of the Thugs.

A grim little scene was then reflected in the river. The Thug jemadar pretended to bargain with the boat captain, who at first flatly refused to lower the price—only when the jemadar and his victims were about to return to the road, was a bargain struck. The wayfarers then embarked and politely were told where in the crowded little cabin to sit. The ropes were cast off and they began their last journey. This typical case of river Thuggee is based on Sleeman's official report:

Hookum Chund, a jewel merchant, and his two bodyguards, sat down inside the cramped cabin of a boat on the Ganges. Chund was on his way home to Murshadabad from a visit to Calcutta. Beside him sat three other wayfarers who had passed him on the road fifteen minutes ago. Opposite, sat the man whom he had met on the road and who had suggested going by boat, with six other men he presumed were passengers. His name was Suroop Dutt. Jemadar of a highly skilled gang, he had found it no more than child's play to entice this merchant with his bodyguards aboard. The other intended three victims were also merchants. Like all river-thug jemadars, Dutt strangled one victim on each trip himself—after nearly twenty years it had become a mechanical operation and he had lost count of the number of his victims.

The vessel drifted away from the landing stage and began its smooth up-river journey. Dutt led the cheerful talk in the cabin—of women, of trade or of the new land annexations in Hindustan which, it was rumoured, the English were going to undertake.

The helmsman steered the vessel clear of other craft and the rope-men ashore heaved it along at a steady pace, past the white-walled villages crowned in wood smoke. They overtook a boat where beneath an awning an Englishman and his wife ate lunch off a white cloth. The Thug craft slowed and stopped twenty yards off the bank, letting the Englishman's vessel pass again. To calm anxieties that his intended victims might feel at the delay, Dutt pretended to be concerned: "Why are we stopping?" he demanded loudly of the helmsman.

"The rope men must rest and eat, sahib. It is tiring work," came the answer.

Dutt spoke across the cabin: "I think I will eat too." He pulled some food from his bundle, whereupon everyone unpacked his lunch. Later, when he had eaten, Dutt leaned out of the porthole and ordered the boatmen in Thug dialect to hurry and start again now that the river was clear of other craft, and safe.

In the burning heat of midday, the passengers began their smooth progress upstream again, lounging drowsily in the heat after their meal. The seven Thugs sat tense and ready to spring, fingers itching on the ruhmals.

Five boatmen now came down from the deck and edged between the victims' backs and the hull, on the pretext of moving heavy baggage. Three sharp staccato taps sounded on the deck above—the signal to kill.

Hookum Chund's wrists were seized—he struggled to try to escape, but there was no escape from the strip of yellow cloth that flashed round his throat and those of his fellow passengers. The struggle lasted less than a minute. Suroop Dutt tucked his ruhmal back into his waistband and surveyed the six sprawling bodies in the cabin as his men bent to strip and pillage them.

Working in pairs the Thugs first broke each victim's spinal cord, jerking head and shoulders against a knee pressed into the small of the back, then thrust a long knife into the armpits, believing these wounds would keep the bodies below the river's surface. Finally, for obscure reasons, they pounded the victim's sexual organs with mallets and then bundled them all out through the portholes into the placid brown waters.

They ripped the heap of clothing to pieces and threw it overboard, swilled the boat from stem to stern and divided the loot—1,200 rupees. The morning's work was complete. The boat was moored at the next landing stage and the Thugs went to sleep. An hour later Dutt and his servant walked the road again, looking for more victims. Thus day after day, year after year, had these sordid tragedies been enacted.

The river Thugs were harder to detect than the land Thugs—the river carried all traces of the crime away and the killers were careful, but Sleeman had a proved and effective organisation with which to ferret them out. A year after starting operations his deputy, Captain Lowis, had arrested 161 of them, had listed thirty-eight others and named them to police in all the areas through which the Ganges and its tribuaries flowed from Calcutta to Patna. Yet further arrests followed only slowly, and Sleeman found out why from an approver named Shumshera—he accused the police and some of the inhabitants of villages on the river banks of conniving at the murders.

From then on Sleeman and Lowis relied mainly upon their forces of *nujeebs* and sepoys who had learned to act swiftly upon confessions obtained from approvers naming fellow Thugs. One of the first approvers among the river Thugs, Bolai Chung, revealed in his recorded confession how treacherously they obtained their victims:

> Early last April a boatman named Nubeendee, whom I know, asked me to trade in rice with him and took me to a boat in which five other men were sitting. Soon the boat stopped and a man named Suroop went ashore and later came back with two weavers with loin cloths for sale. Suroop said to me: "Didn't you want to buy some loin cloths?"
>
> A man named Soobuldam and another man whose name I

> didn't know, then slipped the ruhmal round the necks of the two weavers and threw them to the floor. They then held their heads under water until they were dead and let their bodies go. We set out after this and pulled the boat for 15 days until we found another boat laden with tobacco and hemp. Our boats moved off together next day and we all ate our food upon a sandbank. Nubeendee then said: "I have made a vow to the god Hurry Sote. Let me here fulfil it. Call the captain and his boatmen that they may assist."
>
> When the captain and the four sailors of the tobacco boat arrived, Soobuldam said: "Do you, I pray, sing the song of Hurry Sote."
>
> They had sung one verse and were beginning another when Nubeendee shouted: "Now Hurry—give us your loot!" Five Thugs with twisted ruhmals leapt on the throats of the five singing men and threw them flat on the sand. Others seized them at the same time. . . . They sank the bodies in the water.

But captured river Thugs were usually less ready to betray their comrades than the fraternity ashore. Kali-worship was very strong among them and this faith, a unifying force, doubtless made them stubborn and silent. With various Thug informers revealing their secrets to him, Lowis made rapid progress in suppressing them, despite their greater unity, solidarity and faith in their religion—about which he reported:

> The Western Thugs appear to have been rapidly falling off from the practice and usages of their fathers; and to have constantly committed crimes against their system, such as murdering women, etc. In no one known instance have the Bengalees offended in this way: they are, and consider themselves the purest of all Thugs. . . .
>
> I would notice also the extraordinary audacity and success with which the river Thugs seem to commit their murders—I know of repeated instances in which ten, eleven and twelve persons have been put to death by boats' crews, varying from only fourteen to sixteen in number. I am credibly informed that last year seven men were murdered at one instant by a crew of nine Thugs. In very many instances too, the persons put to death were sepahees (*sepoys*), generally west-country men, who

are notoriously a far stronger and braver race than the inhabitants of Bengal. The small size of the boats, too, is another extraordinary circumstance; so much so that some of the murders stated to have been committed upon them would seem incredible, on any but evidence which it is impossible to resist—it is only another proof of the exceeding dexterity of the murderers.

To conclude, there seems no doubt but that this horrid crime has been fostered by nearly all classes in the community—the land-holders, the native officers of our courts, the police and village authorities—all I think have been more or less guilty; my meaning is not of course that every member of these classes—but that individuals varying in number in each class, were concerned. The Foujdaree Police gomastahs [petty officers] have in many instances been *practising Thugs*; and the chowkedars, or village watchmen, frequently so.

Lowis exposed the sinister power which obedience to Kali's rules and omens had given the river Thugs when combined with the emotional and religious intensity of the Bengali people. Although by the middle of 1838 most of them had been arrested, yet occasional murders still went on and India changes so slowly, they may even occur today.

Sleeman had by now all but stopped the secret ritual murders on India's rivers and roads, though by no means all the Thugs had been captured. At this landmark in his story it is worth again looking at his mental attitude to the grim task that held him from the promotion to the top ranks of government that his abilities merited.

He was fifty an age by which most of his contemporaries had either died from cholera or malaria or were going back home with a comfortable fortune. Twice he had vainly asked to be allowed to return to the normal work of a magistrate. Was he hoping for higher promotion elsewhere? Was he referring to his struggle against Thuggee when he spoke of himself as "weary, so weary of Indian customs"? Did he look back with longing to the Army? Or was his wife tired of the whole evil business of Thuggee, frightened of the threats to kill him and persuading him to resign?

The best evidence about his feelings towards his belief in the worth of his task at this time was given in a letter to his friend Charles Fraser, magistrate in the Jubbulpore district, and involved with the legal side of the campaign. Referring to the unending work it involved, Sleeman wrote to him on 22 February 1838:

> Do not I pray you get tired of the duties—neither you nor any other man can ever be employed in any more interesting or important to humanity. I shall look back with pride to the share I have had in them as long as I live.
>
> They were often fanciful, often even humiliating—but what is that of a soldier ordered to massacre a whole village of innocent beings, and doing it while he believes them innocent merely because he has the order to do it? Believe me Fraser, I would not exchange the share I have had in this work for the most splendid military service that man ever performed in India.
>
> I glory in it and ever shall do.
>
> Go on, I pray you, and be assured that you will recollect with pride and pleasure during the rest of your life the assistance you render to the great cause.

This letter has the ring of truth. There is no moral indecision, unreality of thought or self-deception here. Odious and painful though he found the work, Sleeman had no regrets and was proud of what he had done. There are only two possible explanations for his wish to resign: first, the effect of the hard work and the heat on his failing health; second, his discontent with the Government's failure to reward his services.

He was, of course, seconded to the Civil Service from the Bengal Army; promotion would therefore inevitably be slow, for the Army, as always, looked after its own. Sleeman was consequently a mere major, instead of a brigadier or a general. For the same reason he had failed to be properly rewarded in the Civil Service. And the Governor-General, though he had often praised Sleeman and had spoken of his great esteem for him, had offered him no laurels. No wonder Sleeman, doubtless under pressure from his wife, wanted now to turn his back on Thuggee.

Perhaps the Government could do nothing about his promotion without pressing Sir Harry Fane, the Commander-in-Chief, so far as to cause a rumpus. What is clear is that it was determined at all costs not to lose Sleeman, for there was other important work for him now that the Thuggee Department was not so busy. Meantime, with a clear understanding by the Indian rulers of the independent states that the British Government would tolerate sanctuaries for Thugs neither in their armed forces nor elsewhere in their domains, all their opposition to Sleeman's detachments finally ceased. Thugs were arrested in droves.

Sleeman was able to report early in 1838 that from 1829 to 1837 the total number taken and tried had leapt to 3,266, while several hundred more were in prison awaiting trial. There were now some 600 Thugs in detention at Jubbulpore for life; and the sons of many of them, to prevent their taking up the trade, were detained with them, for the time being. Sleeman had for long felt the need of providing a means by which they might learn trades so that the sons could earn a living when released on security and their fathers could occupy themselves profitably while in prison.

Acting on his own authority, without at first consulting the new Governor-General, Lord Auckland, Sleeman gave Captain Charles Brown, one of his assistants, the task of organising what he believed would meet the need—a trade school for the Thugs in the prison. For this seemingly eccentric scheme Sleeman advanced 1000 rupees to build a workshop, called a "manufactory", in the prison compound; while Brown hired skilled tradesmen to teach carpet-weaving, tent-making, carpentry, cloth-weaving, masonry, brick-making and bricklaying to these professional stranglers and their sons. Sleeman wrote of this scheme:

> The Thugs themselves would have wished their sons to be brought up to their old trade of murder, under the supposed religious sanctions . . . but as they saw no relaxation, or prospect of any, in the efforts of Government effectually to put down the system, they were afraid that the risk of imprisonment or transportation for life was too great; and after a time they acquiesced in our wishes. Those who had sons, with more or less reluctance, by degrees, consented to labour themselves, in order to encourage their sons to do the same.

The scheme prospered, the products being of good quality were easily sold in a country where so few such things were made and Thugs shared in the profits. In February 1838 Sleeman finally reported the scheme and its success to the Governor-General and duly received his sanction. At the same time he went one step further and had these Thug tradesmen build a small walled village near to the jail where those who had served well as approvers and who worked diligently were allowed to keep and visit daily their wives, mothers and children. Trusted prisoners slept with their wives in the village and were given the responsibility of keeping order there. Thus, as far as he could, without endangering society, Sleeman set the imprisoned Thugs on the road to as normal a life as possible. He says of this:

> The boys were delighted to feel that they had now learnt trades that would, with common industry, ensure them a comfortable subsistence for life; and the men to see that their sons were no longer in danger of taking to the old trade. . . . The women too, and their daughters, shared in the happy change of feeling; for they too could add to the general stock of the family comforts by spinning the thread required for the tents, since the cloth was now wove and stamped at the factory. The poles were turned and painted, the ropes and all other materials required for the tents were also prepared by the prisoners.

Sleeman had no hatred for the imprisoned Thugs, no wish to punish these men who willy-nilly had been driven by birth or circumstances to murder their fellow-men. He wanted to destroy Thuggee and to keep them out of harm's way—to give the young a way of earning a living on their entry into the world and the old a profitable and interesting occupation with wives and children in a relaxed and humane prison regime. Even today in Britain we have not yet moved as far.

Thuggee was now all but destroyed, but Dacoity, the organised gang robbery with violence for high stakes throughout central and northern India was rife. On 13 April 1837 Sir Charles Metcalfe, Lieutenant-Governor of the North-Western Provinces, had created the office of Commissioner for the Suppression of Dacoity, appointing Hugh Fraser of the Bengal Civil Service to the post. He was required to seek them out in their haunts, wherever they were, lay open their whole economy and method, punish and suppress them.

But by the end of 1838 Hugh Fraser had made almost no

progress; nor had he acquired any information about Dacoits that would enable him to do so. Lord Auckland, Governor-General, determined to make use of Sleeman's experience by uniting the office of Commissioner for Dacoity to that of General Superintendent of Thuggee throughout India.

17

Dacoity

Sleeman received orders to take over suppression of the Dacoits on 12 February 1839, rather against his will, for he wrote in confidence to his friend Charles Fraser some months earlier on 7 June 1838:

> The matter is out and I must undertake the dacoitee matter in addition to my own. I have got a letter . . . in terms absolutely irresistible—the pill is gilded not with money, but with sweet words and sweet promises and down it goes.

Despite his doubts about Government promises, Sleeman could not refuse, yet the task was formidable, though not comparable with Thuggee, from which Dacoity differed fundamentally, lacking its religious inspiration, its resilience, its power to deceive. The Dacoits were a number of clans with a perfected paramilitary organisation directed towards large-scale robbery with violence. The Budhuk Dacoits were the most notorious.

Information about their precise location and habits was uncertain and vague. Everybody talked of Budhuk Dacoits and their daring robberies, but no one knew whence they came. Some of them lived in isolated colonies in the forests; others together in small towns, where they corrupted society by bribing landholders, merchants, small bankers, farmers and police officers. Perjury and the commission of perjury became a regular trade among their friends and patrons in efforts to screen them from justice. Systematically they drew everyone in their communities into the net and made sure they did well out of it. Goldsmiths were paid generously for melting and disposing of gold and silver ornaments, shopkeepers supplied goods on credit at high prices when raids were being planned for the future, small bankers financed enterprises at huge interest rates, priests received liberal shares of loot for themselves and their temples.

Sleeman soon discovered that their colonies north of the river Jumna were located chiefly in the forest which bordered the Oude dominion to the north, and the Nepal Hills to the south; the districts of Rohilcand and parts of the Dooab, delta of the rivers Ganges and Jumna. He moved his home and his headquarters from Jubbulpore 400 miles north to Moradabad, in Rohilcand, about 100 miles east of Delhi, which was the central point from which he could best direct operations and methods similar to those used with much effect against Thugs.

Eight officers prominent in the attack upon Thuggee were stationed at central points within an area including Indore and Jubbulpore in the south, Meerut in the north, Lucknow and Goruckpur towards the north-east, each of them ready to move to any point within his radius. They were given the power of joint magistrates within the districts in which they were stationed, while in the Indian states they acted under the control of the British Residents accredited to these courts, in the same way as they acted under the control of the judicial authorities in British territories. They commanded the same forces of *nujeebs* and sepoys as for the anti-Thug campaign which they continued while in pursuit of the Dacoits.

As a start, acting under Sleeman's orders, and the authority of the Government and the Princes, his officers collected as many as they could of the Budhuk Dacoits then in prison throughout this region. Captain Paton got fifty from Lucknow, Captain Graham got several from Gwalior, Captain Riddell got some from the prisons of Indore and Bhopaul, and all the other assistants got some. The prisoners, in exchange for the promise of leniency, were invited to tell the story of their exploits, giving the names of all who had acted with them, especially the leaders.

Soon, a vast fund of information was recorded and a general register was formed of all the Budhuk Dacoits at large throughout India, as well as the enterprises in which they had taken part, and in what villages they could be found. Sleeman arrested thirty or forty of them in the parts of the region for which he had made himself responsible—Rohilcund and the delta between the Ganges and the Jumna; and, he wrote:

> Of all who seemed disposed to give me useful information I formed a small colony near my residence at Moradabad, called *Budukpoora*. Here they were comfortably lodged with their wives and families, whom I invited to reside with them. They had a little independent society of their own, and were no longer subject to the taunts and threats of their friends, assured that they would be well fed, clothed and protected, as long as they told me the whole truth. . . . They soon found that the depositions taken by the other officers of the department at distant points, enabled me to detect false statements; and that their status with me in the new colony depended upon their disclosing truly all they knew; and everyone was anxious to attain the highest status.

Some of their narratives—all of which were distributed to magistrates and local authorities in the districts where the Dacoities had occurred—covered as much as fifty years' systematic robbery and bloodshed. Thugs killed in subtle fashion and hid the crime with the burial of the victim, relying upon their power to dissemble and cast suspicion elsewhere to keep them out of the hands of authority. But the violence of the Dacoits, by contrast, was open and undisguised. Sleeman says:

> They had often to seize their spoil from strong, brave and well armed guards, and to enter large towns and scale high walls, and required that every one should be strong, brave and well trained to act his part in the post assigned to him, so that they might, like good soldiers, feel perfect confidence in each other's support under all circumstances of difficulty and danger. If one were left behind in their retreat, he might be seized, and frightened into a confession, dangerous to the safety of all, and they could not venture to take with them any but such as were . . . trained to move rapidly on a long journey of from thirty to forty miles without halting for rest or refreshment.

Dacoits planned their enterprises with meticulous care, studying the terrain carefully first to fix a proper place for attack, estimating the obstacles to be overcome to ensure success, planning their disguises and the systematic deployment of parties to cover and carry out the attack, as well as to protect the retreat. They were all Hindus, and like all whose faith contains animistic beliefs, took the auspices as to the feelings of the gods before an enterprise; but unlike the Thugs they did not see one deity as their sole and especial patron. One Dacoit told Sleeman: "We have nothing to do with Thugs—God forbid that! No, we never wish to murder; but if any one resists us, we strike and kill."

Another explained that when Dacoits were arrested their older women bribed the police with large sums either to release them or get their statements so written that the magistrate ordered their release. If they were brought to court, the old women, dressed in rags, followed three or four miles behind upon ponies, bringing with them one or two thousand rupees, which they distributed among the Indian officers of the court as part of a bargain to get their men released. If these officials could not effect their release they sent the women with letters of introduction to the officials of the higher court, together with advice as to the rate to pay.

Eventually, after months of hard work the names of 118 Dacoit jemadars and 3070 followers appeared on the Dacoit Register. Later their numbers were more accurately estimated at between four and five thousand altogether. Dacoits prided themselves upon remembering all the details of their enterprises. By careful questioning Sleeman and his staff established that from 1803, the earliest enterprise which the oldest man could remember, up to 18 June 1839, the total value of money and goods seized amounted to 2,240,000 rupees (£224,000), a huge sum in India more than a century and a half ago, when half a rupee or less was for millions of people the average weekly wage.

The attacks of gangs from this great family of professional and hereditary robbers were generally bolder and more carefully planned than the best-executed robberies of today, though the comparison is not altogether apt. Dacoits regarded themselves as outside the law, owing allegiance and loyalty to no one but the local landowner who knew of their trade and allowed them to stay in his domains in return for a share of their loot. Moreover, while the police and criminal investigation departments are well organised today, in India then they were rudimentary. Yet in energy and daring the Dacoits were unsurpassed. No district in the vast region of central and northern India was free from them. Sleeman noted:

> Within this vast field hardly any wealthy merchant or manufacturer could feel himself secure for a single night from the depredations of Budhuk Dacoits. They had successfully attacked so many of the treasuries of our Native Collectors of Revenue that it was deemed necessary all over the North Western Provinces to surround them with extensive fortifications. In many cases . . . they carried off our public treasure from strong parties of our regular troops and mounted police; and no one seemed to know whence they came, or whither they fled with the booty acquired. No magistrate who heard of a dacoity, indicating the hand of a Budhuk, could hope that any efforts on his part to catch or trace him, would be successful, whatever means he might have at his command.

A gang of forty Dacoits decided to attack a Government convoy of gold and coinage in a typical enterprise a year or two before Sleeman arrived on the scene. Four armed and mounted troopers and twelve sepoys escorted the cash. The Dacoits discovered the convoy would pass through a jungle and there they decided to attack. They first tied ropes across the road to trees on both sides, and at a short distance behind tied similar ropes to trees on one side of the road, ready to be fastened to the other as soon as the escort of horse and foot were well between. They armed themselves with ten matchlocks, ten swords and twenty-five spears, sent a scout to report on the progress of the convoy, then hid in the trees to wait its arrival. About five a.m. they heard a voice calling the name of Allah not far away. It was the troops of the convoy praying. The Dacoits were ready, their matchlocks thoughtfully loaded not with ball, but with shot "that we might, if possible, avoid killing anybody".

When, unsuspectingly, the troopers, sepoys and treasure-bearers with loaded ponies were all within the space, the ropes at the rear were run across the road and made fast to the trees on the opposite side. Fire was poured into the party. Those who tried to cut the ropes were shot down. When all resistance had ended the

Dacoits seized the cash, amounting to 12,000 rupees, marched continuously with it for the next three days and arrived safely in their headquarters over the border in a neighbouring state.

Against them, Sleeman planned a twin campaign. First, as with the Thugs, he offered pardons to all who came forward, gave themselves up and told the whole story of their enterprises and the names of their associates. At the same time he offered rewards to informers willing to lead troops to their hideouts and enable them to be captured.

Documentation, as always, was painstaking and precise. A separate file was kept for every individual; it was added to from the time when he was first denounced as a gang member until he was finally committed for trial at the sessions. The statement of the person who denounced him was first filed and then those of other Dacoits who had stated anything relevant about him. To these were added reports of local authorities where he resided as to his character, his own defence or confession and the statements of any other witnesses regarding his character.

A separate file was kept of every case of Dacoity described in the confessions, with the report from the local authority confirming that it had in fact occurred, then the statements of all who had taken part in it, those of the victims and those who knew anything about it. Thus, for the first time, everything known about any Dacoit and any particular dacoity in any part of India could quickly and easily be found.

While Sleeman and his staff were collecting and recording this mass of information, the other phase of the campaign—pursuit and attack by sepoys and *nujeebs* upon the gangs—was embarked upon under the same restrictions as those imposed upon the Thug-hunting parties. The detachments showed extraordinary zeal. One of them chased a gang under a noted leader named Bhowanny, in a great semicircle several hundred miles across Rajputana, Malwa and Gujerat, across the Gulf of Kutch down into Hyderabad and then up north again into Bengal before finally catching and arresting them.

In March 1840 Sleeman sent an able spy, Chundal Sing, disguised as a travelling shopkeeper, into the wild and wooded territories of Oude, between Lucknow and the hills of Nepal, to ascertain the exact hideouts of several large gangs. These territories were ruled by the Raja Dan Sing of Tolseepoor, the Rajas of Binga and Bankee, the Ranee of Pudeenaha, the Rajas Gunga Ram Sa of Khyreegur and Arjun Sing of Dhorehra. All were in league with Mungal Sing and other Dacoit leaders, and doing all they could to screen them.

Chundal Sing, the spy, returned in May and reported three extensive Dacoit bivouacs in a forest named *Bunder Baja*, from the number of monkeys that thronged it, and in three hamlets near by on the banks of the Ghogra river. Mungal Sing was the chief leader of these gangs, a man of formidable and attractive personality, who, like the best Dacoit leaders, associated on equal terms with the landed and official aristocracy of the region. So much a part of the country society were Mungal Sing and other leaders that all were formally invited with their attendants to take part in the ceremonies at the wedding of the daughter of the Raja Gungaram Sa to the Raja Arjun Sing in 1839 and to all other functions of the regional elite which their frequent journeys permitted.

This carefree fraternity, living by virtue of their courage and military skill upon the fat of the land, honoured and respected for their prowess for centuries, were now Sleeman's formidable opponents. In one of the first moves, in May 1839, Colonel Roberts, commanding the regular brigade of the King of Oude's troops, was at Sleeman's request ordered to send 500 sepoys and 200 cavalry under the best officer he had to attack the colonies. The King of Oude, having been convinced that he must now cooperate in the destruction of the Dacoits, wrote out his order to his troops thus:

> As it is the anxious desire of the royal presence to seize certain banditti or Dacoits . . . you are commanded, instantly on receiving instruction . . . to proceed to attack these robbers, and to make every possible exertion to capture them, and transmit them, vigilantly guarded, to the palace gates, in our capital at Lucknow.

Captain Barlow commanded the 700-strong detachment. He arrived in the locality of the Bunder Baja half an hour before dawn, drew up his cavalry on the plain near by and moved his infantry round to cut the Dacoits off from the forest behind them.

But he was too late; they had, of course, received information about him, and had fled. Left in their camps were only three old men, five women and nine children. Captain Barlow and his troops marched without resting to their own camp forty miles away and arrived at sunset, somewhat humiliated.

Captain Sturt set out a few days later with another detachment of the same strength and, no less than Barlow, discovered how elusive the Dacoits were in their home territories. Mungal Sing had placed spies among the camp followers of Sturt's force, who sent him information about its movements well in advance. When Sturt reached the village of Munduneea, for example, where the Dacoits were known to reside, the only man he found was their accountant, Bheekun Sing, too busy on their share accounts to bother to run away. He was taken prisoner, together with all the papers relating to recent enterprises.

In response to these determined military advances the Dacoits marched eastward from their hideouts to a strong position on the banks of the Surjoo river in the region. Here they combined in a force of about 1500 men, only 350 of whom, however, were equipped with firearms. The British-led troops, some 1200 in separate detachments under Captains Barlow, Hollings, Need and Worsley, were equipped with the Brown Bess musket and two batteries of six-pounder guns.

But the Dacoits were too wily to be led into a pitched battle against such a force. Receiving strong reinforcements, they feinted by opposing 2000 men to Captain Barlow's force of 300 and sent spies to leak the news in his camp. The British attack was postponed on 10 May 1839 until their forces could be more evenly deployed. At the same time Captain Hollings offered the Dacoits surrender terms. They showed a seeming interest in the offer by sending five of their principal women as ambassadresses, who stayed talking terms for a day, then left promising to prevail upon the leaders to surrender.

Barlow and his colleagues waited until midnight on 12 May for the expected reply. They then advanced into the Dacoit's positions and found them deserted. Villagers told them that for the past two days the Dacoits had been carousing in a marriage feast and several hours earlier had moved off with great noise and pomp. Enjoying themselves in this unworried way, they had then marched across the frontier into Nepal, Mungal Sing having gone on three days before and made terms with the Nepalese.

At this setback, Captain Hollings wrote to the local Nepal Governor asking him to seize and hold them until orders for their surrender came from the King of Nepal at Katmandu. This the Governor agreed to do; Hollings then asked him to turn the Dacoits back into India so that he could surround them. It was then found that they had instead been allowed to enter further into Nepal. The weather had now become too bad for operations in the forest and chagrined at seeing the Dacoits out of his reach Hollings withdrew all his forces and returned to Lucknow.

> There was too much confidence [Sleeman afterwards complained] in the promises of female *ambassadors*, to persuade their husbands and followers to surrender . . . which they had no intention whatever of doing. Their object was to gain time and information, and they succeeded in gaining all that they required of both. . . . Every officer however, did his best; and the result of the best planned movement after such people, in such a forest, must always be very uncertain.

Convinced that his subordinates had tried, Sleeman apportioned blame and praise equally.

Well into August 1840 efforts were made to get the Nepal authorities to expel the Dacoits. Hollings, with fresh troops, waited to seize them when they returned through the pass into Oude. Mungal Sing, hiding in malarial jungle, was himself now reported to be stricken with what was then termed the Turae fever. Eventually, towards the end of August, Hollings was ordered to retire—it was thought improper to expose the troops to risk of sickness there any longer. Finally, in October, spies brought news that many of the Dacoits had died of fever and that the gangs were breaking up, and this was later confirmed.

Subsequently, in October 1840, Colonel Caulfield, Resident at the King of Oude's Court at Lucknow, wrote to the Government in Calcutta claiming that the operation had been a success, that the leaders had been captured and the gangs finally dispersed. Sleeman, who received a copy of the letter, protested that it conveyed "an impression that the work of suppressing these gangs has been completed". He insisted therefore that the King of Oude should continue to supply troops to attack the remnants of the Dacoit force if they returned into India.

Throughout 1841 and during the next three years until 1844 Captain James Sleeman, William Sleeman's nephew, kept up regular pressure on the Dacoits, penned up in the forest bordering Oude and Nepal. Finally, in 1844, those of the original 1500 who had not died of malaria—a mere three leaders, 89 men and 200 women and children—surrendered unconditionally. A lenient and constructive policy was applied to them—they were enlisted into police forces in the areas bordering Oude and Nepal, in the hope that they would earn their subsistence honestly and blend into society.

During this pressure upon the main body, Sleeman's staff elsewhere attacked them with equal energy.

> Their colonies upon the plains of India were like masses of quicksilver upon a table—press the large body ever so slightly, and it instantly separates into numerous small ones, which continue to roll about independently till circumstances are favourable to their reunion, when they combine and act together as if they had never been separated.

Thus, to have attacked one group only would have been useless; they would have separated and reunited with other groups far afield. So Major Graham at Agra, Captain Birch in Rajputana, Major Riddell in Malwa and Gujerat—all led forces of sepoys against the Dacoits with that single-mindedness, that extraordinary conviction in the rightness of their undertakings that then characterised the British.

By the end of 1842 a total of 711 Dacoits had been arrested in these regions and twelve dangerous killers had been sentenced to death. The remainder were transported, or sentenced to varying terms of imprisonment, leniency again being the keynote rather than severity. As an experiment thirty-five chosen Dacoits were in 1841 formed into an agricultural colony and, supplied with the necessary equipment for cultivation, given a grant of land in northern India near Gorruckpoor. But this liberal and constructive effort was only partially successful; the colonists lacked either the skill or the ability to come to terms with peasant life. Most of them eventually drifted into other occupations, only a few settled down permanently.

In the summer of 1841 Sleeman was tired out by the effort he had put into organising and directing every detail of the drive against Thugs and Dacoits simultaneously. His eyesight was also troubling him. For years he had been accustomed to writing long reports by candlelight in the dark tropical evenings after his day's work, but he found it painful to do so now. "I am getting very like yourself," he wrote to Charles Fraser in the late summer of 1841—"write only when I am asked something, or want to ask some other person something."

Home, wife and family had always been a secure base which restored the energy, equability and sanity he needed to sustain his effort to stamp out the hidden sects of Thuggee and Dacoity so elaborately built into Indian society. This was not true of all his contemporaries; many preferred a gregarious club life among colleagues to home. Now suddenly this oasis was threatened. His eldest daughter was repeatedly ill and the two younger girls were not thriving in the superheated climate of central India. Sleeman and his wife decided in 1841 that they could no longer postpone sending them all home to England. At first, Amélie was to go for a year or two as well, but in the end, never having left her husband's side since their marriage, she found herself unable to bear the parting. So the children were to sail from Calcutta in the care of friends in late December.

To his life-long friend Charles Fraser Sleeman wrote on 28 November 1841:

> I am going down so far as Ghazeepore with my three little ones, who are going to England with Captain Bowen on the *Southampton* if they get down in time to sail with him. I shall perhaps remain some short time for my wife, who goes all the way with the little ones. . . . This is what you bachelors escape; but then we have delight with the little ones that you are strangers to.

So in December Sleeman travelled the first 400 miles of the journey, from Moradabad to Ghazeepoor. Here he said goodbye to his three little daughters, who went on to Calcutta with his wife. The parting was bitter—Sleeman was more than tender-hearted towards his children. In another letter he spoke of his feelings without restraint:

> I shall wait for Amélie, who is gone down with the children. She could not bear the idea of separating from them till the last. Their sweet voices still haunt my ear. "Papa dear, Papa dear"—such musick I have never heard from other lips; and much do I fear I have heard this for the last time.
>
> Go, my dear Fraser, and put yourself in the way of hearing the same musick. You will never be a really happy man till you do. I have recommended Amélie to go home with the children, for a change, but she will not be tempted. . . . The house without the little ones will be very dreary.

Ambition, love of India and high hopes for the future held Sleeman there. The "sweet promises" he had referred to in an earlier letter to Fraser were, he hoped, soon to materialise.

By the end of 1841 a total of 3843 Thugs had been arrested and tried; the arrests then slowed almost to a standstill, but another 4000 tyro Thugs, unrelated to the hereditary families, were believed to have escaped when the chase became too hot and to have returned to their former trades. In addition by this time nearly a thousand Dacoits had been either killed in skirmishes with government forces or arrested and sentenced. Before Sleeman's operations began there were thus almost 8000 Thugs and 4000 Dacoits ravaging the roads of India.

The age-old secret society of Thugs was by the end of 1841 practically destroyed, but Sleeman remained prudent, modest and realistic, despite his victory. In a final report attached to a list of the Thugs believed to be still at large though not then practising their trade, he wrote:

> The only parts of India in which there are any Thugs still at large and not entered in these lists are, I believe, the eastern districts of Bengal, where we have reason to believe that the crime still prevails to a small extent, and Midnapore, where Captain Valency and Mr Ewart have recently discovered traces of an isolated colony or two. Measures are being taken to put down these associations should they, on further enquiry, be found really to exist.

> Except in the parts I have mentioned and in Oude, I believe the roads are now from one end of India to the other, free from the depredations of Thug gangs; but there are many leaders and leading members of the old gangs still at large, though they have —for the most part, I believe, found service with the military and police establishments of Native Chiefs.
>
> All these persons would return to their old trade, and teach it to their sons, and to the needy and dissolute of their neighbourhood, and thus reorganise their gangs should our pursuit be soon relaxed. To prevent the system from arising again it will be indispensably necessary to keep up the pursuit for some years till all those leaders and leading members of the old gangs die, or become too old to return to their old trade. Under the pressure of this pursuit their sons will take to honest industry, seeing no prospect of being able to follow successfully that of their ancestors.

Sleeman's belief that the roads were free of Thugs was confirmed during 1840 and '41 in the letters of a number of magistrates, who agreed that for the first years in living memory, no bodies of strangled wayfarers had been found in their districts. Nevertheless, his officers remained active and vigilant and from time to time unearthed Thugs at honest labour. Relentless to the end, Sleeman, knowing that if they had the chance they would return to Thuggee, had them tried and sentenced, but the maximum sentence now was life imprisonment.

Two more small Thug associations outside those of the hereditary families were discovered in the 1840s and both were put down. Mostly, it was these Thugs who brought the number of those convicted in the eight years between 1840 and 1848 to a total of 514.

Thuggee practically ceased after 1848, except for isolated cases in the Punjab for a few years and more persistently on the rivers of Bengal, where it may from time to time still occur, as murder occurs everywhere. The task that nearly everyone but Sleeman believed impossible had been accomplished. For the twenty most important years of his life Sleeman had fought this brotherhood of murderers. For several of these years he had had to fight to convince the East India Company of the very existence of Thuggee and, when he had proved its existence, incredibly, he had been obliged to show that it was desirable to uproot it.

Had he stayed in the Bengal Army, or had he lived the life of a conforming Company official, promotion would doubtless have come earlier and his career would have been materially more profitable for him. But, in his own field, he was a man of destiny. He recognised Thuggee as a remorseless social evil that would, if left alone, dominate the whole of India. One or two other magistrates had chanced before upon it and had tried to fight it, but had felt themselves powerless while the Company followed a policy of *laissez faire*. Not so Sleeman. He resolved to destroy it, whatever the circumstances, and he did so, aided by that remarkable readiness to serve that marked so many of the outstanding men of his time—a spirit that drove them at least as strongly as does mere ambition and love of power their counterparts today.

Epilogue

In 1841, when it was possible to journey through the jungles and plains of India without danger of being strangled, Sleeman received the Government's fulfilment of the promise made three years earlier. He was offered what was then probably the most coveted post in India after that of Governor-General—British Resident at the Lucknow Court of the King of Oude, the then independent kingdom in north-east India. Sleeman accepted this lucrative post, the reward in hard cash no less than prestige for the years of unrecognised work, when throughout India many fellow officials had disdainfully called him "Thuggee" Sleeman.

At the last moment, when he was about to take over from Colonel Low, who had resigned, all Low's money went in a bank failure and he was more or less destitute. There was apparently no other post, at least on the same level, which the Government could give Low instead. Sleeman may either have acted on a generous impulse, or reluctantly after much thought, in declaring himself ready to stand down in favour of Low. Probably it was an almost automatic response to training and to his code of behaviour. There was perhaps, still another factor; his health, which—not to cast doubt on his motives—may well have made him feel unequal to the demands the Lucknow post would have made upon him. "I am not strong and dare not eat and drink like a Christian," he wrote to Charles Fraser at this time. "I ought to be thankful that I am so well as I am at this period of life and in such a country, where so many of my contemporaries have gone to their last long sleep."

Not only many of his contemporaries, but hundreds of Thugs as well. And now, realistically, Sleeman was acknowledging his good fortune in being still alive, but doubtful about how long he would last. Low was enabled to stay on. A few months later Sleeman was given instead the lesser diplomatic post of Resident at Gwalior, while remaining head of the Thuggee and Dacoity Department. At Gwalior during the next few years he remembered the destinies of the former Thugs working in the distant factory at Jubbulpore, visiting it in 1843, in 1844 and for the last time in 1848, satisfying himself that work and rehabilitation were maintained. At first he found the Thugs anxious to talk about the scenes and excitements of their old trade to the young officers who accompanied him and to show them how they strangled and butchered their victims.

At the second visit, next year, he found they would do this only when actually encouraged to and during the last visit in 1848 they were unwilling to answer any questions about it and talked no more together about the scenes of their old trade.

> Their sons . . . were now become able, industrious, well-behaved and well-dressed young men who felt no interest in what their fathers could tell them of a trade so abhorrent to the rest of mankind, and were evidently ashamed to see their fathers asked any questions about it by the European visitors. All had learnt to read and write, as well as to work honestly for their bread at respectable trades; and were proud at the thought of their independent condition.

Some of the most able young men, who had worked in the factory since boyhood and had never been engaged in Thuggee, were helped to set up in business for themselves in the town of Jubbulpore. It was Sleeman's hope that they would add to its industry and form the foundation of a manufacturing community out of people who might well have continued to be hereditary murderers by trade.

His last report to the Government, dated 2 February 1848, about what was then called the Jubbulpore School of Industry, instead of "the factory", noted that its carpets, then considered to be the best in India, were sold widely, that it was paying for itself and providing the sons of Thugs and those Thugs willing to work with a very handsome living. Clearly, Sleeman felt he owed it to the Thugs not to leave them to rot in prison, but to afford them a life as near to normal as possible; and their sons a prosperous future as upright members of society. He seems in this report to be acknowledging this debt and that he had done his best for them.

This year, the Residency at Lucknow again fell vacant. Lord Dalhousie, then Governor-General, offered it to Sleeman on 16 September in these words:

> The high reputation you have earned, your experience of civil administration, your knowledge of the people, and the qualifications you possess as a public man, have led me to submit your name to the Council of India as an officer to whom I could commit this important charge with entire confidence that its duties would be well performed. I do myself, therefore, the honour of proposing to you to accept the office of Resident at Lucknow, with especial reference to the great changes which, in all probability, will take place. Retaining your superintendency of Thuggee affairs, it will be manifestly necessary that you should be relieved from the duty of the trials of Thugs usually condemned at Lucknow.
>
> In the hope that you will not withhold from the Government your services in the capacity I have named, and in the further hope of finding an opportunity of personally making your acquaintance,
>
> I have the honour to be,
> Dear Colonel Sleeman,
> Very Faithfully Yours,
> DALHOUSIE.

Sleeman accepted his reward and became one of the great and influential men in India. Oude was then ruled by a debauched and crazy king who, among other eccentricities, had conferred upon his eunuchs the lucrative honour of administering criminal law and upon his court musicians that of civil law. Sleeman's main task was to induce the King to mitigate the oriental despotism and corruption that was rife in his kingdom.

Lord Dalhousie wished to annex this country on the grounds of the King's misrule. Sleeman urged compulsory reforms instead, with the prophetic words: "The native States I consider to be breakwaters, and when they are swept away we shall be at the mercy of our native army, which may not always be sufficiently under our control."

In 1854 Sleeman, now Major-General, fell victim again to the strain of having toiled non-stop for forty-five years in India. He tried once more to regain his health by rest, up in the cool hills, but his physique failed to respond. He returned to his duties for a year in 1855 and was severely ill. He recovered, but was ordered home.

There was nothing melancholy about his end except that he was worn out. Reaching Calcutta in January 1856, he was informed by Lord Dalhousie that he had been recommended for a knighthood. He replied:

> I cannot adequately express how highly honoured I feel by the mention that you have been pleased to make of my services to Her Majesty. . . . My right hand is so crippled by rheumatism that I am obliged to make use of an amanuensis to write this letter, and my bodily strength is so much reduced, that I cannot hope before embarking for England to pay my personal respects to your Lordship . . .

He and his wife sailed for England on 1 February and she, who had never left his side throughout his fight against the Thugs, later in a letter, quoted him as saying to her: "I feel very happy, happy to know you are with me, and to look at you makes me feel so happy that I should not like to leave you in this world, but I feel that I shall soon leave you unprotected. . . ."

They had two more days together. Sleeman died of a heart attack off the coast of Ceylon on 10 February 1856 and was buried at sea, almost within sight of India, the country which he had served so well.

Appendix

THE THUGS' SECRET DIALECT

Through the centuries the Thugs evolved a dialect of their own to enable them to talk in the presence of strangers without danger. Sleeman listed between five and six hundred words and their meanings, of *Ramasee*, as the Thugs called their dialect, and of this vocabulary he says:

> I am satisfied that there is no term, no rite, no ceremony, no opinion, no omen or usage that they have intentionally concealed from me. . . . Every word entered in this vocabulary is Ramasee in the sense assigned to it; while but few of them are to be found at all in any language with which I am acquainted. Their verbs have all Hindoostanee terminations and auxilaries, such as Kurna to make, Lena to take, Dena to give, Jana to go, Lana to bring, Dalna to throw.

I have selected these words from Sleeman's vocabulary because they throw light on Thug customs and habits of mind:

Adhoreea—Any person who has separated himself from a party whom the Thugs have murdered or intend to murder, and thereby escaped them.
Agasee—A turban. A Thug never moves without his turban, except in Bengal perhaps. If a turban is set on fire it threatens great evil, and the gang must, if near home, return, and wait seven days. . . .
Agureea—Descendants of the Thugs who, after their expulsion from Delhi, resided for a time in the district of Agra, and thence spread over India; in contradistinction to those who went to different parts of India without resting at Agra. Their tradition is that one of the Emperors of the house of Gouree expelled them all

from Delhi after the murder of a *cheyla*, or slave of his, who had been long in league with them, but was murdered in consequence of a threat to betray them, made with a view to extort more money than they thought reasonable. The Emperor had them all marked on the posteriors with the stamp of the copper coin of the Empire.

Ansootore—Literally, "tear drops". Any shower of rain that falls before or after the four usual months of June, July, August and September. If it falls during the first day and night after entering on an expedition the gang must return and open it anew. It is always a bad omen and requires some sacrifices.

Angjhap—A term used by the Thugs of the Deccan for *Rehna*, or a temporary burial of the bodies.

Bajeed—Safe, free from danger. When the Thugs have got their victims at the place where they intend to murder them, they call out *Bajeed* or *Bajeed Khan*, and the work of murder goes on. If the spies see a stranger approach and apprehend danger, they call out *Sheik Mahummud*, or *Luchman Sing*, and the Thugs suspend operations. When one part of the gang advances with the travellers they intend to kill, and on the road meets other travellers, whom the party in the rear may conveniently murder, they tell them to bid their friends *bajeed*, to make haste and overtake this second party. As soon as the gang behind hear this message they may fall upon and murder them, understanding by the signal that in advance the road is clear.

Bae hojana—To become public, viz. the bodies of victims or other traces of their proceedings.

Bugjana—To become aware of the designs of Thugs upon one.

Bojha—The Thug who takes the body of a murdered person to the grave.

Bahleem—One of the seven original Thug clans.

Beylha—The Thug who chooses the place of murder.

Bunij—Literally, merchandise or goods; technically a traveller or any other person whom the Thugs consider worth murdering. He is their stock in trade.

Bhurtote—A strangler. Thugs seldom attain this rank or office till they have been on many expeditions, and acquired the requisite courage or insensibility by slow degrees. At first they are almost always shocked and frightened; but after a time they say they lose all sympathy with their victims.

Baroo—A Thug of respectability, either from the celebrity of his Thug ancestors or from his own character as a Thug.
Burgeela—An accomplice: one who knows the secrets of the Thugs and keeps them.
Burka—A leader or chief of Thugs, or one thoroughly instructed in the art. The Thugs consider a *Burka* as capable of forming a gang of Thugs out of the rude materials around him in any part of India.
Bisul purna—Awkward strangling, with the *rumal* round the head or face instead of the neck. *Soosul purna*—to have it round the neck. Any Thug in whose hands victims have been often *bisull* is excluded from the office of strangler, on the ground of presumed unfitness for duty.
Cheeha—A coward timid Thug, one who shows sympathy or fear.
Chookadena—To cause to sit down and look up, as travellers before strangling them. They direct their attention to the sky or some object above them.
Dada Dheera—A very ancient and canonized Thug of the Bhursote class whom they invoke in drinking spirits at certain religious ceremonies. *Dada Dheera's* tomb is visited as a holy shrine by Thugs at Kumona in Koel, where he was buried.
Dhaga—Finding out the intentions of travellers; or negotiation with chiefs or anyone in authority for protection, or for release when arrested.
Dhokur—A dog; also a man who seizes Thugs.
Dhonkee—A policeman or guard.
Doonr—The loud screams of a victim for help.
Dhurdalna—To strangle.
Gobba—The round grave. This is made circular, and a small pillar of hard ground left in the centre. This they think prevents the dogs, jackals and other animals from digging up the bodies, and at the same time the ground from cracking and emitting that effluvia that often leads to their discovery in the *Kurwa*, or oblong grave. The Thugs about Delhi . . . and many other classes use the *Gobba*. The bodies are closely packed round the pillar of round earth.
Gookhee—The person who is carrying the bones of his relations to the holy river. Thugs may never murder him.

Goneeait—A man who has lost his hand or nose. To murder such a man they consider very unlucky and rarely venture to do it.
Goor Ghaunt—The knot of the gooroo or priest who teaches the use of the *rumal* in strangling. The Thug who has learnt from this man scientifically, as a mark of his college education leaves the end of the *rumal* concealed within the knot, or *ghaunt*. The strangler who has not been so instructed leaves the end out, as more secure for his less skilful hand. The Thug who has had his collegiate education is called the *Goor ponch*.
Hilla—The rank or grade held by three men in every expedition. (1) The man who chooses the place for murdering people and burying the bodies. (2) The man who carries the *kusee*, or consecrated pickaxe. (3) The man who brings the goor or coarse sugar for the sacrifice. All these Thugs are supposed to need peculiar skill and peculiar piety.
Jywaloo—A victim left for dead but found afterwards to have life in him.
Jhummanta—One not a Thug, but to whom Thugs are known and who is to be avoided by them.
Jhora Naek—A celebrated leader of the Multan Thugs, whose name they mention with reverence during their rituals. He was a Musulman and he and his servant are said to have killed a man who had in jewels and other articles property to the value of 160,000 rupees (£16,000) laden upon a mule. They brought home the booty, assembled all the members of their fraternity within reach and honestly divided the whole as if all had been present. Jora Naek, his wife and his slave were all canonized in consequence.
Kucha—Unburied, or imperfectly buried, referring to a dead body. Also a Thug who discloses what he knows regarding his associates.
Kujjee—A woman of any kind not of a Thug family.
Khomusna—To rush in upon travellers when there is no time for the ordinary ceremonies of murder.
Kanthuna or *Kanth dalna*—To cut up the body of a murdered person to prevent its swelling and forming cracks in the soil that covers it. Also, to kill with a knife a person whom they have not time to strangle, on the approach of danger; or to stab a strangled victim in order to prevent the possibility of his recovery.

Karhoo—One who searches after, betrays or molests Thugs.
Khuruk—Noise made by the pickaxe when digging the grave.
Lughae—The office of gravedigger.
Muchhooa—A keeper of a serae for the accommodation of travellers. The greater part of these people are in the interest of the Thugs, often permitting them to perpetrate murders in their seraes, and giving them useful information regarding travellers.
Maulee—The man who takes home money for the subsistence of their families from Thugs engaged in distant expeditions.
Munjwar—A jackal. To prevent jackals digging up the dead bodies, Thugs throw over the grave either very thorny bushes or *ispaghole*, the seeds of the flea-wort, to which they say jackals and dogs have a strong dislike. They say that with the *ispaghole* there is no danger from any animal but the bear and the hyena.
Nizam Oddeen Ouleea—A saint of the Sunni sect of Mahommuduns, said to have been a Thug of great note at some period of his life, and his tomb near Delhi is to this day visited as a place of pilgrimage by Thugs, who make votive offerings to it. He is said to have been . . . born in March, A.D. 1236 and died A.D. 1325. His tomb is visited by Mahommudun pilgrims from all parts as a place of great sanctity . . .; but the Thugs, both Hindu and Mahommudun, visit it as containing the remains of the most celebrated Thug of his day. There are perhaps no sufficient grounds to pronounce him one of the fraternity; but there are some perhaps to suspect that he was so at some period of his life.
Pola—The sign made at a cross-road to guide the gang members who are behind in the direction the others have taken. They draw their feet along the dust in the direction they have taken; and if their friends are to follow quickly they leave the dust piled up at the end of the line where the foot stops, or make a hole in it with the heel. If there is no dust they leave two stones piled one on the other in the line they have taken, and strew a few leaves of trees along the road. If their friends are to make haste they leave a long line of leaves.
Pungoo—A river Thug of Bengal who carries out his murders on his boat, which he calls a *kuntee*.
Phur jharna—To clean the place of murder. After a murder at night, some members of the gang are left behind to remove any signs that may be seen when day appears.

Soon—A Thug by birth who has not yet attained the rank of strangler.
Shumseea—The Thug who sometimes holds the hands or feet of a victim while the *Bhurtote* strangles him.
Saur—Any man who escapes from Thugs when they attempt to strangle him.
Surbalund Khan—The name pronounced by the leader to direct the stranglers to be ready at their posts to fall upon the victims when the final signal or *jhirnee* is given.
Sotha—The Thug who inveigles travellers, always the most eloquent and persuasive man they can find.
Thibana—To cause travellers to sit down on some pretence or other, so that the stranglers may conveniently murder.
Teekula—Any suspicious thing from a murdered person which it is dangerous for a Thug to carry.
Tombako kha lo—Eat or smoke your tobacco; technically "strangle"; one of the signals for murder.
Tonkal—A party of people larger than the gang of Thugs can manage to destroy.
Thap—The place of encampment where the Thugs spend the night, commonly outside a village.
Tuppul or *tupole*—The bye-path into which Thugs lead travellers from the high road to murder them without danger.
Tortunkur—Searching after, seizing or molesting Thugs.

Bibliography

Unpublished

Bengal Political Proceedings, 1829 to 1834; and India Political Proceedings, 1835 to 1842. (India Office Library).

Letters from William Sleeman to the Fraser family in India. (India Office Library).

Collections on Thuggee and Dacoitee. By Captain James Paton. Add. Mss., British Museum.

Published

WILLIAM SLEEMAN. *Ramaseeana*. Calcutta, G. H. Huttmann, 1836.

—— *Report on the Thug Gangs*. Calcutta, G. H. Huttmann, 1840.

—— *Report on the Budhuk Dacoits*. Calcutta, J. C. Sherriff, 1849.

—— *A Journey through the Kingdom of Oude*. London, Richard Bentley, 1858.

—— *Rambles and Recollections*. London, Hatchard, 1884.

WILLIAM BOLT. *Considerations on Indian Affairs*. London, 1772.

The Cambridge History of the British Empire, Vol. 5.

Abbé J. A. DUBOIS, *Hindu Manners and Customs*, 3rd edn. Oxford University Press, 1906.

EMILY EDEN, *Up the Country: Letters to her sister from India, 1837-40*. Oxford University Press, 1937.

M. MONIER WILLIAMS. *Religious Thought and Life in India*. London, Murray, 1891.

G. R. GLEIG, *The Life of Sir Thomas Munro*. London 1830, 3 vols.

G. F. MACMUNN. *Religions and Hidden Cults of India*. London, Sampson Low, 1931.

SIR JOHN MALCOLM. *Memoir of Central India*. London, 1832.

RAJENDRA LALLA MITRA. *Indo-Aryans*. London, Stamford, 1881.

R. V. RUSSELL and HIRA LAL. *Tribes and Castes of the Central Provinces of India*. London, Macmillan, 1916.

VINCENT A. SMITH. *The Oxford History of India*. Oxford University Press, 1920.

PERCIVAL SPEAR. *A History of India*, Vol. 2. Harmondsworth, Penguin Books, 1965.

SIR FRANCIS TUKER. *The Yellow Scarf*. London, Dent, 1961.

Index